Operation Willi

OPERATION WILLI

*The Plot to Kidnap
the Duke of Windsor
July 1940*

Michael Bloch

Weidenfeld and Nicolson
London

To the memory of
General Georges Spillmann

First published in Great Britain in 1984 by
George Weidenfeld & Nicolson Limited
91 Clapham High Street, London SW4

Weidenfeld paperback edition first published in 1986

ISBN 0 297 78462 5 – cased
ISBN 0 297 78757 8 – paper

Typeset and printed in Great Britain
at The Bath Press, Avon

Contents

Illustrations

ILLUSTRATIONS

Colonel Juan Beigbeder (*By special permission of the Spanish Minister for External Relations*)

Don Javier 'Tiger' Bermejillo (*Sr D. Javier Chapa*)

Miguel Primo de Rivera (*The Duque de Primo de Rivera*)

Angel Alcázar de Velasco (*Angel Alcázar de Velasco*)

Dr António Oliveira Salazar (*Diario de Notícias, Lisbon*)

Captain Agostinho Lourenço (*Diario de Notícias, Lisbon*)

The Duke with Ricardo Espírito Santo Silva (*Duchess of Windsor's collection*)

Acknowledgments

___

In writing this book I incurred heavy debts. It would not have been possible without Maître Suzanne Blum's encouragement, and the privileged access she gave me to the Duke of Windsor's files; without Christopher Jackson's advice and moral support and research assistance in the Peninsula; without the kindness of Aline, Countess of Romanones, in putting me on the trail of key Spanish witnesses; without my parents; without Andrew Best; without the limitless patience of John Curtis and Linda Osband; without Michael Day; without James Lees-Milne; without Peter Fleetwood-Hesketh; without Hugo Haig-Thomas's expert translation of endless documents in woolly Nazi German jargon. It would not have been very interesting had I not received the patient co-operation of those persons still living who were intimately involved in the events I set out to describe – Don Angel Alcázar de Velasco, the Viscount Eccles, the Conde de Montarco, Mademoiselle Jeanne-Marguerite Moulichon, Don Ramón Serrano Suñer and Maria-Ursula Baroness von Stohrer. Space prohibits me from listing my other specific debts; I must be content to enumerate my creditors:

In the British Isles: Mr and Mrs Harry Anderson; Dr Toby and Dr Cecilia Bainton; Mrs S. Barnett; Caroline Belgrave; Mark Brockbank; Ernst Brunert; John da Lux Camacho; Michael Chamberlayne; Mrs P.R.T.Chamberlayne; Dr John Charmley; the Hon. Lady Cheke; Sir Michael Cresswell; Michael Crowder; Lord Dacre of Glanton; Dudley Danby; Dr Geoffrey Dymond; Sir Dudley Forwood, Bt; Martin Gilbert; John Grigg; Sir Eric Hallinan; Betty Hanley; Professor F.H.Hinsley; J.A.Hopkins; Ronald Howard; H.Montgomery Hyde; Roy Illingworth; David Irving; Dr Horace King; Mrs Trevor Lamb; Trevor Langford; Sir Robin Mackworth-Young; Brian Masters; Professor R.B.McDowell; Charles Orwin; Lars-Ake Nilsson; Paul Paget; the late Professor Clive Parry; Dr Richard

Robinson; Kenneth Rose; Geoffrey Royston-Isaacs; Ralph Selby; Nicholas Shakespeare; Dr Denis Smyth; Hugh Stewart; Dr W.D. Symington; Professor George West; Nigel West.

In France: the Duque de Baena y de San Lucar Mayor; Jean-Luc Barré; Peter Bloxham; René Brest; Georges Hoffman; Walter Lees; Eric Leins; Marie Marendat; the Hon. Lady Mosley; the Manager of the Hôtel du Palais at Biarritz; François de Panafieu; Stuart Preston; Annette Remond; Georges-Gaston Sanègre; Gerard Watelet.

In Portugal: Dr Ferand d'Almeida; Nuno Brito e Cunha; Anne-Marie Espírito Santo Bustorffe; the Marqueza do Cadaval; Joana Carvalho Meyer; the late Lydia, Princess Clary und Aldringen; Vera Cohen Espírito Santo; Pedro Vieira da Fonseca; the late Conde de Lancastre; Rita Espírito Santo Leite Faria; Peter Lewer; Dr Paulo Marques; Susan Lowndes Marques; Ilidio Matos; Manuel de Melo; António de Mendia; Ambassador Alberto Franco Nogueira; Tomás Pinto Basto; Vera Espírito Santo Ricciardi; Mary Salgado; Mr and Mrs John Shakespeare; John Travis; Dr Zacarias Berenguel Vivas; Alda Wright; the staff at York House.

In Spain: Professor Gonzalo Anes; Rafael Blázquez Godoy; Javier Chapa Bermejillo; Raquel de Concha; Luis Escobar Fitzpatrick; Diane Griffiths; Duarte Pinto Coelho; the Duque de Primo de Rivera; Pilar Primo de Rivera; the manager and staff of the Ritz Madrid; Enrique Rivero; Pedro Sainz Rodriguez; the Marqués de Santo Floro; the Condesa de Velayos.

In the United States of America: Nat Bickford; Peter Ginsberg; Frances Haythe; John Mears; Thomas W. Miller; Robert B. Payn; Senator Claiborne Pell; the Roosevelt Library; Dorothea Scher; Lewis Ufland; Peter Weed; Professor Douglas L. Wheeler.

Elsewhere: Professor W.M. Carlgren; Sebastian Cleaver; the Hon. Neil Hogg; Jakub Gelbart; Dr Kurt Josten; Dr Maria Keipert; Professor Bernd Martin; Madame Jacques Roux; Reinhard Spitzy; Berthold Baron von Stohrer; Dr Hermann Weiss; Richard Baron von Weizsäcker; Dr Werner of the *Bundesarchiv*.

I am most grateful to them all – though had better reserve some of my gratitude for the (I hope not too numerous) people I may inadvertently have left out.

MICHAEL BLOCH
April 1984

Dramatis Personae

DRAMATIS PERSONAE

Sir Samuel Hoare, Bt	recently appointed as British Ambassador to Spain

AT THE BRITISH EMBASSY IN LISBON

Sir Walford Selby	the Ambassador
The Hon. Neil Hogg	Second Secretary
Wing-Commander P.R.T. ('Tanks') Chamberlayne	the Air Attaché
Marcus Cheke	the Press Attaché
Richman Stopford	the Financial Attaché, head of MI6 in Portugal
David Eccles	of the Ministry of Economic Warfare, on a special mission in Lisbon

Herbert C. Pell	US Minister in Lisbon
Renato Bova Scoppa	Italian Minister in Lisbon

THE GERMANS

Adolf Hitler	the Führer
Joachim von Ribbentrop	Reich Foreign Minister
Dr Erich Kordt	his *chef de cabinet*
Ernst Baron von Weizsäcker	State Secretary at the Foreign Ministry
Dr Oswald Baron von Hoyningen-Huene	German Minister in Lisbon
Obergruppenführer Reinhard Heydrich	head of the Reich Main Security Office (*RSHA*)
Brigadeführer Walter Schellenberg	his subordinate in charge of the overseas counter-espionage operations of the Gestapo
Admiral Canaris	head of the *Abwehr*

DRAMATIS PERSONAE

AT THE GERMAN EMBASSY IN MADRID

Dr Eberhard Baron von Stohrer	the Ambassador
Maria-Ursula	his wife, a voluptuous beauty
Dr Erich Gardemann	representing Ribbentrop's private intelligence service in Spain
Kriminalkommissar Paul Winzer	of the Gestapo, in charge of relations between the German and Spanish police

THE SPANIARDS

General Francisco Franco Bahamonde	the caudillo
Don Nicolás	his elder brother, Spanish Ambassador to Portugal
Don Ramón Serrano Suñer	General Franco's brother-in-law, the Interior Minister
Don Eduardo Rojas y Ordoñes, Conde de Montarco	Political Secretary to Don Ramón
Colonel Juan Beigbeder y Atienza	the Foreign Minister
Doña Sol, Condesa de Teba *the Infante Alfonso* }	old Spanish friends of the Duke of Windsor
Don Javier ('Tiger') Bermejillo	of the Spanish Foreign Ministry, another old friend of the Duke
Don Miguel Primo de Rivera, Marqués de Estella	Civil Governor of Madrid, yet another old friend of the Duke
Don Angel Alcázar de Velasco	Press Secretary to the Institute of Political Studies, an agent of the *Abwehr*

DRAMATIS PERSONAE

THE PORTUGUESE

Dr António Oliveira Salazar	Prime Minister and Foreign Minister, effective dictator of Portugal
Dr Luis Teixeira de Sampaio	Secretary-General of the Foreign Ministry, adviser to Dr Salazar
Captain Agostinho Lourenço	Chief of the Secret Police
Captain José Catela	his deputy, a double agent
Dr Zacarias Berenguel Vivas	of the Portuguese consular service
Dr Ricardo Espírito Santo Silva	a banker
Mary Cohen Espírito Santo Silva	his wife

Conde de Lancastre
Vizconde Soveral
Baron Almeida Santos
António Asseca   friends of the
Nuno Brito e Cunha   Espírito Santo Silvas
Tomás Pinto Basto
Alda Wright

Prologue:
The Mystery

Every schoolboy knows that 'something happened' involving the Duke of Windsor and the Germans in July 1940, when he and his Duchess were in Portugal waiting (or, according to some accounts, not waiting) for the ship that was to take them to the Bahamas. It is one of the great spy stories of the Second World War. It is of some historical importance; for Hitler's preoccupation with the Duke of Windsor was one of the factors which caused him to delay – fatally – in launching his attack on Great Britain that summer. Exactly what happened, however, is far from clear. Why were the Germans interested in the Duke – and how far (if at all) was he aware of their interest? How did they plot to bring him under their power – and how close (if at all) did those plots come to success? What long-term plans did they have for him – and to what extent (if at all) was he prepared to go along with such plans? So far there have been few clear answers to these questions from historians, only from novelists.* Nothing stimulates imagination like mystery.

This book – the product of more than four years' research, in the course of which seven countries were visited, dozens of witnesses interviewed, and numerous archives ransacked – is an attempt to break that mystery. I cannot claim to have succeeded entirely: a handful of pieces are still missing from the jigsaw puzzle, and may remain so. But I think I have put together enough of the picture to see it whole – and it is far more complex and extraordinary a picture than I had at first imagined. Moreover, my

---

* While I was writing this book, no less than four novels appeared giving a fictitious reconstruction of the episode. In *To Catch a King* by Harry Patterson (Hutchinson, 1979) – now an uproarious film for American cable television – the Duke of Windsor saves England by pretending to co-operate with the Nazis, obtaining a copy of their invasion plans, and sending it off to Winston Churchill. In *The Windsor Plot* by Pauline Glen Winslow (Arlington Books, 1981) the Duke in order to negotiate his return to the throne enters a German submarine, which sails off with him in it. *Axis* by Clive Irving (Atheneum, 1980) concerns the fictitious spy adventures in England of Walter Schellenberg, leading to his attempt to kidnap the Duke in Portugal, which, the author tells us, 'is part of history'. It is hard to make much sense of *Famous Last Words* by Timothy Findley (Delacorte Press, 1981), the phantasmagorical reminiscences of an unhinged American fascist who keeps bumping into the Duke and Duchess in unlikely situations in Spain, Portugal and the Bahamas.

1

research raised in an acute form certain problems regarding the interpretation of historical sources and the value of human testimony. Before the curtain goes up, therefore, something must be said about the nature of the quest.

The news that the Germans had tried to get their hands on the Duke of Windsor, and that he may have given unwitting encouragement to their plots, broke upon a fascinated world in July 1957* with the much-publicized appearance in London and Washington of Volume X of Series D of *Documents on German Foreign Policy*. This was the latest in a long series of Anglo–American official publications giving selections from captured German diplomatic papers, and it contained indifferent translations of some twenty extraordinary telegrams, many of them several pages long, concerning the Duke of Windsor's adventures in the Iberian Peninsula during the summer of 1940. The captured papers (which have now been returned to Bonn, where they may be freely consulted)† also contain twenty-eight other telegrams on the subject which have not hitherto been published, but which will be extensively quoted here. With a few exceptions, these telegrams, published and unpublished, come from the files of Ernst von Weizsäcker, the highly intelligent former naval officer who administered the German Foreign Office (*Auswärtiges Amt*) from 1938 to 1943 with the rank of State Secretary. The long efforts of the British Government to suppress them, and the curious circumstances of their eventual (partial) publication, will be discussed at the end of this book.‡

In order to understand the telegrams it is first necessary to grasp the movements of their principal subject at this period. In September 1939 the Duke of Windsor – who had abdicated and gone into exile two years and nine months before to marry the woman he loved – was attached with the rank of major-general to the British Military Mission in France, ostensibly as a liaison officer but in reality (as I have described elsewhere)§ to do secret intelligence work. On 10 May 1940 Northern France was successfully invaded by the Germans; and on 19 June the Duke – who was then in the South of France, which had just been unsuccessfully invaded by the

---

* The affair had already been mentioned in Erich Kordt's *Nicht aus den Akten* (1949), Geoffrey Bocca's *She Might Have Been Queen* (1955), *The Schellenberg Memoirs* (1956) and (fleetingly) in the Duchess of Windsor's own memoirs (1956). But it did not receive any great public attention until the 1957 publication.

† As they may also be on microfilm in the Library of the Foreign Office in London.

‡ In Appendix I.

§ *The Duke of Windsor's War* (London, 1982; New York, 1983), pp. 27–65.

Italians – fled to avoid capture to still-neutral (but increasingly pro-Axis) Spain along with his wife, two British Consuls and a number of servants and friends. They crossed the frontier on the 20th, arrived in Madrid on the 23rd (the Duke's forty-sixth birthday), and spent nine days in the Spanish capital before going on to Portugal, where they reached a house at Cascais near Lisbon on 3 July. The original idea was that the Duke should return to England; but this was not possible because of a bitter quarrel with his family, and on Thursday 4 July he was offered and accepted the post of Governor of the Bahamas. Four weeks later, on Thursday 1 August, he and the Duchess of Windsor sailed from Portugal to take up this appointment, in which they remained (with occasional visits to America) until May 1945. Significantly – or coincidentally? – 1 August was also the day Hitler finally issued his Directive No. 17, launching the air war against England.

The drama revealed by the telegrams opens with the Duke's arrival in Madrid, when the Spanish Foreign Minister Beigbeder (who is generally regarded as having been pro-British) asked the German Ambassador Stohrer whether his Government might be interested in getting in touch with the ex-King. Stohrer conveyed this to his chief, the German Foreign Minister Ribbentrop, who asked if the Duke might be kept in Spain for the time being – but without his suspecting that it was the Germans who wanted him to stay there. Beigbeder then suggested to the Duke that he might like to spend the rest of the war in retirement in the South of Spain as the guest of the Spanish Government. The Duke (according to the telegrams) expressed interest in this idea, but nevertheless went on to Portugal. However, while he was in Portugal Beigbeder continued to tempt him with the prospect of a Spanish retreat, first through an unidentified agent, later through the Spanish Ambassador in Lisbon (who happened to be General Franco's brother).

The next act opens in the second week of July, just after the public announcement of the Duke's governorship. Ribbentrop wrote to Stohrer that he wanted the Duke to be lured back to Spain from Portugal, but once again without his being made aware of German interest in him; he suggested, for example, that the Duke might be persuaded by Spanish friends to flee to Spain in order to escape from a mythical British assassination plot. Once in Spain, the Duke would be invited to collaborate with the Germans, who would offer to restore him to the throne. The Spanish Government would be asked to imprison him if he refused.

Stohrer took this matter to the Spanish Interior Minister, Serrano Suñer, who was General Franco's brother-in-law and is generally considered to have been very pro-German. Serrano Suñer agreed to co-operate, and sent out a Spanish emissary to see the Duke in Portugal with a view to drawing him back to Spain. This emissary is eventually identified as Don Miguel Primo de Rivera, who was the son of a former dictator of Spain and an old friend of the Duke of Windsor. Don Miguel returned with the news that the Duke was favourable to the idea of returning to Spain. A second Spanish emissary was then sent out, who is not identified. His task was to give the Duke a letter from Don Miguel stressing the urgency of his coming to Spain as soon as possible, and to suggest a plan whereby he might do so without the knowledge of the British and Portuguese authorities. However, this second emissary returned after a few days with the news that the Duke would not now be coming to Spain after all. On the other hand, he was prepared to play a part in possible future peace negotiations between England and Germany.

There was now only a day to go before the Duke's ship sailed, and the telegrams show that various last-minute efforts were made to keep him in Europe. Don Miguel went out again to plead with him, pressure was put on Salazar, the dictator of Portugal, to keep him there, and a number of frightening incidents were staged to persuade him that it would be dangerous for him to make the journey. Ribbentrop also arranged for the Duke to get a message informing him of German interest in him, of which he was supposed to be unaware till then. This message was delivered by Ricardo Espírito Santo, the Portuguese banker in whose house the Duke was living and who (the telegrams reveal) had been passing regular secret reports about his royal guest to the German Minister in Lisbon, Hoyningen-Huene. In spite of all this, the Duke and Duchess sailed as planned on 1 August. A few days earlier they had been joined by their old friend Sir Walter Monckton, who had been sent by the British Government to stress the need for prompt departure.

The German telegrams also report a number of conversations between the Duke and his Spanish and Portuguese friends, in which he expresses dissatisfaction with his lot and questions the wisdom of Great Britain's continuing to fight Germany against such apparent odds. It is evident that these reports, whether accurate or not, greatly encouraged the Germans in their designs. It is also suggested in the telegrams that the Duke responded quite kindly to the message of German interest which he received just before his departure, and that, although he insisted on sailing, he offered to be in touch at some future date.

Finally, the telegrams contain several highly conspiratorial reports sent in the last week of July 1940 by a thirty-year-old German secret agent called Walter Schellenberg, who had been sent out to the Peninsula for the purpose of bringing the plot to a successful conclusion. This man – whose name was unknown to the public until after the war – was then head of the counter-intelligence section known as *Amt IVE*, and was subsequently to become the last chief of the Nazi German secret service. His role in the affair is revealed by two other sources. First there are the memoirs which bear his name and which were published in London in 1956, four years after his death. In these memoirs – the authenticity and reliability of which have been questioned by some historians* – it is alleged that Schellenberg was ordered to abduct the Duke by force, but that he deliberately circumvented these orders. Secondly there is a log he kept during his mission, now among the papers of the former *Reichsicherheitshauptamt* at Koblenz, which lists his principal daily movements and encounters. In this valuable and hitherto unpublished document – reproduced here for the first time† – the Duke appears under the code-name of *Willi*.‡

This, then, is the basic German source material on the plot – the telegrams (published and unpublished) and the memoirs of Schellenberg (which it is now possible to test against his contemporary log). It is fascinating material, the published part of which has fired the imagination of numerous novelists and journalists and been quoted (though without critical analysis) in dozens of popular historical works.§ Among the annals of the Second World War, there is nothing to touch it for sheer conspiracy. At first glance it appears to give a tantalizingly complete picture, including as it does almost daily reports from the plotters on the spot in the Peninsula. But in fact the picture is anything but complete, and almost nothing can be taken at face value. There are a number of reasons why these sources must be regarded with the greatest caution and suspicion.

First of all there are some glaring inconsistencies. Schellenberg's memoirs (in which he claims to have been sceptical about the plot from

---

* A matter I have discussed in Appendix II.

† In Appendix III.

‡ He is also referred to as *Willi* in at least one of Schellenberg's telegraphic reports from Portugal. See below, pp. 179 and 187.

§ For typical treatments see W. L. Shirer, *The Rise and Fall of the Third Reich* (1960), pp. 785–92; James Graham-Murray, *The Sword and the Umbrella* (1964), pp. 124–44; and Frances Donaldson, *Edward VIII* (1974), pp. 358–77.

the first) do not tell the same story as his reports among the telegrams (in which he seems to have few doubts that the thing will come off). The telegrams themselves are full of unexplained mysteries. Why did Beigbeder, who was to be sacked a few weeks later as Spain's Foreign Minister for being too pro-British, seem so keen on feeding the ducal lamb to the German wolves? How was it that the Duke seemed all eagerness to flee to Spain at one moment, and would not hear of such a thing the next? If, as alleged, he had never wanted to leave Spain in the first place, why had he gone to Portugal at all? Why was Ribbentrop – who apparently believed the Duke to be sympathetic to Germany's cause – so insistent that he should not suspect German interest until he was actually in German hands? The telegrams raise but do not answer such questions.

Secondly, the very nature of the material is such as to cast grave doubts on its reliability. At the best of times, diplomatic documents are to be regarded with caution as historical sources, secret service reports even more so. When they are written by the agents of an ideological dictatorship for the eyes of the mandarins of that dictatorship, nothing in them can be taken for granted. The chances are that they will have been drafted with a view to putting their authors in the best possible light and telling the persons to whom they are addressed (who will probably be immersed in every kind of fantasy and paranoia) what they most want to hear. As Ernst von Weizsäcker, from whose files the telegrams come, wrote after the war:

> Historians ... if they use sources from the Third Reich, must remember that no-one could achieve anything in Germany at that time unless he made concessions to the prevailing style of expressing oneself. Officials and officers who had remained reasonable made their proposals or couched their arguments in terms suited to the person they were addressing; and the historian must beware of using such documents unless he has a thorough knowledge of the people to whom they were addressed and of the persons indirectly concerned. No-one who wanted to accomplish anything in Germany at that time wrote in order to appear later on as one who had uttered wise warnings; nor did he write to save his own soul. He wrote and spoke in competition with psychopaths and for psychopaths.[1]

As for post-war memoirs of the Nazi period such as those of Schellenberg, these must be treated with no less suspicion than the contemporary documents, for obvious reasons.

Finally, the German sources only relate the affair from the alleged points of view of three persons: Stohrer, the Ambassador in Madrid;

Hoyningen-Huene, the Minister in Lisbon; and Schellenberg. (True, all three received detailed instructions from Ribbentrop; but these instructions only reveal the most obvious things about Ribbentrop's attitude and intentions. They do not really give us his point of view. They do not answer the fundamental question of what exactly Ribbentrop meant to do with the Duke of Windsor – or if he knew himself.) Even if one were able to establish the accuracy of the statements contained in the telegrams, therefore, one would still only be able to see things through the eyes of the Germans in the Peninsula – and they were far from being the only individuals involved.

And so, having studied the basic German sources, I put them aside in order to devote the next stage of my research to investigating the affair from other angles. There were three viewpoints in particular which interested me to begin with: that of the British Government in London (and especially Winston Churchill); that of the *Auswärtiges Amt* in Berlin (and especially Ribbentrop); and that of the Portuguese authorities in Lisbon (and especially Lourenço, the secret police chief under whose protection the Duke was). In these quests I was fortunate in being able to profit from the advice and assistance of a great specialist in each field. Martin Gilbert helped me understand Churchill's reactions; David Irving added to my knowledge of Ribbentrop's attitude; and Professor Douglas Wheeler of the University of New Hampshire guided me to the main Portuguese sources. The help I received from these eminent scholars was particularly generous in that they themselves all happened to be writing works of Second World War history which were to deal (in the light of their respective interests) with the Duke of Windsor episode.* I am grateful to them, and also to two retired statesmen who were in Lisbon in July 1940 and gave me much inside information – Ambassador Alberto Franco Nogueira, the former Portuguese Foreign Minister who is now Salazar's official biographer, and Lord Eccles, who played a curious and important role in the affair and whose fascinating volume of wartime correspondence appeared in the middle of my research.† (I was less lucky in my search for Berlin witnesses, the last of whom seemed to have escaped me

---

* The sixth volume of Martin Gilbert's monumental biography of Winston Churchill appeared in London in July 1983 and contains a brilliant chapter on the affair as it affected the Prime Minister (pp. 698–709). David Irving's counterblast to this – which will doubtless live up to his usual high standards of controversy – is eagerly awaited, as is Professor Wheeler's book on wartime secret service operations in Portugal.

† *By Safe Hand* (London, 1983).

by the narrowest of margins;* the nearest I got to a German who had been in the know at the time was Reinhard Spitzy, who had heard about the affair from a brother-in-law at the German Legation in Lisbon.)

Above all, however, I had to try to see things from the point of view of the man who was at the centre of the web – the Duke of Windsor himself. That, in a sense, was the main purpose of my study. And it was here that the greatest difficulty lay. His motives and reactions were shrouded in mystery. Secretive by nature, he had never published his own version of the episode; to the great revelations of 1957 he had replied with no more than a brief press statement. Such clues as existed as to his state of mind at the time only seemed to point to a tumult of conflicting emotions; the only decisive impression that emerged was one of constant and painful indecision. One knew one was dealing with a tortured soul (whose inner conflicts might be interpreted as noble passion or dangerous wavering depending on one's point of view); but one knew little more. The Duke's own papers, however, were likely to shed some light on the matter; and in April 1980 – by which time it was my happy fate to have become assistant to Maître Suzanne Blum, the Duchess of Windsor's lawyer, guardian and friend – I found myself entrusted with a large buff file headed *Governor's Office Bahamas* and labelled *Germans 1940*. I took a long deep breath before opening it.

At first glance, the contents of this *dossier* seemed slightly disappointing. It did, however, contain one amazing item of contemporary evidence – the letter (much referred to in the telegrams) which Miguel Primo de Rivera had sent the Duke (by hand of the mysterious second emissary) urging him to flee to Spain for his life and suggesting a cunning plan whereby he might do so. This document† – which reads like a page from an 1890s' boy's adventure story – carried no suggestion that the Duke was aware of German designs upon him. Otherwise the file contained his correspondence in the summer of 1940 with his London solicitor George Allen, which gave certain important indications as to his intentions and his mood; and a large correspondence with various people in the 1950s on the subject of the German telegrams, from which it appeared that the Duke's reaction on first reading them was one of total astonishment. He had been shown translations of them at 10 Downing Street in

---

* The witnesses – young in 1940 – who I hoped might still be alive to help me were Erich Gardemann (died 1981), Fritz Hesse (died 1980) and Erich Kordt (died 1969).

† Reproduced below, pp. 168–9.

1953 in the form of a confidential paper printed for the British Cabinet; this too was in the file, and in the margin the Duke (rather in the manner of a schoolmaster marking an essay) had ticked off each telegram in pencil and jotted such remarks as 'yes', 'no', 'correct' and 'very interesting'.

Apart from this, I was able to see a number of interesting mementoes in the possession of the Duchess of Windsor, including photographs, the passenger list of the ship on which they sailed, some important letters the Duchess had written at the time to her Aunt Bessie in Washington, and – a valuable and unexpected source – a visitors' book bound in scarlet morocco, begun at Fort Belvedere in January 1935, which, having been taken subsequently by the Duke to wherever he happened to be living, had been signed (with dates) by all of the people who had stayed with him at Cascais in 1940. In addition to this material, file FO 371/24249 at the Public Record Office at Kew – which was declassified in 1972, possibly by accident* – contains a heated telegraphic correspondence between the Duke in Lisbon and the Government in London concerning the arrangements for the Bahamas governorship. Further correspondence with or concerning the Duke at that period is to be found in the papers of Lord Halifax, Lord Monckton, Lord Templewood and Sir Walford Selby†. All this stuff, though interesting, fails to complete a picture which remains in many respects mysterious; on the other hand, it does provide a large number of definite clues. In the text of this book I shall quote extensively from this material in a manner which will, I hope, allow the reader to form his own judgment as to the Duke's conduct and outlook. I shall offer my own interpretation in the Epilogue.

Having made this lengthy excursion, I returned to the basic German material. After studying a subject for some time one acquires a certain sixth sense with regard to it; and re-reading the telegrams in the light of my intermediate researches I had an almost overpowering feeling that there was something fundamentally wrong with many of them, that (quite apart from obvious errors and inconsistencies which one could put one's finger on) they were not telling the truth. I had gone round the telegrams, studied their subject-matter from other aspects. Now I

---

* The material concerning the Duke of Windsor begins with the following extraordinary unsigned handwritten minute dated 1963: 'The attached folder came to light when I was clearing through ancient folders we keep of reference pages. I really do not think American Department is the right place for what appear to be the originals of the telegrams on the appointment of the Duke of Windsor to the Bahamas during the war. Should it not now go into the archives?' (Folio 147)

† Details of these and other archives used are given below, pp. 244–5.

DATE OF ARRIVAL	NAME	DATE OF DEPARTURE	
1940	**BOCCA DO INFERNO** **CASCAES**	*1940*	
July 3rd	*RoaWood*	August	1st
" "	*[signature]*	July	14th
" "	*E. frayMd Phillips*	July	5th
July 8th	*Javier Bermejillo*	July	13th
July 20th	*Ricardo R. de Espiritoauto Silva*	July	21st

DATE OF ARRIVAL	NAME	DATE OF DEPARTURE	
1940		*1940*	
July 21st	*[signature]* *F. Willi*	August	1st
July 27th		July	28th
July 28th	*Walter Monckton.*	August	1st
" "	*E. frayke Phillips*	"	"

The Duke's house guests, July 1940

should have to go behind them, in an attempt to reconstruct the tale they told from other sources. This would involve an intensive study of the protagonists of that tale – that is, of the plotters in the Peninsula. I should have to seek out their surviving friends, relations and papers, establish their histories, learn all I could about their ideas and personalities and what made them tick. In one area of investigation I could not delay too long: I gradually discovered that, apart from the Duchess of Windsor (who, alas, was no longer in a position to answer questions), four persons mentioned in the telegrams (as well as the widow of their principal author) were still living forty-two years after the event.

My first task was to sort out the characters into some kind of order. I quickly decided not to bother too much with Schellenberg. He only came into the affair towards the end, and I already had ample material on his role in the form of his reports, his log and the memoirs (concerning the value of which I had by now reached my own conclusions). That left eight or possibly nine conspirators, whom I divided into four groups. First of all, in Lisbon, there were the German Minister Hoyningen-Huene and the Duke's host Espírito Santo. These two were friends, and Espírito Santo had formed a kind of hidden link between the diplomat and the ex-King, first passing secret reports on the Duke to Hoyningen-Huene, finally passing a cryptic message from Hoyningen-Huene to the Duke. Secondly there were the Spanish Foreign Minister Beigbeder and his Ambassador in Lisbon, Nicolás Franco. Beigbeder it was who had originally suggested to the Germans that they get hold of the Duke; he and Don Nicolás had pressed the Duke to plant himself in Spain, as apparently had an unidentified agent whom Beigbeder had sent to Portugal. Next came Serrano Suñer, the Spanish Interior Minister, and Stohrer, the German Ambassador. Their conclave in Madrid was the crucible of the plot in the Peninsula: Stohrer was the author of most of the telegrams, and it was at his request that Serrano Suñer had sent out the two Spanish emissaries to get the Duke to return. Finally there were the emissaries themselves – Don Miguel Primo de Rivera (whom the Duke knew well) and then the second emissary (as to whose identity there were few clues).

Approaching my first category, I found myself having to rely on fairly distant evidence. Oswald Baron von Hoyningen-Huene died at Estoril in 1956, and a conspiracy of silence seems to surround him. An exceedingly reticent man who rarely, after 1945, spoke of his years in diplomacy, he left few papers,* no memoirs or descendants, and a vague reputation (for which it is hard to find solid evidence) of having been involved in the German 'resistance circle'. His friend Ricardo Espírito Santo Silva predeceased him by two years, leaving four daughters, who were most kind to me when I visited Portugal three decades later.† They shared with me their schoolgirl memories of the Duke and Duchess; they allowed me to roam through the house at Cascais where the Duke and Duchess had stayed (then being converted into flats); and through their wonderful friend Dona Joana Carvalho Meyer I was able to meet quite a number of Portuguese who had enjoyed the ducal company in 1940. But I was informed that the few surviving papers of Ricardo (which were in storage pending the conversion of the house) contained no serious correspondence with the Duke, just a few *recordações*. Anything of consequence would have been destroyed either by Ricardo's widow after his death, or in 1974, when the Banco Espírito Santo was about to be seized by the revolutionary state and its directors thrown in prison.

Turning to the second group, it seemed that there too I would have little archival success. Colonel Juan Beigbeder y Atienza died in 1957, then in disgrace with the regime, and his family know of no private records of his year as Spain's Foreign Minister. As for Don Nicolás Franco, I soon realized that it was futile searching for detailed private information about the activities of that particular family.‡ My great good friend Don Rafael Blázquez Godoy of the Spanish Ministry of Culture, however, spent a considerable amount of time going through the diplomatic records for the period in the Palacio de Santa Cruz – and made a shocking discovery. No archives of real political importance exist for 1940. Everything has disappeared. Only the dregs remain. However, Don Rafael carried on his search with great diligence and went on to look at the archives for 1941 – and there, lo and behold, he discovered a file relating to the distant aftermath of the Duke of Windsor affair,§ which

* They are among the *Nachlasse* at the *Auswärtiges Amt*, and contain nothing about the Duke of Windsor.

† I am grateful to Maria Salgado (and especially her daughter Mary), Vera Ricciardi, Anne-Marie Bustorffe and Rita Leite Faria.

‡ It was only when this book was about to go to press that I learnt of the existence of Ramón Garriga's biography *Nicolás Franco: el hermano brujo* (Madrid, 1980). This work, however, is based on scurrilous gossip and adds nothing.

§ Don Rafael examined all the correspondence between Madrid and the Spanish Embassies in Berlin, Lisbon, London, Paris/Vichy and Rome; the files concerning relations with those capitals; the communications between the Foreign Ministry and other departments; and the papers of Don Juan de las Bárcenas, the permanent head of the Ministry. The papers he discovered consisted of an exchange of suggested that there had indeed been a voluminous correspondence about that affair at the time. All such correspondence, however, has vanished – whether into the bonfires or into some secret repository one can but guess.

But there was a consolation. The Duke's visitors book enabled me to identify the unnamed agent of Beigbeder mentioned in the telegrams,* who had gone out to see the Duke in Portugal ostensibly to repeat the offer of Spanish hospitality. This was Don Javier Bermejillo, a jovial Spanish diplomat who had been an admirer of the Duchess (then Mrs Ernest Simpson) in London in the early 1930s. He had died in 1953, and I discovered that his papers – including a substantial amount of correspondence with the Duke and Duchess in the summer of 1940 – had passed to his nephew, Señor Chapa. Señor Chapa allowed me to see this very interesting material, from which it was clear that Bermejillo's mission had not really been concerned with the Duke's return to Spain at all. Rather it was to do with a domestic affair which presupposed that the Duke and Duchess would *not* be going to Spain – namely their efforts to recover their household possessions from France for shipment to the Bahamas. This seemed absurd and trivial; but it quickly became apparent that the Bermejillo correspondence shed light on a curious sub-plot touched upon in the telegrams. In fact, the telegrams and the correspondence together pointed to the bizarre conclusion that, though the German authorities may not have succeeded in getting hold of the Duke and Duchess that summer, they had nevertheless managed to kidnap the Duchess's French maid, Mademoiselle Moulichon. A few enquiries through Georges Sanègre, the Duchess's major-domo, revealed that Mademoiselle Moulichon had survived this experience and was alive and well in her eighty-fourth year in a *chambre de service* in the *seizième arrondissement*, where I visited her in August 1983. Her lively account of her ordeal provided a fantastic counterpoint to the main drama.

The Bermejillo Papers, dealing as they did with something of a side issue, provided clear documentary evidence that the telegrams were not all they seemed. Meanwhile I had received devastating oral evidence to

---

notes verbales between the British Embassy and the Ministry in April–May 1941 resulting in correspondence between the Ministry and the Spanish Embassy in Paris, all filed under the reference GB 20/61. This concerned the fate of certain funds which the Duchess, through Spanish offices, had sent to Paris the previous summer.

* Not to be confused with the equally unnamed second emissary of Serrano Suñer, as to whom see below p. 17.

the same effect from Don Ramón Serrano Suñer. For Serrano Suñer – who had been described by the British Ambassador in October 1940 as unlikely to live very long,[2] and had fallen from office and into political oblivion two years later – was still very much alive. Through two kind friends, Lady Mosley and the Countess of Romanones, I was able to get in touch with him, and to interview him in Marbella in December 1982 and again in Madrid in May 1983 with the help of Professor C.S.Jackson. (In my Spanish investigations, Christopher Jackson – a bilingual Anglo–Chilean philosopher and sometime British intelligence officer who might well have been the model for Professor Cosmo Saltana in J.B.Priestley's *The Image Men* – was both a dream research assistant and a ceaselessly entertaining guide, philosopher and friend.) Looking very beautiful with his silvery-grey hair, humorous blue eyes and fine gestures, Don Ramón received us most cordially. At eighty-one he was not only entirely lucid but the best sort of historical witness, whose concern for truth and accuracy was equalled only by his awareness of the frailty of human memory.

Serrano Suñer's account was almost entirely at variance with that of the telegrams. To be sure, he had a clear memory of Stohrer (whom he regarded as a friend) coming to tell him that Ribbentrop wanted the Duke brought back to Spain. He also clearly remembered that, in consequence of that interview, he had sent Don Miguel (whom he regarded as a fool) out to the Duke. But those were virtually the only points on which the two accounts agreed. As to what Miguel had reported when he returned from his mission, for example, they differed substantially. What was most interesting, however, was Don Ramón's recollection of the attitude which both he and the Ambassador had taken towards the whole affair. The telegrams show them busily conspiring away together in Ribbentrop's interest, leaving no stone unturned in their zealous efforts to bring a masterly scheme to a triumphant conclusion. But Don Ramón now claimed that both of them had in fact regarded that scheme as mad, puerile and utterly ill-conceived, and that they had gone along with it only to keep Ribbentrop happy and so distract his attention from *another* plot which worried them far more – that of dragging Spain, in her exhausted and impoverished state, into a protracted war. The whole intrigue surrounding the Duke in the Peninsula, Don Ramón seemed to suggest, was really a hollow charade, spun out in order to buy time for Spain.

If this were indeed the case, it would put an entirely new complexion on the telegrams. Could it be that they were no more than a long series of fabrications, designed to dupe Ribbentrop into thinking that all was going according to plan? So enormous were the implications of Serrano Suñer's allegation that I had to find corroborative evidence. The telegrams themselves seemed to provide evidence of a kind: on 2 August 1940, having just learned that the Duke had sailed from Europe and the plot had failed, Ribbentrop wrote to Stohrer: *'What we now want to achieve is Spain's early entry into the war.'*[*3] So if Serrano Suñer and Stohrer had indeed reckoned that the conspiracy, while it lasted, would delay this dreaded instruction, they appear to have been right. But why would the Ambassador have been so keen to frustrate the will of his master? Why would he have acted with Spanish interests in mind rather than the policy of his own Government? It was to Stohrer that I now had to turn.

Dr Eberhard von Stohrer (known socially as the Baron von Stohrer) left Madrid (and the German diplomatic service) in 1943, and died in Germany ten years later. The volumes of the *Genealogisches Handbuch des Adels* directed me to his son Berthold in Rome, who was most helpful and informative and whose own knowledge of the affair corroborated the story of Serrano Suñer.

> I remember my father talking to me about this attempt [he wrote to me in June 1983], which he considered quite unrealistic and an expression of the total misconception that the Wilhelmstrasse had formed of the Duke and leading English personalities in general .... Don Ramón Serrano Suñer and my father agreed that the objective of the German Government to get Spain to join the Axis in the war was totally misconceived and to be avoided in the interests of both Spain and Germany.

Berthold also sent me a note of his father's about the affair from an unfinished work of memoirs, which (though brief and factual) tended to suggest that the Ambassador had not thought much of the plot at the time;[†] and he arranged for me to spend a very pleasant few days with his mother on the *Isola d'Ischia* in March 1984, shortly before this book went

---

* My italics.

† The note read as follows:

Duke of Windsor affair. Ribbentrop wanted the recently abdicated King Edward VIII, who came to Spain on his way to Portugal, to be induced to remain in Spain, for Ribbentrop evidently believed that he could play the Duke off against the new King and the existing British Government. The Spanish Government offered to accommodate the Duke, all assistance, asylum, etc. Nevertheless he went on to Estoril near Lisbon. Berlin sent the SS man who had distinguished himself in the kidnapping on the Dutch border. He flew to Lisbon to try and keep W there. Futile: after some hesitation W proceeded to America and thence to the Bahamas.

to press. Still beautiful and fascinating in her eighty-third year, Maria-Ursula von Stohrer had been her husband's confidante in his diplomatic career; her memories were understandably vague, but she recalled that he had regarded the plan to 'capture' the Duke of Windsor as 'idiotic', as had Don Ramón (whom she had not seen since the war), and that they had 'just pretended' to carry out the plan, 'like two schoolboys'.

All this was very interesting; the pieces in the Spanish part of the puzzle were beginning to fit. But what was even more interesting was the history and personality of Stohrer himself. Remarkably little had been written about this man who had occupied one of the key diplomatic posts of his time – and most of it tended to portray him as a mere cypher of the régime he served.* But Berthold von Stohrer sent me a copy of the judgment of the Denazification Court at Freiburg which had tried (and exonerated) his father in 1949 – an extraordinary encomium.† It credited him with having been an active (though necessarily clandestine) opponent of Nazism; with having carried out a long and cunning resistance to Ribbentrop's policies; with having saved Spain from German occupation; and with having spent the last year of the war in Switzerland as a refugee from the Gestapo. This picture amply explained why the Ambassador would have sought to hoodwink Ribbentrop over the Duke of Windsor episode; and it was confirmed by my Spanish friends. From them I also learned that the Baroness von Stohrer had been a kind of Mata Hari, using her not inconsiderable charms to smuggle people out of Occupied Europe and protect her husband from exposure as an enemy of Nazism; and that she had been a friend of Miguel Primo de Rivera – though she now appeared to have forgotten all about his mission to the Duke in Portugal, if she had ever been aware of it.

Having become a Duke and served for several years as Spanish Ambassador to London,‡ Don Miguel Primo de Rivera died in 1964. Serrano Suñer had spoken of him as a frivolous and irresponsible character, a judgment confirmed by his best friends, so it came as little surprise that his private papers (which his nephew, the present Duque de Primo de Rivera, kindly allowed Rafael Blázquez to search on my behalf) had

---

* See for example Viscount Templewood, *Ambassador on Special Mission* (London, 1946), pp. 44–5; and Frances Donaldson, *Edward VIII* (1974), where she describes Stohrer (pp. 362–3) as 'an orthodox Nazi'.

† Reproduced in Appendix V.

‡ Don Miguel was recalled from this post late in 1957, only a few weeks after the telegrams had been published which spoke of his relations in 1940 with the former King of England.

nothing to say about the episode. However, it turned out that he had spoken of it at the time to his close friend the Conde de Montarco, who was (and is) the owner of the Spanish castle near the Portuguese frontier to which, had the German plan succeeded, the Duke and Duchess were to have been brought. The Conde is now a great traveller in the Far East and elsewhere and not easy to pin down; when, however, I finally saw him in Madrid, he proved to be very jolly and helpful indeed. From what he said, two things were apparent. The first was that Don Miguel had been far from unaware of German plans for the Duke. The second was that he had a plan of his own which did not necessarily coincide with what the Germans (or, for that matter, Stohrer and Serrano Suñer) had in mind.

There remained the other emissary whose mission had followed that of Don Miguel. He was a key figure, for his in effect had been the task of actually bringing the Duke back to Spain. But who was he? For over a year I searched for him in vain, until the problem of his identity came to haunt and obsess me. Serrano Suñer, who had sent him to Portugal in the first place, had forgotten everything about him; nor could the Conde de Montarco think who he might have been. Yet there could be no doubting his existence, for I possessed the letter he had taken out to the Duke, and his doings were described in eleven of the telegrams as well as in Schellenberg's log. These sources provided few clues, however, revealing only that he had been a 'very astute' Spaniard, unknown to the Duke but well-known to Don Ramón and Don Miguel and possibly known also to Schellenberg, one of whose names may have begun with the letter V.* I followed many false trails; and it was not until September 1983 that I learned, lunching with Nigel West at the Gay Hussar, of a Spanish *Abwehr* agent who had carried out an extraordinary operation in England in the autumn and winter of 1940–41 and rejoiced in the name of Angel Alcázar de Velasco. What had he been doing before that? Could this possibly be the man? That evening I raised the subject on the telephone with the Conde de Montarco, who told me that Alcázar de Velasco – who happened to be an old friend of his (as he had also been of Don Miguel) – was still flourishing in Madrid. The Conde could not recall his having been involved in the episode, but agreed to ask him if he knew anything about it. An hour later he rang me back in some excitement. '*C'est lui le second émissaire!*' he cried. '*Venez! C'est lui!*'

And so I set out once more with Christopher Jackson for Madrid. It

* For in Schellenberg's log he was code-named *Viktor*.

being the first week-end in October, the city was packed with *provin-cianos*, and it was only with difficulty (and the help of our friend Enrique Rivero) that we managed to find a hotel, from where we telephoned our quarry. We were mysteriously instructed to appear at the cafeteria on the fifth floor of the *Galerias Preciados* (a well-known department store off the Puerta del Sol) on the following (Saturday) morning at eleven o'clock, and to bring a tape recorder. We would recognize him by his white hair. Arriving at our assignation we indeed had little difficulty in recognizing him: with his searching blue eyes, mephistophelean features, and hair in the manner of the later Franz Liszt, the erstwhile wartime head of the Germans' London network was nothing if not striking. The subtlety of the venue he had chosen was at once apparent: it was evidently one of the few places in the capital where so exotic a figure could escape attention. Having greeted us cordially, he asked us to make sure the tape recorder was switched on, and then (competing for the recorder's attention with a generalized banging of forks and plates) launched out on his startling tale.

So extraordinary were some of Don Angel's assertions that I have thought it best simply to reproduce the text of this interview in the ninth chapter of this book, for the reader to make of it what he will. His most sensational allegation – upon which he insisted with some vehemence – was that both he and Don Miguel had been involved in a conspiracy to bring down the Franco régime, and that they had seen the Duke of Windsor affair (for various complex and peculiar reasons) as a means towards achieving their end. Was this possible? I came away with the feeling that it was entirely possible that Don Angel – a born conspirator – had seen things this way; and I was left with few doubts that he had indeed been the second emissary.

Later, over a lunch of paella and roast suckling pig, Don Angel spoke of some of his other secret service exploits. He proudly displayed the British press cuttings of his great London days, when he had posed with undeniable success as an anglophile Spanish diplomat. He told us how he had seen Hitler during the last days in the bunker, how he had accompanied Martin Bormann to South America in a submarine. Dropping his voice, he informed us that the world was being taken over by an international conspiracy of Jews and Freemasons. The Israeli secret service, he said, was the best in the world, and had infiltrated all other services except the French. He, Don Angel, had fought all his life to prevent such a thing happening, but his philosophy was now 'If you can't beat 'em, join 'em', and he was prepared to put his services at the disposal of *el gran Kaal judío*. To my great delight, he also claimed to have recognized Christopher Jackson as an obvious member of the British Intelligence Service!

My encounter with Alcázar de Velasco highlighted something which was already becoming clear from my research – the extraordinary variety and confusion of motive that existed among the conspirators. There now seemed to be a plot within a plot within a plot. Ribbentrop wanted to use the Duke to realize his designs with regard to England; his agents, Serrano Suñer and Stohrer, were impelled by the desire to save Spain from being sucked into the war; and their agents, Don Miguel and Don Angel, sought (or so it now appeared) to turn the whole affair to very particular purposes of their own. The subject was like a nesting doll; there was no telling what additional complexities, what further layers of meaning, might not be revealed in time. Research might have continued indefinitely – but anxious publishers in various capitals were clamouring for their book, and I had to call a halt to my investigations.

While I believe that I have succeeded in uncovering most of the tapestry, I have no doubt that surprises still lie in store. Important sources remain untapped. There are other files of the Duke of Windsor which, under exceedingly curious circumstances, found their way from Paris to Windsor Castle immediately after his death. There is the huge reservoir of wartime German papers (many of them in America) which I have hardly begun to search. There are the files of the Portuguese secret police in Caxias Fortress, which began to be released to historians after the Revolution but were then (after many of them had vanished) locked up again. There are the missing Spanish archives, which may turn up some time in a strange place; and there are General Franco's and Dr Salazar's papers, which may one day be made public. And who can tell what unsuspected witnesses may yet appear, what new material may yet emerge from archival hibernation? The appearance of the first edition of this work in no way indicates that my own interest in the matter is at an end; and I earnestly invite all who possess any direct or indirect information about the affair to write to me care of my publishers.

The last word, therefore, may still be to come. But I hope this tale may meanwhile be enjoyed not just as a piece of historical detective work but as a cracking good adventure story. In fact, is one not conscious of a faintly familiar flavour, harking back to a rather earlier period? Feuding royal brothers ... scheming German barons ... an abduction ... a hunting trip ... an Englishman caught up in a perilous European destiny

... a castle waiting on a plain .... One ends up asking the following question of Eberhard Baron von Stohrer and Oswald Baron von Hoyningen-Huene, of Don Miguel Primo de Rivera and Don Angel Alcázar de Velasco, of Ramón Serrano Suñer and Ricardo Espírito Santo, of Joachim von Ribbentrop and *Brigadeführer* Walter Schellenberg: had they read *The Prisoner of Zenda*?

1
The Duke and the Germans
June 1940

Bound for the Spanish frontier, the little convoy set out from Antibes around noon. It consisted of four vehicles, containing four dogs and twelve human beings. In front came a Bentley with diplomatic number plates; seated in the back were Major Dodds, H.M. Consul-General at Nice, and his Vice-Consul at Menton, Mr Dean. This was followed by a Buick bearing the Duke and Duchess of Windsor, their comptroller Major Phillips, and their three Cairn terriers; at the wheel was their driver Ladbrook. Next came a Citroën, towing a trailer of luggage and driven by its owner Captain Wood; with him were his wife, her maid and a Sealyham terrier. Bringing up the rear was a hired van containing the luggage of the Duke and Duchess; beside the driver sat the Duchess's maid, Mademoiselle Moulichon.[1]

It was 19 June 1940; and chaos reigned in France. Forty days earlier the long-waited German attack had come – in a brilliant and unexpected form. While the main Allied armies were racing into Belgium to meet what appeared to be the main German advance, Guderian's Panzer divisions had burst through the Ardennes to encircle them in a deadly trap. The 'miracle of Dunkirk' had taken place in the first days of June, followed by a heroic but futile effort to hold the Germans on the Somme and the Aisne. Paris had been abandoned on the 10th – and since then half of France had fallen to the victorious Wehrmacht. The German vanguard had crossed the Loire and was racing towards Bordeaux, where the last government of the Third Republic maintained an increasingly tenuous hold over rapidly diminishing territory and rapidly dissolving armies.

Presided over by the ancient but respected figure of Marshal Pétain, that government had come to power three days before with the avowed intention of making peace with the Germans. On the 17th Pétain had broadcast that 'the fighting must cease'. It was a disastrous statement to make in advance of negotiations, but it was what most Frenchmen wanted to hear. By contrast, General de Gaulle's appeal from London went virtually unnoticed. Meanwhile, Winston Churchill, in a succession of parliamentary speeches, was proclaiming Great Britain's determination to fight on. Once France had left the war, therefore, an alternative of capture by the Germans or internment by the French would await any British troops remaining on French soil. A great evacuation, a miniature Dunkirk, was already underway, as a flotilla of unlikely vessels attempted to ship His Majesty's subjects and His Majesty's forces back to England from the Mediterranean and Biscayan ports. But what of His Majesty's brother?

Since September 1939, the Duke of Windsor had been attached with the rank of major-general to the British Military Mission at French General Headquarters. He had remained with his Mission near Paris until 28 May 1940, when he had been transferred at his own request to an attachment with the *Armée des Alpes* on the Italian frontier. There he had installed himself with his wife at La Cröe, their rented villa at Cap d'Antibes; and there he had been when Italy declared war on France in the second week of June. The Italian invasion had been repulsed; but with the Germans racing down the Rhône Valley, and the French seeking a separate peace, both his friends and the local British consular authorities urged him to get out without delay. For a day or two he dithered, hoping to receive some instructions from London concerning his safety and future; but none came, and so it was that, around noon on 19 June (at roughly the same moment, as it happened, that the French armistice delegates were making contact with the Germans), the Duke and Duchess of Windsor set out in the motor convoy bound for the Spanish frontier.

Whether or not the party would get through was a decided gamble. Roads were choked with troops and refugees and frequently impassable. Even if they reached the frontier, they had no visas; and even if they crossed it, there was a risk that the Duke and Phillips would be interned as serving Allied officers on neutral soil. For that matter, it was not entirely clear whether Spain was still neutral; only the previous week Franco had claimed to alter his country's status to one of 'non-belligerency', and it was widely believed that this presaged Spanish entry into the war on the Axis side.

As it happened, they encountered little trouble on their journey across southern France. Following an inland route, they reached Arles by nightfall and set out again at first light the following morning. Barricades manned by veterans blocked the way at various points; but the Duke, correctly assuming he would be remembered from the First World War, managed to get through each time by announcing: '*Je suis le Prince de Galles. Laissez-moi passer, s'il vous plaît.*' At Perpignan near the Spanish border the Spanish Consul at first refused to grant the party visas on the grounds that they would be 'a charge on the Spanish Government'; but after 'much persuasion' – and telegraphic appeals by the Duke to the Spanish Ambassador at Bordeaux and the British Ambassador to Madrid, both of whom happened to be friends of his – transit papers were finally issued to everyone except the driver of the luggage van (which returned to Antibes with its cargo, to be the subject of future adventures), and they crossed into Spain a little after six o'clock. By midnight they had reached the comparative safety and comfort of a hotel at Barcelona.[2]

The following morning – 21 June – the Duke went to the British Consulate-General in Barcelona and sent the following telegram to the Foreign Office for the attention of the Prime Minister:

> Having received no instructions have arrived in Spain to avoid capture. Proceeding to Madrid. Edward[3]

That day the party rested at Barcelona, where they were joined by Don Javier ('Tiger') Bermejillo, a jovial Spanish diplomat who had been a friend of the Duke and Duchess in London in the early 1930s and had been given permission by his Ministry to act as their unofficial aide-de-camp in Spain. There was one unsettling incident. A party of Spanish journalists came to the hotel, to ask if the Duke would comment on extraordinary press stories concerning him which had appeared that morning in the Madrid paper *Arriba* and the Rome paper *Messagero* – that he was preparing to negotiate an Anglo–German peace, that British troops in France had mutinied and demanded his restoration, that Churchill had threatened to imprison him if he returned to England. The Duke was furious and refused to receive them; it was left to Phillips to deny and ridicule the stories.[4] On 22 June the party left Barcelona for the Spanish capital. Thunderstorms and floods forced them to spend the night at Saragossa; they resumed their journey on the 23rd – midsummer day, which also happened to be the Duke's forty-sixth birthday.

That afternoon the German Ambassador in Madrid, Dr von Stohrer, sent the following telegram to his chief, the German Foreign Minister Ribbentrop:

The Spanish Foreign Minister requests advice with regard to the treatment of the Duke and Duchess of Windsor, who are due to arrive in Madrid today, apparently in order to return to England by way of Lisbon. The Foreign Minister gathers from certain impressions which General Vigón received in Germany that we might perhaps be interested in detaining the Duke of Windsor here and eventually establishing contact with him.

Please telegraph instructions.[5]

The telegram reached Ribbentrop at 9.40 that evening at his field headquarters in the Westwall. We have one eye-witness report of how he reacted to it – that of Erich Kordt, his young *chef-de-cabinet*.* According to Kordt's memoirs (they are self-serving and not wholly reliable, but there is no reason to doubt them on this point) the Nazi *Reichsaussenminister* was 'electrified' by the idea of getting hold of the Duke of Windsor in Spain. 'We must get hold of him!' he cried. 'We must get Franco to detain him!'[6] The next day he sent the following answer to Stohrer, marked 'urgent':

Is it possible to detain the Duke and Duchess in Spain for a couple of weeks to begin with before they are granted an exit visa? It would be necessary to ensure at all events that it did not appear in any way that the suggestion came from Germany. Please telegraph reply.[7]

Edward Albert Christian George Andrew Patrick David, future Prince of Wales, King Edward VIII and Duke of Windsor, was born at Richmond on 23 June 1894. He was brought up in a house on his grandfather's estate in Norfolk by tutors and governesses, under the gaze of an old-fashioned martinet of a father and a discerning (though exceedingly undemonstrative) mother. Like his father, he was to be trained for the navy; at the age of twelve-and-a-half he became a cadet at Dartmouth. There he was treated like any other boy and learned the virtues of social equality. But when he was fifteen an event occurred which set him apart from his fellows. His grandfather, King Edward VII, died, and his parents became King George V and Queen Mary. At seventeen he was invested as Prince of Wales at Caernarvon, by which time he had become very democratic: his main thought during the ceremony was of what his friends would think of him 'in this preposterous rig'.[8]

The Prince's childhood had been typically English; but his ancestral

* In his memoirs, Erich Kordt (1905–69) claimed to have plotted against Ribbentrop, whom he portrayed as a mad buffoon. He was sacked at the end of 1940 and later became the 'father' of the West German diplomatic service.

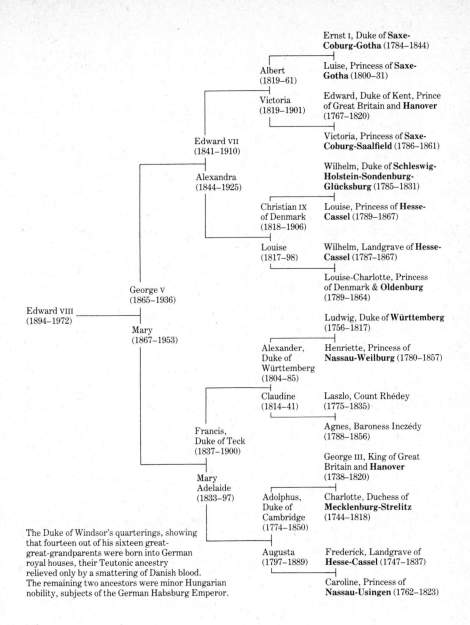

Ernst I, Duke of **Saxe-Coburg-Gotha** (1784–1844)

Luise, Princess of **Saxe-Gotha** (1800–31)

Albert (1819–61)

Edward, Duke of Kent, Prince of Great Britain and **Hanover** (1767–1820)

Victoria (1819–1901)

Victoria, Princess of **Saxe-Coburg-Saalfield** (1786–1861)

Edward VII (1841–1910)

Wilhelm, Duke of **Schleswig-Holstein-Sondenburg-Glücksburg** (1785–1831)

Alexandra (1844–1925)

Louise, Princess of **Hesse-Cassel** (1789–1867)

Christian IX of Denmark (1818–1906)

Wilhelm, Landgrave of **Hesse-Cassel** (1787–1867)

Louise (1817–98)

Louise-Charlotte, Princess of Denmark & **Oldenburg** (1789–1864)

George V (1865–1936)

Ludwig, Duke of **Württemberg** (1756–1817)

Edward VIII (1894–1972)

Mary (1867–1953)

Alexander, Duke of Württemberg (1804–85)

Henriette, Princess of **Nassau-Weilburg** (1780–1857)

Claudine (1814–41)

Laszlo, Count Rhédey (1775–1835)

Agnes, Baroness Inczédy (1788–1856)

Francis, Duke of Teck (1837–1900)

George III, King of Great Britain and **Hanover** (1738–1820)

Mary Adelaide (1833–97)

Adolphus, Duke of Cambridge (1774–1850)

Charlotte, Duchess of **Mecklenburg-Strelitz** (1744–1818)

Augusta (1797–1889)

Frederick, Landgrave of **Hesse-Cassel** (1747–1837)

Caroline, Princess of **Nassau-Usingen** (1762–1823)

The Duke of Windsor's quarterings, showing that fourteen out of his sixteen great-great-grandparents were born into German royal houses, their Teutonic ancestry relieved only by a smattering of Danish blood. The remaining two ancestors were minor Hungarian nobility, subjects of the German Habsburg Emperor.

background was overwhelmingly German. One would need to go back to James I of England, born in 1566, to find an ancestor both of whose parents had been born in the British Isles. Of his sixteen great-great-grandparents, no less than fourteen had been born into German royal houses. His family name was German (Wettin, of the House of Saxe-Coburg-Gotha), and both his grandfathers spoke English with heavy German accents. Little of this German background, however, seemed to manifest itself in the placid Victorian existence of his parents. It was almost as if, in an age of nation states which had seen the rise of a German Empire to rival the British Empire, they went out of their way to present to the world a spectacle of middle-class English ordinariness. If Queen Mary had been influenced to some small degree by the German palace life she had intermittently known during her childhood, George V disliked Germans on principle and prided himself on his unfamiliarity with the German language. 'In all my years', he once remarked, 'I have never met a German gentleman.'[9] But a clever satirist such as Max Beerbohm could make devastating play with the King's heavy Teutonic features and stolid Teutonic character. The stamp of heredity is not easily lost. Was it to mark his son?

In 1913 the Prince, who was then at Oxford, spent his Easter and summer vacations in Germany staying with various royal relations. The idea was his mother's, and the object was to improve his command of German (which he had been learning with a native tutor) and 'to teach me something about these vigorous people whose blood flows so strongly in my veins'.[10] On the first trip, he was the guest of the genial and soporific King and Queen of Württemberg in the south-west of Germany; on the second, of his formidable great-aunt, the Dowager Grand Duchess of Mecklenburg-Strelitz, in the north-east.

Among the Duke of Windsor's papers in Paris exist copies of a diary he kept during these visits, correspondence he exchanged with his parents in the course of them, and letters written from Germany to his Oxford friend James Patterson. Together they give a clear picture of the impression made upon his young mind by Germany and the Germans – and it is not a flattering impression. He was intensely bored by the stiff ritual of the German courts, the endless drives through flat countryside, the long hours (for his upbringing did not dispose him to appreciate the performing arts) at the opera and theatre. He compared Germany unfavourably to France, which he had enjoyed visiting the year before. He disliked the people: 'The Germans as a race are fat, stolid, unsympathetic and intensely military.'[11]

He did not like the fact that they always wore uniform, even if not soldiers; nor was he impressed by their habit of shooting their game at close quarters. On 20 August he wrote to Patterson from Schloss Neustrelitz:

> .... I went south to Thuringia ... which is not unlike parts of Scotland but not half so wild and I would far rather have one day on the hills in Aberdeenshire to 20 in these woods! ... Gracious how glad I shall be to leave this d--d land; I am heartily sick of it and its people and am anxious to hear some decent cockney or broad Scotch accent again .... You have no idea how much one misses that sort of thing, as well as never seeing an English notice in the streets. However it is all experience though I am deuced glad it is over; I couldn't face it all again! ... Good bye old Jack and keep fit and I hope my next letter will be written in Scotland .... [12]

Thirty-five years later, however, when he was writing his memoirs, the Duke of Windsor painted a very different picture of the Germany he had seen before the First World War. Then he wrote of how he had admired 'the industry, the thoroughness, the discipline, the perseverance, and the love of the Fatherland so typical of the German people'; he remembered Germany as 'a prosperous, industrious, agreeable country' which 'echoed with work and song'.[13] Thus are judgments changed with the years, and thus is memory distorted. Nostalgia comes into play. A hitherto unsuspected consciousness of roots emerges.

Less than a year after the Prince's return from Germany, war broke out. 'Thank God the Gov't have decided that France shall not be deserted,' he wrote in his diary. 'Oh!! God; the whole thing is too big to comprehend!! Oh!! that I had a job.'[14] He was commissioned in the Grenadier Guards, and pleaded throughout the months that followed to be sent to the front like any other soldier. In time his wish was fulfilled: he witnessed the carnage and experienced the privations of the trenches, he flirted with death and mixed with all manner of men. He became a mascot, known for his sympathy with the common troops and his determination to share their hardships.

The war had a profound effect on the Prince, as on all his generation who survived the slaughter. It filled him with horror at the idea of future mass conflict, with determination that no such cataclysm should occur again. It caused him to reject the nationalist passions which had led to the fighting and had become hysterical in the course of it. It induced in him feelings of pity and sympathy for the land of his ancestors, where the royal relations he had visited in 1913 now lost their thrones and their subjects faced hardship and shame. It instilled in him a dread of political convulsions as well as an awareness that these could only be avoided if the social aspirations of ordinary people were satisfied. As he wrote to his father a week before the Armistice:

> There seems to be a regular epidemic of revolutions and abdications throughout the enemy countries which certainly makes it a hard & critical time for the remaining monarchies; but of those that remain . . . ours is by far the most solid though it must be kept so & I more than realize that this can only be done by keeping in the closest possible touch with the people & I can promise you this point is always at the back of my mind . . . .[15]

The war had also formed the Prince's character. It had established his extraordinary natural charm and ability to communicate with all classes, his capacity for interesting himself in everything around him and his sympathy with the unfortunate. It showed him to be strong-willed to the point of obstinacy. It also brought out a more sombre side to his nature. As much as he was considerate and a man of the people, he could be selfish and snubbing and stand on his pride. Flair and charm sometimes seemed to be a substitute for inner purpose and serious thought. There was a dash of cynicism and a pronounced escapist streak. Like much of his generation, he was restless and dissatisfied.

Between 1919 and 1931 the Prince made his great series of official overseas tours, strengthening the links of Empire and spreading goodwill abroad. He became an international superstar. He was looked up to as a leader of fashion in speech, manner and dress; he was a model for the post-war cult of hedonistic abandon typified by the Bright Young Things. But he had serious concerns – above all the welfare of the common man in a crisis-ridden industrial society. When a new-fangled nationalist movement came to power in Germany committed to large-scale social reform, he was not alone in viewing it with more interest than apprehension.

In *Mein Kampf*, in his conversation and speeches, Adolf Hitler only ever had one consistent foreign political idea. It was that the future of international society depended on Anglo–German co-operation. Filled with romantic notions about the British (of whom he knew little, but whom he considered to be akin to the German *Herrenvolk*), he had a vision of Germany dominating Europe while her British ally continued to rule the seas and her glorious overseas Empire. In the light of this dream, the Führer was greatly excited by reports received from Leopold von Hoesch, the German Ambassador in London, about the pro-German inclinations of the heir to the English throne. By 1935, Hoesch (a personal friend of the Prince of Wales and an old-guard diplomat who was not a Nazi) was regularly informing Berlin of the Prince's sentimental attachment to Germany, his approval of Hitler's anti-communism and of Nazi economic and social welfare policies, his sympathy with Germany's desire for a revision of the Versailles Treaty, his abhorrence of war and belief that European peace depended on Anglo–German *rapprochement*.[16]

Such views were in fact commonplace in England in 1935, before Hitler had become aggressively expansionist and the full horror of his internal policies had become apparent. Conservative opinion viewed Nazi Germany as a bulwark against the menace of Soviet Russia, while liberal opinion tended to take an indulgent view of German nationalist grievances. Disillusionment with France as an ally contributed to these attitudes. It was fashionable to regret and try to forget the First World War: appeasement was in the air. National Socialism tended to be regarded as a bizarre but interesting political experiment with positive as well as repugnant aspects: at a time when parliamentary democracy seemed to be coping indifferently with the problems of the depression, it was easy to admire from a distance the practical achievements of authoritarian regimes. The private opinions which the Prince expressed to Hoesch were therefore not unusual. But would he give public expression to them? And would he, as King, seek actively to further the cause of closer Anglo–German relations?

One episode encouraged the Nazis to believe that he would. Speaking at the Annual Conference of the British Legion on 11 June 1935, the Prince declared his support for the idea that 'a deputation or a visit might be paid by representative members of the Legion to Germany at some future time'; and he added: 'I feel that there could be no more suitable body or organization of men to stretch forth the hand of friendship to the Germans than we ex-service men, who fought them and have now forgotten all about it and the Great War.' The promotion of such Anglo–German exchanges was in fact already a part of British Legion policy, and the Prince had been specifically asked to make this reference by the Legion's President. It was nevertheless interpreted both in Britain and abroad as an expression of his own political views made on his own initiative. It aroused disapproval from a number of English quarters (including his father) – and it caused a sensation in Germany, where it was publicized out of all proportion to its real significance.[17]

In January 1936, Edward VIII came to the throne. Hoesch assessed the importance to Germany of the new reign in terms of cautious optimism: the King would 'naturally have to impose restrictions on himself ... in questions of foreign policy', though 'his friendly attitude towards Germany might in time come to exercise a certain amount of influence in the shaping of British foreign policy', and 'we should at least be able to rely on a ruler who is not lacking in understanding for Germany and the desire to see good relations established between Germany and Britain.'[18] Other, less orthodox reports reaching Hitler went further. The Duke of Saxe-Coburg, a royal Nazi eager to ingratiate himself with the Führer, claimed that the King (who was his first cousin once removed) was 'determined to concentrate the business of government on himself' and fired above all by the personal ambition of forging an alliance with Germany. Saxe-Coburg put into the King's mouth the following improbable comment: 'Who is King here? Baldwin or I? I myself wish to talk to Hitler, and will do so either here or in Germany. Tell him that, please.'[19] It is hardly necessary to point out that the Nazis – even the better educated of them – had very little understanding of, or did not wish to believe in, the constitutional position of the British Sovereign. They tended to assume as a matter of course that the Government took its line from the King: during the Second World War, for example, they imagined George VI to be responsible for his Government's refusal to contemplate peace negotiations.

Only a few weeks after King Edward's accession, an event occurred which convinced Nazi observers that he was indeed the key to *rapprochement* and intended to play an active foreign political role. In the Rhineland crisis of March 1936, he urged the Government not to take action against Germany's reoccupation of her demilitarized province. This was entirely within his constitutional rights: indeed, only a few months earlier his father had similarly warned ministers not to act against Italy over Abyssinia.[20] But the German Embassy reported the King's attitude in such a way that, when the democracies acquiesced in the German move, it seemed in Berlin that the King had prevailed over the policy of his Government.[21]

Once again, the signs were wrongly interpreted. Edward VIII had in reality done no more than to encourage his Government in the only policy it had felt able to take. It was not the case that the King was determined to increase his political power, or that Anglo–German relations were his overriding preoccupation; the matter which most filled his mind was not political but domestic, and he was in fact prepared to give up his position altogether. Since 1934 he had been deeply in love with an American woman, Mrs Ernest Simpson.* In the summer of 1936, with his encouragement, she was preparing to divorce her husband, a London businessman. As soon as she was free, the King was determined to marry her, even at the price of his throne: his passion for her, and the strain of his lonely position, were such that he felt he could no longer continue without her constant support.

On 27 October 1936, Mrs Simpson received her decree *nisi* at Ipswich. Three days later, the King received the new German Ambassador to London, Joachim von Ribbentrop, who had been appointed with the express object of realizing, with Edward VIII' s help, Hitler's desire for Anglo–German 'understanding'. In his memoirs the Duke of Windsor recalled that formal occasion:†

> At the stroke of 11.30 the double doors of the audience room opened, and there advanced towards me a tall, rigid figure in faultless tail coat and white tie. The Nazi salute with which the Ambassador was to outrage the officials of the next reign was not employed. He bowed, we shook hands, and he handed me his letters of credence, which I passed to Mr Anthony Eden . . . . Herr von Ribbentrop spoke of his Führer's desire for peace; I wished him a successful mission to my country . . . .[22]

That was the last Ribbentrop was to see of Edward VIII as King of England. Exactly six weeks later, to the Ambassador's horror, the King – whom the Nazis had imagined might 'concentrate the business of government on himself' and conclude an Anglo–German alliance – accepted his constitutional position and gave up the throne to marry the woman he loved.

Joachim Ribbentrop (he obtained his noble particle at the age of thirty-two by having himself adopted by the widow of a distant cousin) was born

---

* After the Abdication, there were rumours in London that Mrs Simpson had been a Nazi agent, or at least that she had tried to influence the King in a pro-German direction. There is no evidence whatever for this, or indeed that she had any strong political interests. Her name is barely mentioned in the many official and unofficial German reports on the King. It is evident that the Nazis failed to appreciate his feelings towards her both during and after his reign.

† According to Ribbentrop's memoirs, they had only previously met at large diplomatic receptions and had had no significant private conversations.

at Wesel-am-Rhein in 1893, the son of an artillery officer. As a young man he emigrated to Canada, but returned to Germany to fight in the First World War. Afterwards he entered the wine trade, his success being assured by his marriage to the daughter of Otto Henkel, the German champagne magnate. He was a late recruit to Nazism, only joining the Party in August 1932; but his rise was rapid. Hitler was impressed by his easy salesman's prattle, his *haut bourgeois* style of living, and his apparent familiarity with foreign countries. It was at his villa in the Berlin suburb of Dahlem that the political negotiations took place which led to Hitler's becoming Chancellor in January 1933. In the early days of the new regime, Ribbentrop was appointed Hitler's private foreign affairs adviser and put in charge of the Party's Foreign Affairs Bureau (*Dienststelle Ribbentrop*), which sought to rival the conservative and as yet un-nazified German Foreign Ministry (*Auswärtiges Amt*). Further posts followed – Commissioner for Disarmament Questions, Ambassador-at-Large and Personal Envoy of the Führer. In the spring of 1935 he negotiated the Anglo–German Naval Agreement, which was hailed in Germany as a great diplomatic triumph.

Ribbentrop possessed polished manners, a command of foreign languages, a certain political cunning and a remarkable talent for persistence; but few statesmen have been the object of greater contempt and derision on the part of their contemporaries both at home and abroad. He was regarded as a pretentious *parvenu* whose arrogance concealed a deep sense of insecurity, a bombastic bore who talked and never listened. His lack of tact ('Brickendrop') was proverbial, and his capacity for talking and believing nonsense was legendary. 'He was difficult to like,' recalled Serrano Suñer. 'Everything about him was affected, every look and gesture seemed artificial.'[23] To many he seemed not so much a thinking human being as an actor reciting his lines, a dehumanized gramophone record spouting claptrap. Goering called him 'Germany's number one parrot'. To say that he was despised as an ignorant amateur by the old German diplomatic establishment would be an understatement. 'I honestly hated him,' wrote Ernst von Weizsäcker, who was his State Secretary at the *Auswärtiges Amt*; 'but when I left Berlin I had got so far as to pity him. For if one were to visit any mental home one would find a number of people of the same type as Ribbentrop.'[24]

Ribbentrop had no personal following in the Party, where he was regarded as an upstart. He owed his position to one thing and one thing alone – the support of Hitler. The special technique he developed for winning and retaining the Führer's favour has been described in a number of memoirs. It consisted of

> listening religiously to his master's monologues and committing to memory the ideas expressed by Hitler .... Then, after Hitler had forgotten ever discussing them with Ribbentrop, the courtier passed them off as his own, unfolding them with great warmth. Struck by this coincidence, Hitler attributed to his collaborator a sureness of judgment and a trenchant foresight singularly in agreement with his own.[25]

Ribbentrop was the complete court toady, always flattering, never contradicting, forever thinking up projects likely to appeal to his master. But this was not mere calculation. He was firmly under the mesmeric spell cast by Hitler, and possessed an almost sacred faith in the infallibility of Hitler's decisions. His value lay in the fact that he was a pliant, subservient creature with a love of power and little independence of mind who could be relied on to carry out Hitler's will in the diplomatic sphere. And this applied particularly to England. What had most impressed Hitler about Ribbentrop from the outset was his good knowledge of English and apparent familiarity with English Society. The naval treaty seemed to indicate that Ribbentrop was the man to bring about an Anglo–German agreement, and Hitler's high hopes of Edward VIII suggested that the moment for an approach had arrived. So Ribbentrop was sent to England in the autumn of 1936.

When, soon after his arrival in London, the new Ambassador heard of 'the King's matter' and the possibility of abdication, he could not believe it; it was inconceivable that England's dictator-in-waiting should give up his throne for a woman. He tried to obtain a private interview with the King – and was astonished when he was rebuffed. Only one explanation presented itself to his mind – that sinister anti-German elements were seeking to bring down the pro-German sovereign before Ribbentrop could make his overtures. When his Press Secretary Fritz Hesse, who was in close touch with London newspaper editors, tried to tell him what was really going on, he angrily expostulated:

> Don't you know what expectations the Führer has based on the King's support in the coming negotiations? He's our greatest hope! Don't you think the whole affair is an intrigue of our enemies to rob us of one of the last big positions we hold in this country? ... You'll see, the King will marry Wally and the two will tell Baldwin and his whole gang to go to the devil.[26]

Hesse also tells us that at first Hitler too 'refused to believe in the Abdication and regarded the whole affair as a piece of make believe.'

As the crisis drew to a close, it was only with the greatest difficulty that Ribbentrop could be prevailed upon by his staff to inform Hitler of the Abdication in advance of the public announcement,[27] and to send a sensible telegram to Berlin reporting Baldwin's statement to Parliament about the affair on 10 December. It was humiliating for the Ambassador to have to admit that the King had slipped from his grasp, that he and the Führer had been wrong in discounting abdication as something that could not happen. At least, in his telegram of 10 December, he could add a touch of conspiracy theory – that there had been 'other reasons' for the tragedy apart from those mentioned by Baldwin, that 'his friendly attitude towards Germany undoubtedly gained the King very powerful enemies in this country', that 'a systematic agitation has been fomented in England against the King, on which I would like to report later orally' and that 'there is no doubt that communist agitation, both in the British Empire and elsewhere, will make great use of the Abdication'.[28]

Yet even now, Ribbentrop seemed reluctant to accept the Abdication as a *fait accompli*. The following day, as the Abdication Bill was before Parliament, he lunched with John Davidson, Chancellor of the Duchy of Lancaster and Baldwin's closest political confidant. Davidson was amazed to hear Ribbentrop express the view

> that this was the end of Baldwin, that there would be shooting in the streets, that the King's Party would eventually restore Edward VIII to the throne. Indeed, he said that he had been extremely nervous coming out to lunch on a day like this! He talked more nonsense than I have ever heard from anybody in a responsible position of the level of Ambassador . . . . It was quite obvious that he had been stuffing Hitler with the idea that the Bill and the Government would be defeated and that a more pacifist Government would replace it . . . . I had some pleasure in disabusing Ribbentrop of these illusions, and the Ambassador was not gratified by what I had to say.[29]

Hitler, writes Erich Kordt, 'believed that the renunciation of the throne was nothing other than the result of the machinations of a decadent clique, behind which lay the usual enemies of National Socialism – communists, freemasons, Judaeo–Christian circles. This reinforced the illusion that a Great Britain led by the "social" King Edward would have ranged itself with the Axis.'[30] Ribbentrop did everything to foster that illusion. His mission in London was not a success. It was easy for him to take the view that his failure was in no way due to his defects as an envoy or his efforts to carry out an unrealistic policy; that there was an anti-Germany conspiracy in the British Government; that Edward VIII too had been the victim of that conspiracy; that, if only he had remained on the throne, everything would have been different. Perhaps one day he would return – and then everything *would* be different.

There is a striking and hitherto unpublished document which reveals the extent of Ribbentrop's fantasies on the subject of Edward VIII. On 19 October 1943, in his sixth year as German Foreign Minister, he treated the Prince Regent Cyrill of Bulgaria to a lecture on the causes of the Second World War. He explained that, when he had arrived in London as Ambassador, he had been 'warmly greeted by the press and encouraged to hope that an [Anglo–German] Understanding would be possible. This hope was especially based on the attitude of the then King Edward VIII, who had been a kind of English National Socialist, with strong concern for the social problems of his country and warm sympathy for an Understanding with Germany.' According to the notes made by the translator, the Foreign Minister went on:

> Seldom in history has greater baseness been shown than by the circles around Edward VIII whose work finally led to his being deprived of the English throne. The *Reichsaussenminister* had noticed even after a short time that Edward's influence was being frustrated by dark forces hostile to Anglo–German Understanding. The Foreign Office and anti-German English circles had done everything for three or four months [*sic*] to prevent a private conversation between the King and the *Reichsaussenminister*.
>
> The *Reichsaussenminister* then proceeded to discuss the Mrs Simpson affair. The fact was that Edward VIII never really wanted to marry her at all. However, by his candid talk to English ex-servicemen and his speech in Welsh distressed areas to the workers there he had incurred the enmity of certain English circles. Thereupon the wife of Duff Cooper befriended Mrs Simpson and took her and Edward on a Mediterranean cruise, during which she talked them into believing that the English people would accept Mrs Simpson as Queen. So Edward on his return was thus goaded into declaring to Baldwin: 'No coronation without Simpson.' This was just what Edward's enemies had been waiting for, and with the help of the press and whisky they wore him down until he signed his Abdication. The *Reichsaussenminister* was advancing these details merely to show how strong the powers in England had been who were against an Understanding with Germany.[31]

In October 1937 – ten months after the Abdication and four months after their marriage in France – the Duke and Duchess of Windsor spent twelve days in Nazi Germany on what was described as a tour of workers' social conditions.

There can be no doubt of the Duke's personal curiosity to visit the Third Reich and meet its leaders, or of his genuine interest in schemes to improve the welfare of industrial workers. He also later claimed (and there is no reason to doubt his claim, which says as much about his naïvety as about his good intentions) that, by going to Germany in 1937, he had hoped in a vague way to help defuse the growing tensions between England and Germany and so lessen the risk of war.[32] He had, however, a special reason for wishing to make the trip: he wanted to give the Duchess a royal progress.[33] He had been deeply hurt by the refusal of his family to allow her to share his royal rank or so much as acknowledge her existence. Here, he felt, was a chance to give her a taste of the red carpet treatment she would have enjoyed had he been able to marry her without abdicating.*

The visit was organized and paid for by the German Government, but was the brainchild of Charles Bedaux, the expansive French–American time-and-motion tycoon who had lent his castle to the Duke and Duchess for their wedding. Though described as a private study tour, it caused embarrassment both to the German *Auswärtiges Amt* and the British Foreign Office.[34] It was arranged at short notice and announced at the last moment, when a number of the Duke's friends, including Churchill and Beaverbrook, unsuccessfully tried to dissuade him from going. The British Ambassador in Paris warned him that 'the Germans were past masters in the art of propaganda and would be quick to turn anything he might say or do to suit their own purposes', to which he replied that he was 'well aware of this' and 'would be very careful and would not make any speeches'.†[35]

The tour did not prove a comfortable experience for the Duke and Duchess. Their guide, Dr Ley of the Reich Labour Front, turned out to be a boisterous drunkard addicted to high-speed driving. With this unedifying companion, they were raced round Germany on an exhausting (and, to the Duchess, mortally boring) schedule of visits to factories and model

---

* Interestingly enough, it was for the same reason that the Archduke Franz Ferdinand visited Sarajevo in June 1914; it was a rare opportunity to give some recognition to his morganatic and much-humiliated wife. The local commander, uncertain of how to react, reduced precautions to a minimum – and the result was the First World War.

† Dudley Forwood, the Duke's ADC, also recalls the Duke telling him 'to take special care not to make any gesture that might be interpreted as a stretched arm salute'.

housing developments. Their trip was given no official character and was reported without comment in the German press, but they were privately and enthusiastically entertained by Goebbels, Goering, Hess and Ribbentrop. Like other foreign visitors, the Duke seems to have formed the impression that the Nazi leaders were idealists and potentially reasonable men with whom the democracies could reach an accommodation; William Shirer, an American correspondent following the tour, had the impression that he had little real idea of what his hosts were like.[36] The British Embassy in Berlin ignored him on instructions from London, but submitted a report on his movements to the Foreign Office.

On 22 October, the day before their departure from Germany, they had tea with Hitler at Berchtesgaden. The Duke had an hour of private conversation with the Führer, in which the latter did most of the talking. The interpreter, Paul Schmidt, recalled:

> Hitler was evidently making an effort to be as amiable as possible towards the Duke, whom he regarded as Germany's friend, having especially in mind a speech the Duke had made several years before, extending the hand of friendship to German ex-servicemen's associations. In these conversations there was, so far as I could see, nothing whatever to indicate whether the Duke of Windsor really sympathized with the ideology and practices of the Third Reich, as Hitler seemed to assume he did. Apart from some appreciative words for the measures taken in Germany in the field of social welfare the Duke did not discuss political questions.* He was frank and friendly with Hitler, and displayed the social charm for which he is known throughout the world.

When they had left, Hitler remarked: 'She would have made a good Queen.'[37]

The tour was criticized in England as an attempt on the Duke's part to seek the limelight – but there was nothing unusual about a prominent Englishman visiting Germany in 1937 as a guest of the Government. Such visits were commonplace, for war was still two years away and curiosity about the Nazis was intense. Lloyd George had gone to see Hitler the previous year, and numerous people (including respectable liberals) had accepted invitations to the Berlin Olympics and other junketings. Conservative cabinet ministers such as Halifax and Londonderry were visitors, as were socialists such as James Maxton. It was fashionable to go to Germany in the mid-1930s and meet Hitler just as it was to go to

---

* However, Dudley Forwood, who was present at the interview, recalls that the Duke did in fact make some critical remarks about the tendencies of the régime. The Duke (who had a good knowledge of German) noticed that these were being modified by the translator, and cried out: '*Falsch übersetzt!*'

China in the mid-1960s and meet Mao Tse-tung. Churchill wrote to the Duke after his return from Germany that the tour did 'not seem to have had the effect' of offending anti-Nazi public opinion and that he was 'glad it all passed off with such distinction and success'. The Duke replied that he had gone to Germany 'without any political considerations and merely as an independent observer studying industrial and housing conditions', and that the world could not ignore what was happening in Germany, 'even though it may not have one's entire approval'.[38]

If the tour had no significant effect in England, however, it had fateful effects elsewhere. It created a disastrous impression in America, where it received widespread unfavourable press publicity and was attacked by the labour unions, who were opposed to Bedaux's industrial efficiency schemes; this damaged the Duke's reputation in the United States and forced him to cancel an American tour which he had planned to make under Bedaux's auspices in the last six weeks of the year. On the other hand, the impression created in Germany was all too excellent. The Duke's friendliness and charm, his enthusiastic comments on the projects he inspected, his evident affection for the German language and people, delighted his hosts. So did his wife. 'What a pity that England lost not just such a clever King but such a splendid person as Queen,' wrote Frau Hess in a letter to Egypt which was intercepted that autumn by British intelligence – adding that it must rankle with the Duchess that her husband had been 'brought down by underhand intrigues, not least because of his sound social and pro-German attitude'.[39] The Nazi leaders, lower-middle-class republicans, were not the men to realize that well-trained royalty is charming to everyone, that it always appears to be in sympathy with whomever it is talking to, that its expressions of appreciation are automatic and meaningless. In their minds, the ducal visit confirmed the illusions which had been fostered by the Abdication – that King Edward had been Germany's best friend and one of nature's National Socialists, that he had been deposed by an anti-German clique, that his marriage had been a mere pretext to get rid of him, that it would be a good thing for Germany if he were to resume his throne one day, which no doubt represented the cherished desires both of the British people and of himself.

No one felt this more strongly now than Ribbentrop, who returned from England especially so that the Duke might dine with him in Germany. His mission to London had by this time proved a fiasco; soon he would be recalled in order to take up the duties of Reich Foreign Minister.

In his final report to the Führer of January 1938, he stated (untruthfully) that he had never been optimistic about Anglo–German *rapprochement*, but that 'seeing that Edward VIII was on the throne, a last attempt [had] seemed advisable'. England was in fact 'our most dangerous enemy', and 'Edward VIII [had] had to abdicate because it was not certain whether he would co-operate in an anti-German policy'.[40]

After the failure of his American plans, the Duke of Windsor withdrew altogether from the public eye and retreated with his wife into domestic life in France. Two subjects continued to haunt him, however. The first concerned his deteriorating relations with his family and his frustrated desire to return to his country. There are two views about the treatment of the Duke of Windsor after the Abdication. The first is that, after he had given up the throne in circumstances which dismayed his people, and handed over to a reluctant and embarrassed successor, the only future which could await him was one of permanent exile accompanied by a measure of disgrace. This has always been the view of the Court. The second view is that, given the circumstances, King Edward had behaved honourably by abdicating; that there was no reason why, after a suitable interval, he should not return to live in and serve again his country (which was what most people expected); but that instead he was submitted to a campaign of vindictive persecution. The Duke of Windsor looked upon things this way, as did many of his friends and admirers. The refusal of the Court to recognize his wife or allow her to share his royal status; their denial to him of the courtesies to which he still considered himself entitled; their determination to keep him out of England, even by attempting to make his annual allowance (£21,000) dependent on his remaining abroad; the conspiracy of silence surrounding his name in England; a host of real or imagined slights – all of this filled him with bitterness towards what he called 'Official England' and led to a feuding relationship with his family.

The Duke's second preoccupation was the drift to war. He watched with grave anxiety the deteriorating European situation. At the time of Munich he momentarily considered going to Germany again to reason with the Nazi leaders – but this time was firmly dissuaded by his friends.[41] In May 1939 he broadcast an international peace appeal from Verdun:

> I speak simply as a soldier of the last war, whose most earnest prayer is that such cruel and destructive madness shall never again overtake mankind .... The grave anxieties of the time compel me to raise my voice in expression of the universal longing to be delivered from the fears that beset us.

Finally, in August 1939, he sent a telegram to Hitler urging him not to plunge the world into war. The Führer replied, on 31 August:

> You may rest assured that my attitude towards Britain and my desire to avoid another war between our two peoples remains unchanged. It depends on Britain, however, whether my wishes for the future development of German–British relations can be realized.[42]

The following morning, Germany invaded Poland at dawn.*

The Duke considered the outbreak of war a disaster. His overwhelming desire, however, was to serve his country in this emergency; and his hope was that wartime circumstances would make possible his return there and reconciliation with his family. This hope was to be dashed. True, his old friend and supporter Winston Churchill, now First Lord of the Admiralty, sent a destroyer to fetch him and the Duchess; but they arrived in England to find themselves totally ignored by his family, who refused to accommodate him or even to have him met when he landed at Portsmouth. The Duke was offered the choice of two jobs – that of Assistant Regional Commissioner in Wales or of liaison officer with the British Military Mission at French General Headquarters. He chose the former: it was immediately withdrawn, and he was left with the latter. As a palliative, he was told he might tour the Home Commands before taking up his post: this prospect too was withdrawn. By the end of September the Duke and Duchess were back in France. The wretchedness of this brief homecoming profoundly affected the Duke. It explains his reluctance to return to England the following summer.

The Duke's war work in France – attached to the Howard–Vyse Mission at General Gamelin's Headquarters – at first appeared to give him a real chance to serve his country. He was immensely popular with the French Army. Officially he was to make a series of goodwill tours of the French front, where he was uniquely granted permission to go wherever he liked. This gave a tremendous opportunity to the Howard–Vyse Mission, the real object of which was to spy on the Maginot Line and other defences, about which the French were immensely secretive and which had hitherto been prohibited to the scrutiny of British military personnel. It was decided to use the Duke as a secret intelligence officer, preparing detailed reports on the frontal defences he saw in the course of his morale-boosting tours. The ruse worked; the Duke turned

* For details of the Duke's activities between the summers of 1939 and 1940, see my account in *The Duke of Windsor's War*, pp. 1–75.

out to have a flair for his undercover job; and his five secret reports[43] give a devastating picture of French unpreparedness, particularly in the Meuse Valley where the breakthrough was eventually to occur. Had these warnings been heeded in London, the course of the war might well have been different; but they were ignored. Meanwhile, the Court was making extraordinary efforts to restrict his role and keep his profile low. He was forbidden to visit the British Expeditionary Force in France. (It was ironical that the one Englishman with a free run of the French Army was not to go near the British Army.) Eventually even his French tours were curtailed, and he found himself with little to do. He resented the régime of petty Court restrictions to which he was subjected; his attitude towards his family hardened. As he wrote to his brother in 1943:

> Granted that the first year or two cannot have been too easy for you – I can see that – but ever since I returned to England in 1939 to offer my services and you continued to persecute [me] and then frustrate my modest efforts to serve you and my country in war, I must frankly admit that I have become very bitter indeed.[44]

Among the German diplomatic archives captured at the end of the Second World War are two curious letters concerning the Duke of Windsor during the first weeks of 1940. They are from Julius Count von Zech-Burkesroda, German Minister to the neutral Netherlands, to Ernst Baron von Weizsäcker, State Secretary of the *Auswärtiges Amt* in Berlin.

In the first of these, dated 27 January, Zech writes that, through a channel of (presumably neutral) contacts, he 'might have the opportunity to establish certain lines leading to the Duke of Windsor'. Through this channel he had already learned that the Duke was 'not entirely satisfied' with his war post in France and sought 'a field of activity which would permit him a more active role'. (This was true.) He had also heard that 'there seems to be something like the beginning of a Fronde forming around W which for the moment of course still has nothing to say, but which at some time under favourable circumstances might acquire a certain significance'.[45] Weizsäcker showed this letter to Ribbentrop.

In the second letter, dated 19 February, Zech writes that the Duke of Windsor had 'said' (to whom or in what circumstances is not stated) that the Allied High Command had decided not to send troops into Belgium should that country be invaded by the Germans, but to hold a line on the Franco–Belgian frontier.*[46] (If the Duke had said this, it would have been

---

* This was after the Venlo incident, in which the Allies came into possession of German plans for the invasion of France through Belgium.

a clever piece of deception: what had been decided was in fact exactly the opposite.) Ribbentrop showed this letter to Hitler.[47]

Whether Zech was merely passing on some inflated scraps of gossip, or whether he really did have contacts (reliable or otherwise) 'leading to the Duke of Windsor', is difficult to determine. What is certain is that Ribbentrop and Hitler were encouraged to believe that – even in wartime – the Duke might be their man.

The Duke became increasingly worried about the Allied conduct of the war. He was appalled by the corruption and incompetence he witnessed in France, in political as well as military life. On 3 May he wrote to his friend Philip Guedalla that

> things are going very badly indeed for us at the moment, and they can't possibly go any better until we have purged ourselves of many of the old lot of politicians and much of our out-of-date system of government.
>
> We are up against a formidable foe, not only formidable in the military sense but politically as well. If we are forced to spend millions each day arming and equipping our forces to match Germany's, surely it is equally necessary to equip ourselves politically in order to match ourselves against the calculating shrewdness and freedom of action of the Nazi chiefs?[48]

One week later, the Germans attacked. For some days the Duke visited the front: his position as liaison officer between the British military missions at French General and Frontal Headquarters enabled him to appreciate the extent of the Allied military collapse. The only consolation was that Churchill, who might still give the Allied war effort the dynamism it so desperately needed, was now Prime Minister. 'The news that you have accepted to form a Government at this supreme hour of trial for our nation', the Duke wrote to him, 'is dramatic indeed.'[49]

The armies in the north-east were cut off by the advancing Panzers. In Paris, the Duke found himself with nothing to do. Towards the end of May, at the time of Dunkirk, he obtained leave to go south; picking up the Duchess at her refuge in Biarritz, he drove with her to Antibes through roads choked with refugees – mostly travelling in the opposite direction, since an Italian invasion was daily expected. They reached La Cröe on the 29th. The Duke attached himself to the *Armée des Alpes* – though he seems to have meant to return to Paris. But Paris was abandoned by the Allies on 10 June – and the same day war was declared by the Italians. The following day the Duchess wrote from La Cröe to her Aunt Bessie in Washington:

It really is becoming a most awful mess. We haven't decided what we will do exactly but will stay here for a few days anyway. You can imagine how difficult it is to make a real plan. I had just taken 2 Italian servants .... The Duke is with the army here for the moment but can do more or less as he likes .... France is having a tough time. I can't believe they will go for the Island – and I believe you will be in it before long. It is 'the old order changeth giving place to new' I am afraid .... The battle is supposed to start tonight here. The Duke thinks the defences in the Alps excellent. Everyone is calm and the gardeners (all Italian) are busy planting flowers for the summer. The sky is blue, the sea smooth – but the mind ruffled ....[50]

The Italians were repulsed on the Riviera – but the Germans were racing down the Rhône Valley. What was the Duke to do? Not for the last time that summer, he showed himself irresolute. He was reluctant to leave Antibes until he had some definite sign from the British Government inviting him to return. It was not until the evening of the 16th that he sought the advice of the British Consul–General at Nice, Major Hugh Dodds.* 'I expressed the very definite opinion', Dodds reported the following week to London, 'that he should leave France without delay, as with the rapid advance of German troops he might find himself cut off. I had visions of HRH being held as a hostage by the enemy.'[51] Dodds (who had received instructions to close his Consulate) would soon be leaving for Spain along with his colleague from Menton (which had been overrun by the Italians). He advised the Duke to join them on the journey.

Others also counselled flight. Major Gray Phillips of the Black Watch, the charming fifty-four-year-old soldier-aesthete who had become the Duke's comptroller in October 1939, joined his master in Antibes after a nightmare hitch-hike from Paris; he painted a graphic picture of a France which had lost all will to resist and lay prostrate before the Germans. The final persuasion was delivered by the neighbours of the Duke and Duchess at Antibes, the rich and handsome George Wood and his Hungarian wife Rosa, whom they had befriended some years before when Wood had been attached to the British Legation at Vienna. Their daughter, married to a Habsburg Duke, had been arrested with her husband by the Nazis in Vienna and sent to a concentration camp; nothing had been heard of her since. The New Order was no respecter of royalty. One would have to get out without delay.

And so, around noon on Wednesday 19 June, the Duke and Duchess set

* A veteran of the Boer War, Major J. H. H. Dodds-Crewe served as H.M. Consul-General in Addis Ababa (1911–24), Tripoli (1924–8), Palermo (1928–36) and Nice (1936–40). He was fifty-nine in June 1940.

out for the Spanish frontier accompanied by the Consuls, Gray Phillips and the Woods. No word had been received from England about the Duke's future.* There was no guarantee that the party would get through to Spain. In her memoirs, the Duchess described their departure from La Cröe, where she had spent the year before the war creating a domestic idyll for her husband and herself:

> The staff was grouped around the entrance to say goodbye. As I was about to enter the car, the gardener stepped forward to press into my arms a huge bunch of tuberoses. 'Your birthday present, darling,' whispered David. In the confusion I had forgotten the date.† I buried my face in the sweet-smelling mass, grateful for being able to take away with me at least this lovely reminder of La Cröe. Our staff wept as we left; and so did I.[52]

The same day that the Duke and his party set out for the Spanish frontier, the Germans and Italians met at Munich to discuss the French Armistice. Ciano, Mussolini's Foreign Minister, was struck by Hitler's anxiety for a peaceful settlement with England. The Führer was like 'a gambler who has made a big scoop and now wants to get up from the table without losing more'. He did not wish to harm the British Empire, which he regarded 'even now' as 'an important factor in world equilibrium'. He was confident that Anglo–German understanding could be achieved. (He had in fact already issued orders for the German army to begin demobilizing.) The normally bellicose Ribbentrop, echoing as ever his master's voice, was also all for peace. And he revealed to Ciano that there already existed 'tentative contacts between London and Berlin via Sweden . . .'.[53]

For something had happened which, for a brief moment, seemed to justify Hitler's confidence that there would soon be Anglo–German negotiations. On 17 June the Swedish Minister in London, Björn Prytz, had been called to the Foreign Office to receive what sounded like a strong hint that the British Government might be grateful for Swedish good offices in starting talks with Germany. The Under-Secretary, R.A. Butler, said that Churchill 'did not have the last word' and that 'no occasion would be missed to reach a compromise peace if reasonable conditions could be obtained'. The Secretary of State, Lord Halifax,

---

* In fact, instructions were sent to the British Consulates–General at Nice, Marseilles and Bordeaux that same afternoon. Despatched at 2pm, the telegram from Lord Halifax read: 'Please send me any information you have or can get from consular offices under your supervision regarding Duke of Windsor's whereabouts and do anything you can to facilitate his return to this country' (FO 800/326/183).

† The Duchess was forty-four.

added the message that 'common sense and not bravado' would govern British policy. Prytz telegraphed these remarks to the Swedish Foreign Minister, Christian Günther – who that same day had been treated to similar comments by the British Minister in Stockholm, Sir Victor Mallet. This apparent peace initiative was reported to the Germans.[54]

But the 'contacts' vaunted to Ciano by Ribbentrop never materialized. Nothing more was heard through the Swedish channel. By the time the Franco–German Armistice was signed on 22 June, no direct sign had been received of willingness to talk on the part of England. Another way would have to be found.

That was why Ribbentrop was 'electrified' the following day when he received from the Spanish Foreign Minister the suggestion that the Duke of Windsor – who had always favoured *rapprochement* and always regretted the war, who was at loggerheads with his successor and who was regarded by Hitler as Germany's best friend among Englishmen – might 'perhaps' be kept in Spain with a view to the Germans 'eventually' getting in touch with him. That was why he at once responded by asking that the Duke and Duchess be detained there 'for a couple of weeks to begin with' – but without their being aware that the Germans lay behind such detention. The Spanish reply – contained in a telegram of Stohrer of 25 June – was brief and satisfactory. 'The Foreign Minister', it read, 'promised he would do everything possible to detain Windsor here for a time.'[55]

2
Nine Days in Madrid
23 June–2 July

The arrival of the Duke in Madrid was awaited with particular attention by three men: the British Ambassador, Sir Samuel Hoare; the German Ambassador, Dr Eberhard Baron von Stohrer; and the Spanish Foreign Minister, Colonel Juan Beigbeder y Atienza.

Sir Samuel Hoare, Bt

At 8 pm on Thursday 20 June, Sir Samuel Hoare sent the following wire from Madrid to the Foreign Office in London:

> Duke of Windsor has telegraphed asking me to facilitate his passage across the frontier. I am doing so and propose to show His Royal Highness the usual courtesies. In view of press articles here saying that it is intended to arrest him on arrival in England, please confirm by telegram that I am acting correctly.[1]

One of the best-known careerists of the Conservative party, one of the pillars of the National Government which had ruled Britain in the 1930s, Hoare was sixty when he arrived in Madrid to take up the duties of British Ambassador on 1 June 1940. The clever and ambitious son of a famous banking family, he had made his reputation as Air Minister in the 1920s and had subsequently occupied most of the great offices of state – Secretary of State for India (1931–5), Foreign Secretary (1935–6), First Lord of the Admiralty (1936–7), Home Secretary (1937–9), Lord Privy Seal with a seat in the War Cabinet (1939–40), Air Secretary once again in the last weeks of the Chamberlain Government. He was a man of many gifts, reinforced by the support of a single-minded and aristocratic wife. He was hardworking; he had a quick brain; and he was an outstanding administrator. But above all he was a pure politician, whose reputation for being calculating and devious had earned him the sobriquet 'Slippery

Sam'. His unpopularity had been enhanced by an unattractive streak of old-maidishness and cowardice, and by the understanding he had reached with Laval in 1935 to acquiesce in Mussolini's conquest of Abyssinia – an understanding which had been repudiated by the British Cabinet and had led to his resignation as Foreign Secretary. He was an obvious scapegoat for Appeasement, and Churchill, his political rival, had no hesitation in sacking him from the Government when he became Prime Minister on 10 May 1940.[2]

Less than two weeks after this apparent end to his political career, Hoare found himself appointed Ambassador to Spain on Special Mission – the mission being to keep Spain neutral during the critical period which lay ahead. Though Hoare (whose virtues did not include modesty) later exaggerated the part he had played in keeping Franco out of the Axis camp,[3] there can be no doubt that he was ideally suited to his role and performed in it brilliantly. Sensing the mood, playing for time, putting on a bold front, beating his adversaries at games of intrigue and manoeuvre – these were arts at which he was past master. That June, when British fortunes seemed so low and Spanish opinion so hostile, he set himself to persuade the Spanish Government that Great Britain would not be defeated, and to identify and play up to her potential friends in Madrid. He was in the midst of this task when the news came that the Duke and Duchess of Windsor were about to cross into Spain – news which added to his worries.

The Duke was no stranger to Hoare. They had come to know each other well in the 1920s, when Hoare was Air Minister and the Prince of Wales had a passion for aviation; and they had seen much of each other in 1936, when Hoare was First Lord of the Admiralty and King Edward was deeply interested in naval questions. In November 1936 Hoare had accompanied the King on his visit to the Home Fleet at Portland (his account of that visit remains one of the most moving memoirs of the short reign[4]); and, later that same month, he was one of two cabinet ministers (the other was Duff Cooper) whose support the King sought in the Abdication Crisis.[5] But Hoare was not the man to ask. Cautious and old-fashioned, a devout Anglo–Catholic who disapproved of divorce, above all concerned for his own political career which had already been compromised by the Abyssinian affair, he expressed sympathy but felt unable to give his support either then or two years later when, as Home Secretary, he was asked by the Duke of Windsor to help solve the family difficulties which stood in the way of his return to England.

It will become apparent that the ex-Minister still harboured feelings of loyalty and friendship towards the ex-King. Nevertheless, the Duke's arrival in Spain caused Hoare (who had been less than three weeks in his new post) considerable anxiety. Not only did he dread getting involved once again in the quarrel between the Duke and his family, but German propaganda showed every sign of making mischief over the Duke's presence in the Peninsula. As Hoare wrote to Churchill, before the Duke arrived in Madrid

> every kind of rumour was spread by the German Embassy. Under the pressure of the German machine the Spanish press declared that you had ordered his arrest if he set foot in England, that he had come here to make a separate peace behind your back, that he had always disapproved of the war and considered it an even greater mistake to go on with it etc., etc.[6]

These were the reports which had so incensed the Duke at Barcelona; and they had sufficiently worried Hoare for him to ask London for reassurance that he was 'acting correctly' in extending to the Duke 'the usual courtesies'. Hoare would do his best to ridicule such stories, and he would also try to use the Duke to stimulate pro-British feeling in Madrid; but above all he wanted to see the Duke and Duchess safely out of Spain as soon as possible. It was therefore with relief that he received a telegram from the Foreign Office on the evening of 22 June, twenty-four hours before the Duke's arrival in Madrid, asking him to 'inform His Royal Highness that a Flying Boat is leaving the United Kingdom for Lisbon on June 24th' and to 'invite Their Royal Highnesses [sic] to proceed to Lisbon.'*[7]

At the last moment, however, there was a change of plan.

It so happened that, on 24 June, the Duke of Windsor's younger brother, the mysterious and ill-fated Prince George Duke of Kent, was due to arrive in Lisbon as leader of the British delegation to the eight hundredth anniversary celebrations of Portuguese independence. It was a visit of some symbolic significance, affirming in effect that the ancient friendship of England and Portugal had not been unduly affected by Great Britain's critical war situation. It meant much to the Portuguese dictator Salazar, whose private sympathies (in spite of his strictly neutral policy) were for England and whose sense of history gave him a deep reverence for the Anglo–Portuguese Alliance of 1373. Concerned that nothing should detract from the public effect of Prince George's

---

* The Foreign Office official who described the Duke and Duchess as 'Their Royal Highnesses' was actually reprimanded by the Court (FO 800/326/195).

mission, Salazar told the British Ambassador to Lisbon on 21 June that 'it would be inconvenient and undesirable for several reasons if the Duke of Windsor were to be present at the same time as the Duke of Kent' – a point also pressed at the Foreign Office by the Portuguese Ambassador to London.[8]

So new instructions went out to Hoare – to hold the Duke of Windsor in Madrid until his brother had left Lisbon. The Ambassador did not relish the prospect of having the ex-King and his wife on his hands for a week or more; but he would do his best with them and for them.

Dr Eberhard Baron von Stohrer

As it happened, the Duke's arrival in Madrid was viewed with concern not only by the British Ambassador but also by the German Ambassador.

Fifty-seven years old in June 1940, a great giant of a man and a South German, the son of an infantry general who had been ennobled by the last King of Württemberg,* Dr Eberhard von Stohrer was a career diplomat of long experience. As a young attaché he had served in London, where he acquired an understanding of England; and during the First World War he had been posted to Madrid, where he acquired an affection for Spain. For nine years (1927–36) he was the highly popular German Minister in Cairo, where he made many friends among the local British establishment. Like Sir Samuel Hoare, his success owed much to a remarkable wife: Maria-Ursula von Stohrer, who was twenty years his junior, was a woman of strong will, passionate temperament and sirenesque beauty. It may have been partly through her influence that, in 1936, he was promoted to be Ambassador to the Spanish Republic (he had originally been earmarked as Minister to Romania); but no sooner had he presented his credentials in Madrid than the Civil War broke out, and Stohrer (whose Government quickly decided to support Franco against the Republic) was hastily recalled.[9]

Stohrer was not a Nazi.† (Few senior German diplomats were: their task, after all, was to give the impression abroad that Germany was still the gracious, civilized land of yore.) Though he served the Third Reich with the same loyalty as he had shown the German Empire and the German Republic, and was made to join the Party in September 1936, he

---

* This noble creation was of a kind which entitled Stohrer to call himself Baron abroad but not in Germany.

† See the judgment of the Denazification Court of Freiburg in Appendix v.

had openly disapproved of Hitler before 1933 and was known to be unhappy about many aspects of the new régime. He had also aroused Party hostility through his efforts to protect the German Jews in Egypt – though he managed to ward off this antagonism through his close friendship with the parents of Rudolf Hess, prominent German residents of Alexandria. Nevertheless, after his recall from Madrid he found himself on the reserve list and might have faced premature retirement, but for a fortunate circumstance. The first German missions to the Spanish Nationalists were made up of fanatical Nazis, who behaved with gross lack of tact. They meddled in local politics; they attacked the Catholic Church; they even proclaimed the Spaniards to be racially inferior. Franco protested about this behaviour and asked for the Nazi envoy Faupel to be replaced by a non-political figure. Stohrer's lack of close identification with the régime therefore turned out to his advantage, and by the late summer of 1937 he found himself back in Spain as Ambassador to the Nationalist Government at Burgos.

Stohrer served his country well in Spain. He quickly brought the local German rabble under control, and re-established harmonious relations between Berlin and Burgos. He made an excellent impression on the Spaniards, and formed a close friendship with Franco's powerful brother-in-law and Interior Minister, Ramón Serrano Suñer. It was largely his work that German aid to the Nationalists was so effective, and that Spanish neutrality, when the Second World War broke out, was so strongly slanted in favour of Germany. But his own position was never comfortable. The Party always regarded him as a suspect figure. His Embassy was filled with Gestapo men who spied on him. He paid lip-service to Nazi ideology; but to his Spanish intimates he confided his strong reservations about the German régime and its policies both at home and abroad.[10] He hated Ribbentrop, whom he privately described as 'that cold-blooded cad' (*eiskalter Schuft*) and whose long-term aim of bringing Spain into the war he considered fundamentally unsound. He became adept at humouring the German Foreign Minister while side-stepping his wilder instructions. But what of the latest instructions?

In a sketch for his never-completed memoirs, Stohrer wrote that Ribbentrop wanted the Duke 'to be kept in Spain, for Ribbentrop evidently believed that he could play the Duke off against the new King and the existing British Government'.[11] Stohrer did not share this belief. In his view the whole idea was based on false assumptions and manifestly unwise – as was the propaganda concerning the Duke which emanated from his Embassy, the work of Goebbels' men over whom he had little control. Having for long years been the intimate of the British rulers of Egypt, Stohrer considered it most unlikely that the former King of England, whatever his private views, would agree to collaborate with his country's enemies as long as the war continued.[12] Personally he would be relieved to know that the Duke had safely departed from Spain; but meanwhile he had no choice but to impress Ribbentrop's wishes on the Spanish Government. After all, the original suggestion that the Germans 'might perhaps be interested in keeping the Duke of Windsor here and eventually establishing contact' had come from none other than the Spanish Foreign Minister.

Colonel Juan Beigbeder y Atienza

Colonel Beigbeder – who was fifty-two in June 1940 – is one of the mystery men of modern Spanish history: he was shortly to fall into disgrace and hence into oblivion. He had become Foreign Minister on the eve of the Second World War, partly because of his popularity in the Spanish army, partly because of the great services he had rendered the Nationalist cause as High Commissioner of Spanish Morocco. Morocco was his greatest love and the scene of his military career; he was steeped in Arab culture, kept an open copy of the Koran on his table, and enjoyed dressing up in Moorish robes. *Somos todos moros* was his motto: we are all Moors. He was in fact a highly original, cultivated, brilliant and eccentric character, very unpredictable and considered by some to be more than a trifle mad. His fine drooping portrait in the *piano nobile* of the Spanish Ministry of Foreign Affairs shows a mixture of scholar, aesthete, soldier and visionary.[13]

Beigbeder's task during the Second World War was to put into effect what Franco, in a speech delivered during the summer of 1939, had described as a foreign policy of 'skilful prudence' (*hábil prudencia*). Franco wanted the Germans to win, for purely practical reasons. He had nothing to gain from the victory of the democracies, where public opinion was hostile to him; he had everything to gain from their defeat, which might bring two coveted prizes tumbling into his lap – Gibraltar and French Morocco. But while modelling his régime on that of Hitler in some respects (such as police methods), and admitting large numbers of German technicians and advisers, Franco could not afford to involve his exhausted and impoverished country in a real war against the Allies. Nor was he eager to harness Spain too closely to so voracious a power as the Third Reich. Only if two things happened could he consider aligning himself openly with the Axis – if the prizes to be won were certain to be very great, and the fighting to be done was likely to be very short. Until such conditions prevailed, Beigbeder had to walk a tightrope in the conduct of Spain's foreign relations, quietly favouring the Germans while doing nothing to antagonize the Allies, with whom he signed an economic agreement in March 1940. Both sides, indeed, came to feel he slightly favoured their interests. (Married to a Frenchwoman, he was believed to be an admirer of French civilization; while the fact that he had once been Spanish Military Attaché in Berlin enabled him to pose as an admirer of the German army.)

Then came the German victories in the West. For a moment events seemed propitious for Spain to reconsider her neutrality. In a curious announcement, Franco declared that his country's status was now merely one of 'non-belligerency'. Amidst a fanfare of pro-German propaganda, he sent General Juan Vigón, the germanophile Chief of the Army Staff, to see Hitler and Ribbentrop in the second week of June, to congratulate them on their triumphs and assure them of the Caudillo's desire to join them in their struggle. On 16 June, Beigbeder communicated to the Germans Spain's price for a military alliance – Gibraltar and French Morocco, large tracts of Algeria and French West Africa, extensive military and economic aid. These terms were politely but firmly rejected in Berlin: they would have led to the failure of the Franco–German armistice talks, and it was far more important to Hitler to have France at peace than Spain at war.[14]

That June, the views of Beigbeder – that wayward romantic – seem to have undergone a profound change. At first he had been mesmerized by the prospect of Spain acquiring a great new empire across the Mediterranean in the wake of a German victory. With his mystic belief that Spain's destiny lay with the Moors, that was his greatest dream. He believed that the Franco–German talks (which in fact took place through his own good offices) might founder; that Germany's conflict with France and England would then continue for a few weeks; and that last-minute Spanish participation would bring in these rich colonial spoils.[15] The German reply to the Spanish terms shattered this dream. Meanwhile Beigbeder – who had been influenced by his pro-British adviser Mamblas, and his anglophile Ambassador to London, the Duke of Alba – appears to have been deeply impressed by the British decision to fight on.[16] As he told Sir Samuel Hoare (whom he showered with kind attentions): 'The British bull has yet to come into the ring. Will it fight? And if so, how will it fight? No one can say that it is dead until the *corrida* is over.'[17] As that summer progressed, it became increasingly clear that his own personal sympathies lay with the bull. And his policy turned round completely. Having failed to make Spain the ally of Germany, he became passionate in his desire to keep the Germans out of Spain. He was determined that Spain should never fight with Germany against England. But at the same time he wondered whether Spain might not gain prestige – and save herself from getting dragged into the affray – by helping bring about peace between Germany and England. When he said as much to Hoare, the Ambassador significantly replied: 'It is possible that it may one day come to that . . . .'[18]

That Beigbeder, having just turned pro-British, should have proceeded to invite the Germans to get hold of the Duke of Windsor in Spain may seem paradoxical. But it becomes explicable in the light of two facts. First, it would appear that the romantic visionary in Beigbeder hoped and believed that the Duke might be the agent of a Spanish-sponsored peace. Secondly, the practical statesman in Beigbeder realized how keen the Germans would be to make contact with the Duke. Beigbeder's policy was now to prevent the Germans from making any sort of demands on Spain by means of skilful appeasement. 'We have a monster on our frontier,' he told Hoare. 'We have to humour that monster.'[19] And what better way of keeping the monster happy than by offering to put it in touch (or just pretending to put it in touch) with the man who (so Beigbeder had learned from Vigón) was regarded by Hitler and Ribbentrop as their best friend among Englishmen? Even if the Duke were not the man to restore peace to Europe, at least he could be used to tantalize the Germans for a few weeks.

Ribbentrop's instant response confirmed Beigbeder's view. It remained for him to try to induce the Duke to stay on in Spain – without mentioning the Germans. For this he would need a go-between – and he had one at his disposal in the person of Javier Bermejillo, the Spanish diplomat who had joined the Duke at Barcelona on 21 June.

Don Javier Bermejillo y Schmidtlein

Don Javier 'Tiger' Bermejillo – who owed his feral nickname partly to the inability of the English to pronounce 'Javier', partly to his feline good looks and bright-green Mexican eyes – was forty-two in June 1940 and had known the Duke and Duchess of Windsor for nine years, almost longer than they had known each other. He was a lighthearted, romantic character with a colourful background: his father was the son of a Basque who had made a fortune in mid-nineteenth-century Mexico, his mother the daughter of a German army doctor who had accompanied the Mexican expedition of the ill-fated Emperor Maximilian. In 1931 he had become Secretary to the Spanish Embassy in London where, by a curious coincidence, he had independently befriended the Prince of Wales and the Ernest Simpsons long before the heir to the throne fell in love with his future wife. As one of the common denominators between the Prince and Mrs Simpson, Tiger was subsequently cherished by both of them and was a regular week-end visitor at Fort Belvedere – until he was abruptly recalled in 1935 and demoted to a minor consular post. Why this happened is not entirely clear, but there was some sort of scandal, from which Tiger's career was never to recover. There was a rumour at the time that he had outraged the English Court by allowing the Spanish Embassy to be used for secret assignations between the Prince and Mrs Simpson: but this would hardly account for the cloud which hung over the remaining twenty years of his professional life.[20]

In July 1936 Bermejillo was back in Madrid serving at the Spanish Foreign Ministry when the Civil War broke out. A massacre began of all persons connected with money or titles or the old régime. Tiger (whose father, though no longer rich, was a marquis and a sometime hunting friend of the exiled King of Spain) fled to seek sanctuary in the Mexican Legation, later transferring to the Romanian Legation, where he remained miserably for a year with other refugees. It was there that he heard of the Abdication, and of the marriage in June 1937 of his two old friends. He managed to smuggle out to the British Embassy a letter in his colourful English addressed to the Duke of Windsor:

> Unable up to now to communicate with the outside world, I avail myself to this first opportunity to send my sincere congratulations and all imaginable good wishes for the happiness of Your Royal Highness and the Duchess. The moral and physical suffering we are going through is indescribable, over two stones of weight have I lost, but my real agony is not the fear of being shot, like over 70,000 in Madrid alone, but not to be able to be on the side that fights and dies for one's ideals. I realize Sir that the very great favour I am taking the liberty of begging Your Royal Highness is possibly beyond all reason, but, dear Sir, remembering that your Ambassador for Spain, Sir Henry Chilton, who resides

at Hendaye, has been honoured with your friendship, would it be too much if Your Royal Highness could send him a word (or to Mr Leche, Chargé d'Affaires in Valencia) so as to take me out of Red Spain, in the same way as many other Spaniards in my condition have been evacuated thanks to the chivalry of representatives of the British Government? They can drop me anywhere as I shall soon find my way to die with honour and in any case demonstrate my eternal gratitude.

The Duke wrote to Chilton, and Tiger was evacuated shortly afterwards in a refugee exchange.

I do not know how to thank Your Royal Highness for the interest shown towards me [he wrote on the eve of his liberation]. I have always been so deeply grateful to you Sir for all the favours with which you honoured me but this last one which I dared beg Your Royal Highness was too great in the extreme ever to be granted were it not, Sir, for your extreme kindness and great heart . . . . With the kindest of thoughts and love to the Duchess and thanking Your Royal Highness millions and millions of times again . . . .[21]

Now, three years later, Tiger was reunited with his benefactor, and sought to repay something of the great debt. In the weeks to come, he was to be given ample opportunity to do so.

Guided by Tiger, and still accompanied by Major Phillips, the George Woods and the two Consuls,* the Duke and Duchess arrived in Madrid – a half-starving and half-ruined city which bore the scars of the Civil War which had ended fifteen months before – on the evening of Sunday 23 June. Rooms had been booked for them at the Ritz, the only good hotel; and it was there that Hoare called on them soon after their arrival. The meeting, wrote the Duchess, 'came off very well, with the past scrupulously ignored by both parties'; and 'for the first time in a month we had news we could trust about the war – bad news to be sure'.[22] The Duke now learned that the British Government wanted him to return to England; Hoare handed him a telegram from Churchill to say that 'we should like Your Royal Highness to come home as soon as possible' and that the Ambassador would explain the arrangements.[23]

The Duke reacted to this news with mixed feelings. It was all very well for the Government to ask him to return; but what would he be returning to? He remembered with pain his homecoming in September 1939, when

---

* The Consuls subsequently returned to the French frontier to assist in the evacuation of British personnel. Phillips and the Woods remained with the Duke and Duchess.

his family had practically ignored his existence and he had quickly been ordered back to France. At the very least he wanted to be assured that, on his return, there would be a job for him to do. Hoare, however, was able to tell him nothing about the future which awaited him in England, except that Saighton Grange, a house near Chester belonging to the Duke of Westminster, might be made available to him as a private residence.*

The following day – 24 June – Hoare telegraphed Churchill that the Duke was 'ready to leave Madrid provided his stay in Lisbon does not overlap with the Duke of Kent's. He would like an aeroplane at Lisbon on Tuesday 2nd July.' However, before leaving Madrid the Duke was 'most anxious' to know if he was to have a job in England. As Hoare explained: 'He does not want to appear to be returning as a refugee with nothing to do. I hope you can help him with a friendly answer as soon as possible. I have told him that if he fails to return to England within a few days, all sorts of mischievous rumours will circulate about him.'[24]

As the Duke settled down in Madrid to await his brother's departure from the Peninsula, Hoare had to face two worrying problems. First there was the Axis propaganda which insinuated that the Duke had broken with his Government and been threatened with arrest – and the risk that the Duke himself might unwittingly lend credibility to such a story through some casual indiscretion. Hoare knew how to deal with this. As he wrote to the Foreign Secretary, Lord Halifax, on 26 June:

. . . . All sorts of rumours were being spread about his visit, that he had come to make a British peace negotiation, that he had come to make trouble against the British etc., etc. I felt the only possible course was to take him as much as I could under my wing and to make it as clear as I could to the whole world that he was in friendly relations with all of us and merely stopping in Madrid on his way to England.† I think I have been able to edge him out of a number of difficult situations. For instance, he wished to give an interview to the American press. I told him that this was impossible as the British press would be furious and I eventually got him to see both the British and American press in a room at the Embassy rather than in his spy-haunted room at the hotel, and to say nothing but platitudes.‡ I am now doing my best with him to get him off to Lisbon at the

* Not Eaton Hall, as the Duchess writes in her memoirs. The offer of Saighton Grange was withdrawn on 1 July since the Duke of Westminster had decided to use the house to accommodate friends of his who had come over from France (Monckton Papers).

† Axis propaganda then put it about that Hoare had joined the Duke in his schemes to conclude a peace behind Churchill's back (FO 371/24407/74).

‡ The press conference was in fact interesting for what the Duke said about his flight to Spain and the causes of the French defeat (*New York Times*, 26 June 1940).

end of the week. There is not the least chance of his getting to Lisbon before the Duke of Kent has left. I am also having him from time to time to lunch and dinner to keep him on the rails. . . .[25]

The other problem was more serious. Hoare feared that, unless the Duke were given some encouragement about his future, he might in the end refuse to return to England. As he wrote to Churchill on 27 June:

> . . . . May I say a word about our friend, the Duke of Windsor . . . . Whenever I see him – and this is very often – he returns to the charge about being given a job in England. I know as well as you do the difficulties of the position. Nonetheless I feel that you will never have peace and perhaps I shall never get him away from here unless you can find something for him. Could you not give him a naval command of some kind? He still loves the sea better than anything else and anything actually in Great Britain might be troublesome to the Palace and you. I do feel strongly that this is the moment to get them both back to England and to clear up the situation. If the chance is lost, there will be a prince over the water who will be a nuisance and possibly an embarrassment . . . .[26]

'I do feel strongly that this is the moment to get them both back to England and to clear up the situation.' In effect, Hoare took the Duke's side. At this critical moment in wartime there was no room for a feud within Great Britain's ruling family. A gesture would have to be made; a place would have to be found for the former King of England. The Germans were putting it around that the Duke was at loggerheads with his native land. Unless he were welcomed home, they might be proved right.

Hoare would have been even more alarmed had he been aware of certain secret contacts of the Duke during his first days in Madrid. The first of these was with the Spanish Foreign Minister.*

Ribbentrop's telegram asking that the Duke and Duchess be detained in Spain – but without it appearing that the Germans were responsible – arrived in Madrid on 25 June. Through Tiger, Beigbeder thereupon invited the Duke to remain in Spain for as long as he wished as the guest of the Spanish Government.[27] The romantic Foreign Minister, with his love of Arab culture, proposed to put at his disposal the small but exquisite Palace of the Moorish Kings (*casa del rey moro*) in the remote mountain fastness of Ronda in Andalusia.[28] There can be no doubt that this offer greatly interested the Duke. If Spain were to remain neutral – and if

---

* What makes this whole affair even more bizarre is that Hoare was at this time in the process of forming a warm and somewhat conspiratorial friendship with Beigbeder; and one wonders whether the Colonel may not have tipped off the Ambassador at some stage as to what was going on.

he were to have no British war job to do – then Spanish retirement seemed in many respects a more tempting prospect than that of being ignored and cold-shouldered in his own country. On 26 June he went so far as to send a telegram to Churchill asking if there were any hurry for him to return to England.[29]

It seems unlikely, in view of Ribbentrop's wishes, that Beigbeder had made the Duke aware of German interest in him. At most he may have suggested to the Duke (as he was also around this time suggesting to Hoare) that he might eventually play a role for peace. But meanwhile the Duke was engaging in another initiative which did involve contact with the Axis and which, if not exactly sinister, was indiscreet in the extreme. He got Tiger to ask the Germans and Italians – through their embassies in Madrid – if they would agree to protect the two houses in France in which he and the Duchess had abandoned all their possessions and to which they hoped to return after the war – their Paris residence on the Boulevard Suchet and La Cröe at Cap d'Antibes.

Having received Tiger's visits, the Axis envoys reported the matter to their respective capitals. Stohrer's telegram to Berlin has not been found, but it is referred to in a captured minute from Ribbentrop's private office to the Protocol Department of the Foreign Ministry, dated 30 June:

> With reference to telegram No. 2140 of 29 June from Madrid, concerning protection of the residence of the Duke of Windsor, the Foreign Minister requests (1) that Abetz* be instructed to take unofficial and discreet measures for an unobtrusive watch on the Duke's residence, and (2) that Ambassador von Stohrer be instructed to let the Duke know confidentially through a Spanish intermediary that the Foreign Minister is looking out for its protection. However, no written statement whatever should be made.[30]

The telegram sent to Rome on 28 June by the Italian *chargé*, Count Zoppi, is particularly interesting since it shows how far the Duke had been influenced by the suggestion that he remain in Spain:

> The Duke of Windsor has been in Madrid with his wife for three days.† An official of the Spanish Ministry of Foreign Affairs who is a friend of his has told me that the Duke is not certain he will be returning to Great Britain in spite of the pressure of the British Government upon him to do so. Rather he seems to

---

* Ribbentrop's personal representative in occupied Paris, subsequently German 'Ambassador' to France.

† In fact for five days.

wish to keep himself outside events, following developments from afar. Through the said official, the Duke has asked if he may commend his villa at Cap d'Antibes, La Cröe, to the protection of the Italian Government in the event of that district being taken over by Italian troops.

and Zoppi added that he had learned that the German Embassy had been instructed 'to make it known to the Spanish Ministry of Foreign Affairs that the German Government is not averse to the Duke of Windsor remaining in Madrid'.[31]

Although the Duke may not have known it, his properties were in no danger in 1940. Antibes was well outside that tiny area of France occupied by the Italians under their armistice of 24 June; and the house in Paris had been entrusted to American protection along with British diplomatic property. Three years later, however, the Americans were no longer there, and Italian armies stood all along the Riviera. With hindsight it then seemed prudent of the Duke to have arranged some security for his possessions, which included his family memorabilia and his private archives.* But his requests, if not exactly superfluous, were extremely unwise. Albeit in a purely domestic matter, he had put himself under an obligation to his country's enemies. And the Axis envoys had learned a number of interesting things about his state of mind as a result of Tiger's visits. A link had been forged, however tenuous; and it was to have fateful consequences.

Throughout his stay in Madrid, the Duke found himself preoccupied and depressed by the war. As to his attitude at that moment there can be no doubt. He believed that Great Britain faced a catastrophic military defeat, which could only be avoided through a peace settlement with Germany. Even if successful resistance were possible for a period, there was little point in continuing a struggle which could no longer attain any of its original objectives and which could only lead to prolonged destruction and suffering.

There was nothing either unpatriotic or unusual about such views in the summer of 1940. Recent research has finally exploded the war propaganda myth that the British establishment was unreservedly behind

---

* When the Duke and Duchess finally returned to France in the autumn of 1945 they discovered the contents of both of their houses virtually intact. Minefields, however, had been laid in the garden and along the shorefront at La Cröe (*The Heart has its Reasons*, p. 361); and there had been an awkward moment in October 1940 when the sign 'German Property' had appeared outside the house in Paris, which the Duke had the Foreign Office remove through the US Embassy (FO 800/326/210).

Churchill in his determination to fight on come what may. On 17 June –
less than a week before the Duke's arrival in Madrid – R. A. Butler had
told the Swedish Minister that 'no chance would be missed to reach a
compromise peace if reasonable conditions could be obtained'.[32] At the
time of Dunkirk, Halifax had urged the War Cabinet to seek a peace
'which would save the country from avoidable disaster'.[33] Hoare admitted
to Beigbeder that Great Britain might one day have to come to terms
with Germany[34] – and this was certainly an understatement of his private
opinions about the war. Even Churchill himself had said at the end of May
that he was 'prepared to consider' such German terms as might be put to
him, and that the aim was 'no longer to crush Germany but rather to
preserve our own integrity and independence', and that 'the time might
come when we felt that we had to put an end to the struggle' – though for
the time being it was essential to make a stand against Germany.[35]

However, it was one thing to share the widespread private view that
there would eventually have to be negotiations with Germany, and quite
another to give any public hint of this while resistance was continuing. So
long as Great Britain was fighting for her life, it was essential to show a
bold and united front and subscribe to the official policy of no compromise.
For a man like the Duke of Windsor, whose every utterance was liable to
be picked up and repeated and exploited for enemy purposes, it was
especially important to guard against making imprudent statements.
And on the whole he did. He had refused to talk about the war to the
Spanish journalists at Barcelona. When his Spanish cousin, Prince
Alfonso, spoke to him about the invincibility of the German army, he
listened in stony silence and merely replied: 'There's still the Channel to
cross, remember that.'[36] Nevertheless, Hoare was fearful that the Duke
might drop some remark to a Spanish friend, or be persuaded into making
some admission, which would reveal his own strongly held preference for
a negotiated peace and tend to lend support to the Axis rumours that he
had broken with Churchill and wanted to find an independent settlement.
Hence Hoare's anxiety that the Duke should not receive American journalists in his hotel room, and that he should spend much of his time at the
British Embassy where the Ambassador could keep an eye on him.

Hoare's fears were well-founded. In public or at social gatherings the
Duke could be relied upon to be discreet; but off his guard with a sympathetic listener he was all too prone to disburden himself of his feelings.
Alexander Weddell, the United States Ambassador to Madrid, reported
to Washington that one of his Embassy staff had been told by the Duke

that 'the most important thing to be done now was to end the war before thousands more were killed or maimed to save the faces of a few politicians'. The Duke had gone on to say that

> stories that the French troops would not fight were not true. They had fought magnificently, but the organization behind them was totally inadequate. In the past ten years Germany had totally reorganized the order of its society in preparation for this war. Countries which were unwilling to accept such a reorganization of society and concomitant sacrifices should direct their policies accordingly and thereby avoid dangerous adventures. He stated that this applied not only to Europe but to the United States also. The Duchess put the same thing somewhat more directly by declaring that France had lost because it was internally diseased and that a country which was not in a condition to fight a war should not have declared war.[37]

The Duke can hardly be blamed for holding such views at that time. He had, after all, witnessed the appalling morale and eventual collapse of the French army, while he had seen nothing of wartime England and next to nothing of the British army. He could not know of the spirit of defiance which had arisen in his own country, or of Churchill's efforts to forge a war machine to match Hitler's. Even Hoare, who also received from Weddell an account of this conversation, found the Duke's words 'harmless and understandable in themselves' – though he knew they would 'make trouble' if the Germans got to hear of them.[38]

The Germans indeed appear to have been made aware of the Duke's views while he was in Madrid. They would have agreed with Weddell, who concluded in his report that such views reflected those 'of an element in England, possibly a growing one, who find in Windsor and his circle a group who are realists in world politics and who hope to come into their own in the event of peace'. And their picture of the Duke as the natural leader of a peace party in England would have been reinforced by the knowledge of a strange quarrel then in progress between the ex-King and the British Government.

In London, Churchill had been unable to arrange a job for the Duke in advance of his return to England. He would probably have liked to do so; but he was obstructed by the hostility of the Court, and the fear that the hesitant and uncharismatic George VI – built up by propaganda to symbolize England's struggle – would be unable to function in the shadow of his glamorous elder brother. The King's Private Secretary, Sir Alexander Hardinge – who had once and with questionable loyalty served

Edward VIII – told the Prime Minister that he did not see how it was possible for the Duke 'as an ex-King to perform any useful service in this country'.[39] To the Duke's plea for work, therefore, Churchill was only able to reply: 'It will be better for Your Royal Highness to come to England as arranged, when everything can be considered.'[40]

This, however, did not satisfy the Duke, whose position had now changed in two respects. First, he seemed to have been presented with an alternative future to returning to England in the form of Beigbeder's offer of a castle in the south of Spain. Secondly, he had come to the conclusion that, as a matter of honour, he could only go back to his own country if some gesture of recognition were made towards his wife. As he later wrote:

> His [Churchill's] personal advice to me was not to quibble about terms but to come home and wait patiently while he worked things out. But I could not in honour take this line. The year before, while we had been in England, the presence of the Duchess at my side had never been acknowledged, even perfunctorily. Before going back I wanted an assurance that simple courtesies would be forthcoming.... From a distance, what I insisted on may look to be of small value. But the perspectives of my life had changed, and the matter loomed mighty large for me.[41]

Contrary to what is often supposed, the Duke did not ask that the Duchess be given royal status, merely that she be received with him by the King and Queen in order to dispel the public impression that they were in disgrace. He did not imagine there could be an immediate reconciliation with his family; a mere gesture for the sake of appearances was what he sought. 'In the light of past experience', he wrote to Churchill on 27 June, 'my wife and myself must not risk finding ourselves once more regarded by the British public as in a different status to other members of my family.'[42]

The Court, however, would not consider the Duke's request. In a fierce exchange of telegrams lasting two days, Churchill continued to urge the Duke to return without conditions. The Duke would not yield, but declared his willingness – should his terms not be acceded to – to serve his country anywhere in the British Empire.[43]

Hoare was appalled at this dissension in time of strife. He tried to reason with both sides and bring about a settlement. On 29 June he wrote to Churchill that he had managed to get the Duke to whittle down his demands to very little. He had now dropped his request for a job in

England. As for the other matter, it 'boiled down to both of them being received only once for quite a short meeting by the King and Queen, and notice of this fact appearing in the Court Circular'. All that was at issue, Hoare stressed, was a 'once only' meeting of 'a quarter of an hour'.[44] Hoare earnestly hoped the Court would agree to this. But no reply came while the Duke was in Madrid; and when one eventually reached him, it was to be far from conciliatory. Meanwhile the quarrel put his future in doubt; it further embittered his relations with his country; and it encouraged those outside observers who got to hear of it – who included the Germans[45] – to believe that he might be willing to cast himself adrift from the policy of the British Government.

The Duke and Duchess did not spend all their time in Madrid thinking about their future. Accompanied by Tiger, they went sightseeing – to Toledo, the Escorial, the Civil War ruins outside the capital.[46] They saw something of their Spanish friends. The Duke was popular in Spain, which he had visited in the spring of 1927 at the invitation of his cousin-by-marriage King Alfonso XIII – now dying in exile. He enjoyed the company of Spaniards, and spoke tolerably good Spanish which he had picked up on his tours of South America. Among the old friends he saw in Madrid that summer were the beautiful Countess of Teba, whose brother had become Spanish Ambassador to London;[47] Prince Alfonso, another cousin-by-marriage, one of the flying heroes of the Civil War;[48] and Don Miguel Primo de Rivera, Civil Governor of Madrid, who had been the Duke's Spanish guide in 1927 and of whom he was to see a great deal more in the weeks to follow.[49]

Hoare was uneasy about some of these friends. 'If not actively pro-German, their memories of the Civil War made them anti-English.'[50] He suspected they might be encouraging the Duke in his hopeless view of the war – if not to stay on in Spain and make a stand for peace. On the other hand he saw definite advantages in the Duke's social round. The presence of so legendary an Englishman (with a romantic history likely to appeal to Spaniards) stimulated pro-British feeling in the capital: the Duke was the only Englishman to be cheered in the streets of Madrid that summer. And the Ambassador, who had not been in Spain long enough to make friends, saw a way through the Duke to get in touch with an influential section of Spanish society.

On 28 June, Hoare had a moment of triumph which made up for all the annoyance caused by the ducal visit. He gave a huge cocktail party in honour of the Duke and Duchess, using them as bait to draw over five hundred Spaniards to the British Embassy. They 'rose in every way to the occasion', he wrote afterwards. They 'could not have been more helpful' to him. 'Far from making any defeatist remarks, they went out of their way to show their belief in our final victory.'[51] It was a good mark for the Duke. But would it be enough to solve the problems still in the way of his return to England? Or to disabuse the Germans of the idea that he might be willing to break with his country?

On 1 July, as the Duke of Kent prepared to leave Lisbon, Hoare informed the Foreign Office that the Duke and Duchess of Windsor would be leaving the next day for Portugal. Their stay in Madrid, he said, had 'stimulated pro-German propaganda but otherwise it has done good in extending our personal contacts. They have both been very discreet and have made a good impression on the Spaniards. They took my advice on several points, e.g. interview with press.'[52] He warned, however, that he did 'not believe they will return to England without further assurances'.[53]

What then were the Duke's intentions when he left Spain for Portugal? The evidence is confused. Hoare wrote in his memoirs that, rather than return to England immediately, the Duke intended 'to await the reply in Lisbon to the questions about his future'.[54] The Duchess told Mrs Weddell that they were on their way back to England;[55] but she sent a telegram to her Aunt Bessie in Washington saying that their plans were still uncertain.[56] Beigbeder told Stohrer that the Duke had indicated (presumably through Tiger) that he meant eventually to return not to England but to Spain*[57] – in which case one might wonder why he was going to Portugal at all. Count Zoppi, on the other hand, informed Rome that he had heard from 'a reliable source' (again presumably Tiger) 'that the Duke of Windsor has removed himself to Lisbon in order to show the British Government – which continues to insist on his return to his own country – that he is not opposed in principle to going back to London. But he has not yet made up his mind and may possibly remain on the Continent.'[58]

Zoppi's report would appear to express the situation correctly. True to character, the Duke was hedging his bets, adopting a policy of wait-and-see. He had now made his return to England conditional on a single concession – that the King and Queen receive the Duchess for a quarter of

---

* But in a farewell note to Tiger, Gray Phillips gave no hint that the party might be returning: 'I don't know what we should have done without you and I hope some time in London we shall have the opportunity of repaying you' (Bermejillo Papers).

an hour. Failing that, he had offered to serve anywhere in the Empire. But what if neither the concession nor an imperial post were forthcoming? In that case, he would still have the Spanish Government's invitation up his sleeve (and there is nothing to suggest that he was aware that the Germans were behind that invitation). That was his insurance policy – so he would have taken care to give Beigbeder the impression that he was still thinking seriously about his offer, that he had not ruled out return to Spain.

Hoare's principal reaction to the departure of the Duke and Duchess was one of overwhelming relief.[59] Now that they were gone, he looked back with satisfaction on their visit. They had, he reported to Halifax,

> behaved admirably during their stay here. They have made themselves extremely popular with the many Spaniards whom they have met and apart from the family row in which once again I have been unwillingly involved, they have been both easy and affable. We have seen a good deal of them, having them to dinner and luncheon and at a big party we gave at the Embassy . . . the biggest cocktail party that there has been for years. . . . Several hundred came and it was generally adjudged to be a great success. You can however imagine what a trouble it is to have this kind of thing on one's back when the world is crashing. I think, however, that it can be said that we have already created a great body of goodwill here that may stand us in good stead if real trouble comes. . . .[60]

But to Churchill, Hoare wrote differently, and with a sense of urgency:

> I did my best with them while they were here and I greatly hoped that you would come to some accommodation over the offer. I am certain that this is the moment to end the trouble and if it is not ended now, the rift between them and the rest of the Family will become deeper and possibly more dangerous. The trouble is that he has no one who knows anything about England to advise him. As it was, I argued with him and with her for hours on end that this was not the moment for bargaining over details. They replied that they agreed provided both sides in the controversy behaved in the same way. . . .[61]

3
The Bahamas Appointment
2–4 July

The news that the Duke had been invited to remain in Spain by the Spanish Government, but had nevertheless proceeded to Portugal, reached Berlin around midnight on 2 July in the form of a telegram from Stohrer reporting a conversation with Beigbeder. It put an interesting construction on events. The Duke had told Beigbeder that he would not be returning to England unless 'his wife were recognized as a member of the Royal Family and he were given an influential post of a military or civil nature'. (The Duke wrote 'Correct' against this when he saw it for the first time in 1953.) He had also expressed himself 'in strong terms against Churchill and against this war'. (Against this the Duke wrote: 'No'.) He therefore intended to return to Spain, where Beigbeder had offered him the palace at Ronda for an indefinite period. Why then was he going to Portugal at all? Stohrer's telegram gave two answers: 'to confer with the Duke of Kent' and 'to replenish himself with money'.[1]

This is nonsense, and shows the care which must be taken with the German telegrams. Prince George was by this time safely back in London, and the Duke of Windsor had gone out of his way to ensure that his own presence in Portugal did not coincide with his brother's. As for extra funds, there was no greater prospect of touching these in Portugal than in Spain: the Duke was travelling with quite a large sum in cash, and apart from this had only his bank account in Paris (frozen on the occupation) and his liquid assets in London (upon which he could not draw abroad without permission). Either the Duke had spread a deliberately misleading account of the motives for his journey – or else Beigbeder or Stohrer had concocted a cock-and-bull story to explain away their failure to keep him in Spain.

At all events, this was the despatch by which Ribbentrop learned that the Duke had left Spain and gone on to Portugal. What were his reactions to it? The only account is again that of his young aide Erich Kordt – not the most reliable of witnesses, but the only one we have. According to Kordt, the Reich Foreign Minister was not taken in by the reassuring language of Stohrer's telegram. To him it was a simple case of the fish escaping the net. He was furious. He ranted and raved. 'The Embassy has failed us completely in letting him get away!' he thundered. 'And so has Franco!' He cursed himself for not having asked the Spanish Government to intern the Duke. Would this not have been simple, seeing he was a British officer on neutral soil? Pulling himself together, the fuming *Reichsaussenminister* proceeded to issue 'new instructions'. But we may leave the reminiscing Kordt at this point, for his recollections as to what those instructions may have been are hopelessly muddled.[2]

All that is known for certain is that Dr Erich Gardemann now went to see Ribbentrop in Berlin on the matter of the Duke of Windsor.[3] Gardemann (who was thirty-four in July 1940) was the Madrid agent of Ribbentrop's private intelligence service (*Dienststelle Ribbentrop*), with the rank of Counsellor at the German Embassy. He was a shifty and common Westphalian who before the war had been a shady businessman in Latin America. No one quite knew what he was doing in Madrid (it was generally assumed he was spying on Stohrer for Ribbentrop), and he was cordially disliked both by the Embassy staff and by the Spaniards. The records tell us nothing about whatever discussions he may have had with Ribbentrop on the subject of the Duke, nor did he wish to divulge anything when interviewed by a German historian in 1970.[4]

Meanwhile, on the morning of Wednesday 3 July, the Duke and Duchess – still accompanied by Gray Phillips and the George Woods – had crossed safely into Portugal after spending the night at the *Parador Nacional* at Mérida. They were met at the frontier by Neil Hogg, Second Secretary at the Lisbon Embassy, a rubicund young man who was thirty in July 1940 and whose father had been Edward VIII's Lord Chancellor. He recalls:

I met the ducal party at the Badajoz/Elvas frontier on a blazing day in July.... Both posts had been informed in advance that the Duke would be coming, for the formalities were brief; even so, I was left at the Spanish post to tie up loose ends, while the party went on towards Lisbon in two cars and a trailer. As they did not know their way, they went right into the fortified town of Elvas instead of round it, and found themselves unable to turn in the narrow streets. From their account I gathered that they were quickly recognized by the enthusiastically pro-British inhabitants, who manhandled the cars in the right direction and showered the party which boxes and boxes of the preserved fruits for which the region is famous. When I caught up with them I found them facing the right way, astonished, gratified and somewhat bewildered.

I had arranged for lunch at the country house of an old-established English family in the neighbourhood of Vila Viçosa, but they would have nothing of it. Instead, we picnicked under a cork oak in the middle of the burning Alentejo plain known to the Portuguese as Africa. There we sat, eating sardines from the tin with our fingers and making the kind of conversation that you hear at Embassy luncheons. You could not have guessed that Europe was falling in ruins at the time. As we finished, two of the Duke's small terriers, who had been skirmishing round us while we ate, discovered a deposit of some unidentifiable filth, rolled in it lavishly, and presented themselves reeking and full of self-satisfaction. In that state it would have been impossible to tolerate their presence in a car. An attempt by the Duchess to cleanse them with Vichy water had no success at all. Fortunately, to my utter astonishment, there proved to be a copious spring nearby; this, in a notoriously waterless region, still seems to me nothing short of a miracle. To his great credit, the Duke insisted on washing his dogs himself.

The onward journey to Lisbon was uneventful.[5]

The Duke (who had been in Portugal once before, on a brief state visit to Lisbon in April 1931) now breathed a new atmosphere, for Portugal in July 1940 was a very different place to Spain. Despite some sympathy for Italy and Germany within the dictatorship, the general feeling in the country was decidedly anglophile. British influence had always been strong in Portugal, who was England's 'oldest ally' and had recently been her ally in the 1914–18 War. Salazar, though determined to remain strictly neutral, harboured a deep historical reverence for the Anglo–Portuguese Alliance and privately wanted Great Britain to win.

In the late afternoon the party crossed the Tagus Estuary, in the ferry from Cacilhas to Cais do Sodré, where a friendly local press was waiting in force to meet them. There they had their first glimpse of Lisbon – a city which, in spite of its great beauty and its being the last Western European capital to have an abundance of food and drink, was a nervous and uncomfortable place in July 1940. It had been inundated by a wave of desperate refugees from France and the Low Countries (along with large numbers of homeward-bound journalists and diplomatists), who competed for a strictly limited number of hotel beds, residence permits, and visas and passages to foreign destinations. The Portuguese Secret Police – the dreaded PVDE* – were widely and often brutally in evidence

* Subsequently and better known as PIDE.

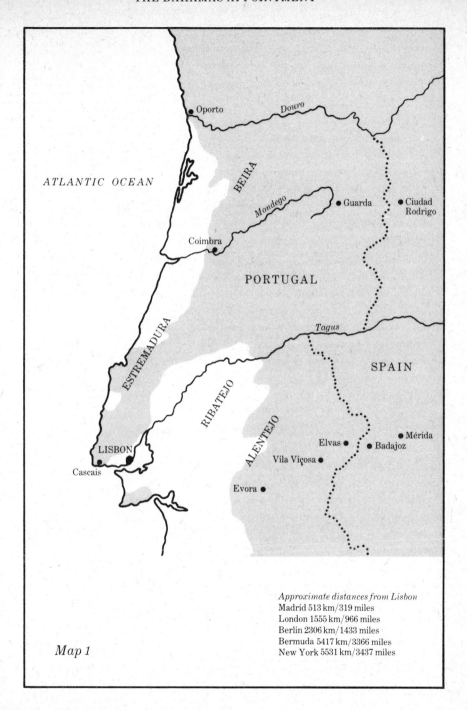

ATLANTIC OCEAN

Oporto

Douro

BEIRA

Mondego

Guarda

Ciudad Rodrigo

Coimbra

PORTUGAL

ESTREMADURA

Tagus

SPAIN

RIBATEJO

ALENTEJO

Mérida

Elvas

Badajoz

Vila Viçosa

LISBON

Cascais

Evora

Approximate distances from Lisbon
Madrid 513 km/319 miles
London 1555 km/966 miles
Berlin 2306 km/1433 miles
Bermuda 5417 km/3366 miles
New York 5531 km/3437 miles

Map 1

as they tried to control this influx. To the chorus of tragedy was added one of conspiracy, for Lisbon had become Europe's most active centre of international espionage; great numbers of Portuguese were bribed to spy on the would-be emigrants, the ships in the harbour, and other nations' diplomats and spies. The city buzzed with rumours that the Germans were about to occupy Portugal to forestall a British landing.

This spy-ridden and refugee-infested capital was not, however, the final destination of the Duke and his party on 3 July. They were heading for a house on the sea outside the fashionable fishing town of Cascais, some seventeen miles to the west of Lisbon. Originally they had been due to stay at the British Embassy;[6] but instructions had arrived from London that they were not to receive official hospitality,* and so it had become necessary to find somewhere else to put them.

The member of the Embassy responsible for finding alternative accommodation for the Duke and Duchess – in fact for making all the practical arrangements in connection with their stay in Portugal – was the Air Attaché, Wing-Commander P. R. Tankerville ('Tanks') Chamberlayne. The son of an Anglo–Irish landowner and an Italian princess, Chamberlayne (who was forty-two in July 1940) had had a legendary career during the First World War, both as an aviator (he was a pilot at seventeen) and an intelligence officer. 'In defeat fear me most' was his family motto. In 1937 he had joined the Air Intelligence Branch, serving as Assistant Attaché in Paris before going on to Lisbon. His numerous official and clandestine duties in Portugal included the evacuation of British refugees, and the task of seeing the Duke and Duchess of Windsor safely off to wherever they were going came within this category of operations. Faced with the problem of accommodation, Chamberlayne booked the ducal party into the Hotel Palacio at Estoril, that celebrated establishment which since opening its doors in 1930 had already become something of a haunt of royalty on the run. However, shortly before the party was due to arrive the manager rang the Embassy to say that the hotel could no longer take them owing to shortage of space and problems of security, and that he had arranged instead for them to stay at the nearby villa of the banker Ricardo Espírito Santo Silva.[7]

The man who thus became the Duke's host was thirty-nine in July 1940,

---

* Presumably to emphasize the distinction between the Duke of Windsor's private visit and the Duke of Kent's official mission. There were also general instructions which had gone out after the Abdication to British missions overseas that the Duke of Windsor and his consort were not to be treated as official personages or entertained officially (see FO 954/33).

and had become one of the richest and most influential figures in Portugal under Salazar, with whom he claimed to be on intimate terms. He was an expansive, engaging, strikingly good-looking individual, noted both as a sportsman and a lady-killer. His origins were romantically obscure: he was said to be the grandson of a foundling child who had been abandoned on the steps of the Church of the Holy Ghost (*Igreja do Espírito Santo*) in Lisbon. At the age of fifteen he had inherited a small family bank with his elder brother José, a somewhat retiring youth who turned out to be a financial genius. The brothers married sisters, the heiresses Mary and Vera Cohen; for José it was a second marriage, and the stigma of divorce obliged him in the 1930s to hand Ricardo control of what was now well on the way to becoming a colossal business empire. As a rapidly rising young man in a country noted for its class distinctions, Ricardo sought to acquire social credentials. The hallmark of a great family in Portugal was its art collection and, having inherited no heirlooms, he built up one of the finest twentieth-century collections of silver, porcelain, furniture and *objets de vertu*, much of which filled his summer villa at Cascais. He also became known for his generous benefactions (the British Council owed much to him in Portugal); and he sought to establish himself as a famous host and entertainer. The Duke of Windsor was a magnificent catch for him – as the manager of the Palacio doubtless realized.

When he heard that the ducal party had been redirected to the Espírito Santo villa, Chamberlayne was dismayed. Ricardo was a close friend of the German Minister in Lisbon, and though he had strong English as well as German connections and had entertained the Duke of Kent on his recent visit, British Intelligence was increasingly coming to regard him as pro-German.* (The Nazis had been cultivating him as a useful man close to the régime; they would soon have a very special use for him indeed.) However, Chamberlayne came to the conclusion (as he later wrote) 'that it would do more harm than good if an attempt were made at that late stage to put things into reverse, particularly as the Windsors were then expected to stay in Portugal for no more than a couple of days'.[8] So the villa it was. On the afternoon of Wednesday 3 July Chamberlayne went out there to make sure all was in readiness for the ducal arrival, and was alarmed to discover Ricardo and his wife ('Mr and Mrs Holy Ghost', as he called them) waiting to greet the party as host and hostess: he had previously been led to believe that the loan of the villa was purely a

---

* On the other hand, his two brothers were regarded as pro-British – a fact which enabled the *Banco Espírito Santo* to trade with both sides throughout the war.

business transaction.[9] They were joined by another who wished to welcome the ex-King and his entourage in person – the British Ambassador to Portugal, Sir Walford Selby.

Selby (who was fifty-nine in July 1940) was a Foreign Office hand of the old school whom the Duke of Windsor knew well. He owed much to a fine, old-fashioned appearance, and had been Principal Private Secretary to a succession of British Foreign Secretaries from 1924 to 1932, finally resigning in disgust at the weak and vacillating policy of Sir John Simon. He was then packed off as British Minister to Vienna, a post which was minor when he took it on but soon became important because of Nazi Germany's annexationist designs on Austria. Selby was probably the most popular British envoy there has ever been in the Austrian capital. He believed passionately in Austrian independence, and that its maintenance was a paramount British interest; he was distressed by the British policy of appeasing Germany and alienating Italy, which he rightly feared would seal Austria's fate. He also charmed the Austrians socially, and his hour of glory came in 1935 when – to Austrian rapture – he twice persuaded the Prince of Wales to take a holiday in Austria. The following year as King he came again, and after the Abdication it was in Austria that he chose to spend the first months of exile. 'The Austrians were unquestionably grateful to HRH', wrote Selby in his memoirs,* 'for his presence in Vienna at a time when they were under so much pressure from Hitler.'[10] Bonds of affection and respect had grown up between the two men; and when they met at Cascais on 3 July 1940, the Duke of Windsor could count himself in the presence of an old friend.

Unfortunately, the Selby of 1940 was not the same Selby as the Duke had last seen in Vienna in April 1937. Only shortly after that time, fear and trepidation at the awful destiny dangling over Austria, coupled with the traumatic effects of an accident sustained while disembarking from a ship, had affected poor Selby's mind. The once able and cheerful envoy suddenly seemed to lose his touch; he became nervous and inarticulate; and the Foreign Office quickly transferred him from the ultra-sensitive

---

* Selby's memoirs are a somewhat pathetic work, dealing with the social rather than the political events of his career. Of the ducal sojourn in Portugal, he has only this to say:

Shortly after the departure of the Duke of Kent, HRH the Duke of Windsor and the Duchess of Windsor arrived. They made a relatively prolonged stay at Estoril [sic] before proceeding to the Bahamas, and met numerous Portuguese who were very glad to welcome them.... I had the impression that both the Duke and Duchess enjoyed their stay in Portugal, where they made numerous friends (Diplomatic Twilight, p. 122).

Vienna Legation to the comfortable but unimportant Embassy at Lisbon, a convenient backwater, it was thought, for a once distinguished diplomatist, now a mere shadow of his former self, to await retirement. But though Lisbon may have been a backwater when Selby arrived there in December 1937, it rapidly ceased to be one after the outbreak of war; and the fall of France gave it a critical importance as Great Britain's last listening-post in Western Europe. Selby, nervous wreck that he had become, was unable to cope. Rather than recall him for the time being, the Foreign Office chose to keep him on as a kind of mascot while sending out a number of astute men to take over most of his diplomatic functions. One such was David Eccles, who was struck by the pathos of Selby's decline. 'Here we have a minor tragedy in the failure of Walford – and he is *so* nice – to carry out his own good ideas, to act up to his own sense of his own role. . . . What a tragedy, quite a tiny tragedy, but exquisite in its completeness.'[11]

The impending arrival of the Duke and Duchess at so tense a moment filled Selby with nervousness. He told Salazar that, 'though a friend of the Duke, he would put personal feelings aside and simply follow whatever instructions he was given'.[12] It fell to him to receive the ex-King at the end of his journey; and he was on the steps of the villa to greet him on the evening of 3 July, flanked by Chamberlayne and a somewhat resented Espírito Santo.

The greetings over, the practicalities were raised of the party's imminent repatriation. Chamberlayne explained that two flying boats of RAF Coastal Command were waiting in the Tagus to take them back to England.* These would be leaving the following day – or at the latest the day after, under the Portuguese neutrality regulations. However, before leaving Spain the Duke had still been laying down conditions for his return to England – albeit rapidly diminishing ones. What would be his attitude now?† Would he – as Hoare had warned London the previous day – refuse to return 'without further assurances'? Or would he – as the Duchess had told the US Ambassador in Madrid – embark with her for England without delay?

---

* The Duchess appears to have imagined Chamberlayne to be one of the captains of the Flying Boats.

† The Duchess's memoirs are somewhat muddled at this point. She writes that the Duke refused to return to England and 'requested Sir Walford to have the Flying Boats sent home immediately', then engaging in a two-day telegraphic battle with London concerning the status of the Duchess. What the Duchess almost certainly had in mind were events which had in fact taken place the previous week in Madrid, when the Duke was having traumatic interviews on the subject of his return not with Selby but with Hoare.

In the event, he was given little choice. Selby handed him a telegram from Winston Churchill dated 1 July, which had been addressed to him in Madrid but missed him there and so been sent to Lisbon. It read:

> Your Royal Highness has taken active military rank and refusal to obey direct orders of competent military authority would create a serious situation. I hope it will not be necessary for such orders to be sent. I must strongly urge immediate compliance with wishes of the Government.[13]

In other words, he was now being ordered back to England on pain of court martial. The curt and threatening language of this message distressed the Duke terribly. As he wrote to Churchill the following October:

> I used to have your support until you reached the supreme power of PM, since when you seem to have subscribed to the Court's hostile attitude towards me. Due to the negligence of both our military and diplomatic authorities in France I got lost in the shuffle of war and, left to my own devices to avoid capture by the enemy, I duly informed you when I had reached a neutral country. You thereupon summoned me back to England, and when I felt bound in my interests to make my compliance with this summons contingent upon a fair and simple request which my brother evidently turned down, you threatened me with what amounted to arrest, thus descending to dictator methods in your treatment of your old friend and former King. . . .*[14]

However, for all the bitterness he may have felt, the Duke did not resist this final command of the Prime Minister. He now agreed to return to England without delay and without conditions. After a hasty consultation with Chamberlayne, a travel schedule was worked out. The party would leave Lisbon on the flying boats at 11.40 the following (Thursday) night; they would be due to arrive at Poole Harbour at 5.50 on the morning of Friday 5 July. Chamberlayne conveyed this flight information to London in a *Most Urgent* telegram which reached the Air Ministry shortly before midnight on Wednesday.[15] But by then a new wartime destiny had been worked out for the Duke of Windsor. This he discovered when he drove to the British Embassy the following morning,† where he was

---

* In the draft of this letter, the Duke originally wrote of 'gangster methods', which the Duchess changed in her own hand to read 'dictator methods'.

† A fine rose-tinted palace, the Embassy was situated in the western part of the capital, on the hill of Lapa overlooking the harbour. It would have taken about forty-five minutes to drive there from Cascais in 1940. Owing to the wartime expansion of the Embassy, the chancery moved the following year to a larger building nearby, and the original Embassy became the private residence of the British Ambassador, which it still is.

received not by the Ambassador but by David Eccles, who gave him unexpected news.

David Eccles (now the Right Honourable Viscount Eccles, PC, CH, KCVO) was thirty-five in July 1940. His official rank was that of Economic Counsellor to the Embassy, but the influence which he exercised was far greater than this title suggested. A highly educated Wykehamist and a lover of the arts, his marriage to Sybil, the remarkable daughter of the royal physician Lord Dawson of Penn, had given him an ally in life and powerful social connections, including connections at Court. Before 1939 he had travelled widely in the Peninsula and made a fortune in financial operations connected with the construction of a railway in Northern Spain; and on the outbreak of war he was sent to Madrid by the newly-created Ministry of Economic Warfare to persuade the Franco régime to accept a trade agreement which would encourage its economic dependence on the Allies and hence its neutrality in the Second World War. Not only was the mission crowned with success, but the young plenipotentiary – with his intelligence and charm and familiarity with the language, temperament and civilization of the Spaniards – turned out to have a surer touch than any of the British diplomatists in the Peninsula. In April 1940 he was sent out again, this time to Lisbon. His official brief was to reorganize the economic side of the Embassy, but he quickly took over from the faltering Selby the whole conduct of relations with the one man who really mattered in Portugal, Dr Salazar. Eccles got on splendidly with the donnish dictator, sharing his love of philosophy and of Europe's conservative traditions. 'Salazar really is a wonder,' wrote Eccles to his wife (for he was not just the *eminence grise* but also the Creevy of British policy in the Peninsula); 'so quiet, so romantic, so efficient and, I can't help adding, so extraordinarily fond of me.'[16]

Among the numerous subjects they discussed in late June of 1940 was the impending visit of the Duke of Windsor.[17] Salazar (whose principal concern, it has been noted, was that the Duke of Windsor's stay should not 'clash' with the mission of the Duke of Kent) regarded the ex-King as something of an embarrassment, but nevertheless wished to make him welcome and secure in Portugal.[18] The Duke was not a stranger to Eccles, who had come into contact with him on several occasions before and during his reign, not only through Court connections but also through their mutual friend Victor Cazalet. A Nonconformist upbringing now caused him to take a somewhat disapproving view of his former sovereign; when he heard he was coming to Lisbon (which he appears to

75

have done before anyone else), he resolved to 'watch him at breakfast, lunch and dinner with a critical eye'.[19] It seems likely, indeed, that Eccles had been asked to keep a critical eye on the Duke on behalf of certain important quarters. But when they finally met that Thursday morning, it was under peculiar circumstances.

The following telegram had arrived from London:

> Foreign Office, 4th July 1940, 2.10 a.m. MOST IMMEDIATE
> Following for Duke of Windsor from Prime Minister.
> I am authorized by the King and Cabinet to offer you the appointment of Governor and Commander-in-Chief of the Bahamas. If you accept, it may be possible to take you and the Duchess direct from Lisbon dependent on the military situation. Please let me know without delay whether this proposal is satisfactory to Your Royal Highness. Personally I feel sure it is the best open in the grievous situation in which we all stand. At any rate I have done my best.[20]

The precise origins of the idea of sending the Duke to the Bahamas are not entirely clear.[21] Churchill told Beaverbrook that he had thought it up himself; while Lord Lloyd, the Colonial Secretary, told a friend that the appointment was 'the King's own idea, to keep him at all costs out of England'.[22] But the source does not greatly matter. By the end of June it had become clear that, if the Duke was not going to return to England, it was essential to find a niche for him outside Europe.* As Churchill wrote in a personal telegram to Roosevelt:

> The position of the Duke of Windsor in recent months has been causing his Majesty and His Majesty's Government some embarrassment as though his loyalties are unimpeachable there is always a backwash of Nazi intrigue which seeks to make trouble about him now that the greater part of the continent is in enemy hands. There are personal and family difficulties about his return to this country. In all the circumstances it was felt that an appointment abroad might appeal to him, and the Prime Minister has with His Majesty's cordial approval offered him the Governorship of the Bahamas.[23]

The irony was that the telegram containing the offer came only a few hours after the Duke had actually agreed to return to England without

---

* While the Duke was in Madrid, Hardinge had suggested to Churchill that he might be made a staff officer in Egypt (which was about to be invaded by the Italians); while the Prime Minister's Private Secretary had telephoned the Colonial Office to ask: 'Are there any spare governorships going?' The Bahamas may have been suggested by Sir Bede Clifford – a former Governor of that Colony and friend of the Duke – who was then in London on leave from his post in Mauritius.

delay and without conditions: the two despatches had in fact crossed.* It was too much for poor Selby. His nerve failed him; he could not face breaking the news to the Duke; and, as so often in those wild, those incomprehensible days, he sought out the cool and masterful Eccles, thrust the telegram into his hands, and uttered that weak and desperate phrase which Eccles invariably heard when any delicate or complicated matter cropped up at the Embassy: '*You deal with it!*' And so it was Eccles and not Selby who received the Duke that Thursday morning, and presented him with the telegram.[24]

The Duke stared at the telegram in astonishment for some minutes, unable to decide what to make of it. He was still smarting from the effect of Churchill's previous telegram threatening arrest. As he wrote to Churchill four months later: 'I will never forget that telegram you sent me via Madrid and which I received in Lisbon, nor can I describe my surprise upon going to the British Embassy the next morning to find another telegram offering me the governorship of the Bahamas.'[25] Well might the offer of the Bahamas have given the Duke pause for thought. In modern British history no member of the Royal Family had been a colonial governor or indeed occupied any post involving political responsibility – and this post was a notorious grave of reputations.†

The Bahamas – a coral archipelago strung out between Florida and Cuba – was one of the smallest and least important of all British Colonies. Its population of 72,000 was descended from pirates and slaves. The main island of New Providence had recently acquired a reputation as a smart winter resort for American tourists; before that, the principal economic activity had been bootlegging. The islands were stony and infertile and produced next to nothing. There was constant political warfare between the colonial authorities and the corrupt white merchants who controlled the House of Assembly, and posts there were generally regarded as the most undesirable in the colonial service.

Eventually the Duke said to Eccles: 'What would you advise me to do?'

'I'd take it, Sir,' replied Eccles. 'You'll be safe there. You'd get blown up here.' He pointed out that the post, however minor and remote, would enable the Duke to serve his country in war, and that it would mean some

---

* A Foreign Office official minuted on the copy of Churchill's telegram: 'A message has just been received by the Air Ministry to the effect that the Duke will leave Lisbon tonight by air for England. The above telegram may, possibly, affect his decision.'

† I have described the constitutional peculiarity of the Duke's appointment, and the history and geography of the Bahamas, in some detail in *The Duke of Windsor's War*, pp. 95–6 and 107ff.

recognition for the Duchess. The Duke seemed to agree. They discussed the post for half an hour. Finally the Duke declared that he would send his reply to Churchill after lunch accepting the appointment.[26]

Eccles accompanied the Duke back to Cascais. On arrival at the house, the Duke gave the news to the Duchess. 'Governor of the Colony of the Bahamas,' he said (according to the Duchess's memoirs). 'One of the few parts of the Empire which I missed on my travels. Well, Winston said he was sorry, but it was the best he could do, and I shall keep my side of the bargain.'[27] (The 'bargain' was a reference to the Duke's earlier assurance to Churchill that, if family circumstances made it impossible for him to return to England, he would be willing to serve in any part of the Empire.) Gray Phillips and George Wood were also informed, and both offered to accompany the Duke to the Bahamas – Wood as his ADC, Phillips as his Private Secretary. It was arranged that Phillips should go to England that night with the returning flying boats: he would be the Duke's agent in London in the weeks that followed in the long and complex preparations for the unprecedented appointment.

And so they proceeded to lunch. Being a tremendous ladies' man and student of women, Eccles was interested to see the Duchess again: they had last met in the autumn of 1936 when Eccles, accompanied by Victor Cazalet, had called on Mrs Simpson at Cumberland Terrace. His impressions now were disappointing. 'I wouldn't give ten shillings for Wallis,' he wrote that evening in a facetious letter to his wife. 'She is a poor creature.' (He was later to revise this opinion.) In the same letter he wrote that the Duke – who 'adores her and is in fine health' – had been offered a job, 'a very cunning solution'; that he had accepted it 'under great pressure from your affectionate DE'; and that he was 'pretty fifth column – but that's only for you'.[28] This was, of course, humorous exaggeration. The Duke had required little persuasion to accept his post, and (Lord Eccles is today at pains to point out) in no way was he 'fifth column' in the sense of being on the side of his country's enemies. But he did strike Eccles as something of a faint heart. He said that in his view it was hopeless to carry on the struggle, and that the best thing to do would be to negotiate a peace which would end the fighting and enable Britain to avoid the worst.* Otherwise all that lay ahead was endless suffering, defeat and occupation. What was Britain fighting for now? To save

---

* The previous day, the Royal Navy had attacked the French fleet at Oran. Though this tragic act was the result of diplomatic muddle and misguided strategic anxieties, it was widely interpreted as an act of vengeance against a renegade ally and a symbol of Great Britain's determination to fight on.

Poland? To save face? Eccles was astonished: less than six months earlier he had heard the same things said across a lunch table – almost exactly the same words, though applied to the fate of France rather than of England – by ... Marshal Pétain, then French Ambassador to Spain, now head of the French Government which had signed the Armistice with Germany.* Eccles tried strenuously (and not entirely without success) to convince the Duke of a contrary view, that the situation was far from hopeless, that any peace would make England a vassal of Germany. But he did not doubt the Duke's patriotism. 'No one can understand the Duke's attitude at that time', he says, 'unless they realize that he honestly believed the war was lost. He did not want the Germans to win, but he thought that, if the war carried on, they would.'†[29]

After lunch they returned to the Embassy, where the Duke installed himself in a private sitting-room and ordered a typewriter to be brought. Using two fingers, he typed out his reply to the Prime Minister: 'I will accept appointment as Governor of Bahamas as I am sure you have done your best for me in a difficult situation.'[30] This he handed to Eccles to take to the cipher clerk. Eccles promptly showed it to Selby, who was gratified and relieved. 'But this won't be the end of it,' added Eccles. 'You'll see.'[31]

---

* The armistice with Germany was signed on 22 June, that with Italy on the 24th. Both came into effect in the early hours of the 25th. The Third Republic was to be replaced by the new 'Etat Français' at Vichy on 10 July.

† By the end of the month, however, the Duke appears to have taken a somewhat rosier view of Great Britain's prospects, which he described to a Spanish visitor on the 31st as 'still by no means hopeless'. See below, p. 188.

4
In the Jaws of Hell
July 1940

If one drives west out of Lisbon along the southern coast of the
Estremadura Peninsula, past Belem, from where the Renaissance
navigators sailed, past the point where the Tagus Estuary becomes the
Atlantic Ocean, one comes after fifteen miles to a wide bay terminating in
a quiet cove. The long shore of the bay contains the scenically dull bathing
resort of Estoril, which sprang up between the wars, noted for its Hotel
Palacio, its beach and its casino. Above the cove rises Cascais, a pretty
eighteenth-century town with a fishing harbour, fashionable since the
1870s, when the Portuguese Court chose it as a summer residence. Continuing along the coast road, past the former royal palace, one next comes
to an isolated promontory jutting southwards into the Atlantic, its pine
forest protected from the gales by one headland further to the west. At
its edge lies a spectacular rock formation known as *o boca do inferno* – the
jaws of hell – a steep gulley created by marine erosion into which the
waves crash violently in stormy weather. Beyond this there is really
nothing. One is at the extremity of the Old World. Turning north at the
tip of Estremadura one finds a desolate coast, the windswept sands of
Guincho, rising suddenly to the barren heights of Cabo da Roca, the
westernmost point of Europe.

Taking its name from the *boca do inferno*, Ricardo Espírito Santo's
estate occupied most of the wooded promontory; and his house, being then
the last along that stretch of coast, was in a sense the last house in
Western Europe. It is still there, though now divided into flats for his
descendants; and it is now almost part of metroland. Little roads inter-
sect what remains of the pine forest, giving access to a new suburb of
fashionable modern dwellings. Even the walled garden of the house has
been turned into building lots. The road dividing the house from the rocky
shore, once a quiet lane, is now busy with tourist traffic and loud with the

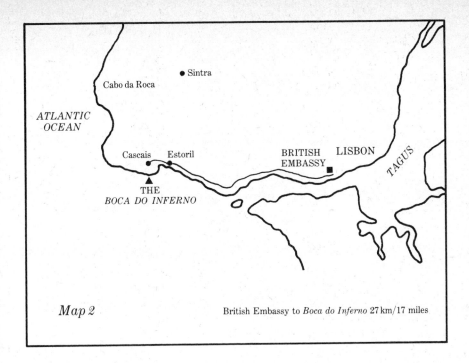

Map 2   British Embassy to *Boca do Inferno* 27 km / 17 miles

roar of motor cycles. The *boca* itself, three hundred yards away, has become a well-established tourist attraction, complete with car park, cafeteria, souvenir shops and disregarded litter-bins. On fine days there is a flotilla of pleasure craft out at sea where once only a few fishing boats were to be seen. And yet, as one stands on the terrace on a quiet morning out of season, it is not hard to recapture the seclusion of this place, or see it as the Duke of Windsor would have seen it in July 1940 – as a rugged stretch of coastline sharply disappearing to left and right, an eighteenth-century villa and a little coastguard station providing the only other signs of human life, and all around the vast expanse of ocean, bare and blue, broken only by a thin grey line of hills faintly visible on the south-east horizon beyond the Tagus Estuary.

The house – set in a few acres of walled gardens, which included a swimming-pool terrace – was a typical rich man's seaside villa of the 1920s. It was a roomy, rambling, unremarkable edifice in pink stucco, with a gabled roof and a colonnade. The south-facing apartments consisted of a huge plush bedroom suite with a terrace on the first floor, and a

81

heavily gilded ballroom, dining-room and drawing-room on the ground floor, filled with eighteenth-century furniture and *Compagnie des Indes* porcelain of sensational quality. It was a house which spoke eloquently of the character of its owner – a comfortable family house, a showy collector's house, a house where one might give splendid dinner parties but not have many guests to stay. There were a dozen indoor servants, including a chef of international reputation.

This was to be the home of the Duke and Duchess until they left for the Bahamas – or wherever they were going. It was a pleasant refuge, where they wanted for no material comfort. But they had little peace of mind there, and it was not long before they came to regard it both as a haunted house and a prison. To begin with, there was security.

Throughout his stay in Portugal, the Duke (as he was uncomfortably aware) was under the surveillance of Great Britain's Secret Intelligence Service, MI6. Its agents attempted to obtain information about him by bribing the Portuguese guards and servants by whom he was surrounded; by talking to those who visited or received visits from him; and through the occasional tip-off from the Portuguese secret police.[1] With the exception of this last source, it is unlikely that the information thus secured was of much value. Though it somehow succeeded in impressing the Germans, the Lisbon station of MI6 in the summer of 1940 was straight out of Graham Greene. Its first wartime head, an elderly, alcoholic ex-naval officer, had recently been replaced by Richman Stopford, an Anglo–Brazilian former MI5 officer who was new to intelligence work and who within a few weeks had succeeded in quarrelling with almost every member of the British Embassy, where his cover was that of Financial Attaché.[2] When it came to getting a picture of the Duke and what he was saying and thinking, it is far more likely that the British authorities would have relied on a man like David Eccles, who knew the Duke personally and saw him frequently and was in direct touch with Lord Halifax and other leading figures in London. 'As I kept saying at the time,' says Eccles, 'we could have done without the secret service in Portugal. They were always getting it wrong, and they were always getting into trouble.'[3]

The Duke's safety was another matter. As there were no British guards locally available, Chamberlayne had to arrange for him to be protected by the Portuguese authorities. Astonishingly, it never seems to have crossed Chamberlayne's mind that it might be necessary to guard against a German undercover plot to kidnap the Duke in Portugal. 'Our only fear', he

Hitler greets the Duke of Windsor at the Obersalzberg, 22 October 1937. According to the interpreter Paul Schmidt (seen on the left of the picture, beside the Duke's bibulous German guide Dr Ley in the belted raincoat) the Duke was 'frank and friendly' with the Führer, but 'there was nothing whatever to indicate whether he really sympathized with the ideology and practices of the Third Reich, as Hitler seemed to assume he did'.

In uniform, November 1939

Arriving at the Ritz Madrid, 23 June 1940

In Madrid

The villa at the *Boca do Inferno* as it is today, a photograph taken from over the sea. The swimming-pool terrace is on the right. The Duke and Duchess occupied the suite of rooms on the first floor giving out onto the terrace above the colonnade.

At the *Boca do Inferno*

Garden party at the *Boca do Inferno*, 30 July 1940. From left to right: the Baroness Almeida Santos; Madame Ricardo Espírito Santo Silva; Walter Monckton (obscured); Viscountess Soveral; Madame Tomás Pinto Basto; Madame José Espírito Santo Silva; the Duchess; Madame Melo Breyner.

Sir Samuel Hoare: with King Edward VIII as First Lord of the Admiralty, November 1936; and arriving in Spain as Ambassador on Special Mission, June 1940. Hoare suspected the existence of a German plot, and considered it essential that the Duke of Windsor return to England in the summer of 1940 and be reconciled to his family.

Sir Walford Selby, British Ambassador to Portugal. An old friend of the Duke, he was deeply embarrassed by the instructions he received regarding the ex-King's treatment.

David Eccles. A special British agent responsible for keeping Spain and Portugal under economic pressure, one of his duties that July was to keep an eye on the Duke of Windsor.

Mademoiselle Marguerite Moulichon, the Duchess of Windsor's French maid. By kidnapping her in France together with her mistress's luggage, the Germans imagined that they might detain the Duke and Duchess in Europe.

Sir Walter Monckton, the Duke's old friend. Having got wind of the German plot, Churchill sent him to Portugal to tell the Duke to get out fast.

Hailed by cheering crowds and scarcely aware of the danger from which he is escaping, the Duke embarks on the SS *Excalibur*, 1 August 1940. Behind him, Walter Monckton.

The Palacio de Montarco at Ciudad Rodrigo, where the Duke and Duchess were to have been brought – and **kept** – had they come to Spain.

wrote in the 1950s, 'was that Hitler might launch his long-awaited attack on Spain and Portugal. . . . Paratroops, fast-moving light armour and the inevitable confusion that such an attack would cause might well have resulted in the capture of the Duke, if not worse.'[4] Apart from the Duke's physical security, there were other fears of a rather different order: that a flood of journalists and refugees would try to get near him with a view to writing embarrassing stories or asking embarrassing favours; that he might drop some indiscretion which could be magnified into an incident; that he might make too great an impression on the Portuguese and so steal the thunder from the successful recent mission of the Duke of Kent. These considerations weighed just as heavily with the Portuguese as with the British: Salazar was anxious not to spoil the effect of the official Kent visit, and wished to avoid all embarrassments. Accordingly, a régime of virtual protective custody was envisaged for the Duke, accompanied by a total news blackout; and it was decided to put him under the personal protection of the head of the Portuguese secret police, Captain Lourenço.

Capitão de Infantaria Agostinho Lourenço da Conceição Pereira was fifty-four in July 1940. He was a small, unremarkable-looking man with an egg-shaped skull and a passion for orderliness. For ten years his had been the task of rooting out and crushing the opposition to the New State, a task he had accomplished with ruthless determination. By 1940 little opposition remained; his problem now was to control the great mass of foreign agents and refugees inside Portugal. To this task he addressed himself conscientiously. The Germans suspected that his personal inclinations were pro-British (he had fought with the Portuguese contingent on the Western Front in 1917–18); and there is substantial evidence that this was so. But now that Portugal had become a precarious neutral enclave on the edge of a Nazi-dominated Europe, he pursued a skilful and realistic policy of doing nothing to offend the Germans and little to interfere with the web of rival secret service activity which was rampant in the Portuguese capital. Quiet observation was his method. Knowledge was power. Thousands of Portuguese were recruited as paid agents into the belligerent intelligent services; many of these men were Lourenço's agents as well.[5]

In the interests of prudence, Lourenço was often willing to accommodate the Germans over the treatment of particular refugees that summer – but the most notable of those refugees was a decided exception. Salazar was concerned that nothing should happen to the Duke of Windsor in Portugal, that no incidents should arise from his presence there, and that everything should be done to fulfil the wishes of the British Embassy in the matter of his visit. Moreover, it happened that Lourenço himself had twice been in close contact with the Duke as Prince of Wales, in circumstances which gave him a sense of personal loyalty towards that personage – at the Battle of Passchendaele in June 1917, and during the Prince's brief official visit to Lisbon in April 1931. On the latter occasion Lourenço had been responsible for the Prince's security, and had subsequently been created an Honorary Commander of the Royal Victorian Order – a decoration given for personal service to the British Royal Family. The task of ensuring that nothing befall the Duke in Portugal, and that nothing untoward arise from his stay, therefore represented even more to Lourenço than the will of his political master. It was for him a matter of personal honour.

In the long run, the Duke would have cause to be grateful for Lourenço's vigilance. In the short term, however, the Captain seemed more of a gaoler than a protector. The *Boca do Inferno*, with its numerous drives and entrances, with a dense forest behind it and a bare undefended coast in front of it, was a problem to guard, so Lourenço simply flooded the whole locality with scores of his agents, mingling with the servants inside the house, patrolling the gardens and the road outside, cruising around in cars and boats, stopping anyone who came within half a mile of the residence. The Duke and Duchess were instructed to leave the house as little as possible, and only with an armed escort.[6] A Portuguese visitor was astonished to find Lourenço with the Duke one afternoon, upbraiding him for having slipped away for a long solitary walk in the woods. A search party had found him and escorted him back to the house, where he was warned by the hastily summoned chief that he must never go out without first informing the captain of the guard and only walk along the shore road where he would be under constant watch from land and sea.[7]

The Duke was used to detectives; but restrictions of this order put him increasingly on edge. They made him feel anything but secure. His confinement, week after week, in an isolated place – coupled with his anxieties about the war and his own future, his feeling that he had been shabbily treated by his country, and his sensation that he was constantly being spied upon (which he was) – gradually caused him to lose his sense of reality, and induced in him a state of mind which bordered on paranoia. This was to be an important factor in the events which were to develop.

To the terrors of isolation were added those of enforced inactivity. Condemned as he was to virtual house imprisonment, the Duke found himself with little to do during his first days in Portugal. The appointment of Governor of the Bahamas which he had accepted on 4 July remained top secret until its public announcement, which was not due to take place until the 10th of the month. Until then he could neither discuss it with anyone* nor make any practical arrangements for taking it up: he could only brood upon it in the uncomfortable atmosphere of the *Boca do Inferno*. Meanwhile there was no news from Gray Phillips, whom he had sent as his agent to London. Tension and boredom filled the days of waiting.

If the Duke and Duchess could not go out, however, it was still possible for other people (carefully scrutinized on arrival and departure) to come to them. In this connection, Ricardo and Mary Espírito Santo proved to be excellent hosts. Though they themselves had moved with their four daughters to one of their Lisbon houses to make way for the ducal party, they got together a group of their Portuguese friends who might be congenial company for their royal guests. These included Ricardo's brother José and his wife Vera; the Conde de Lancastre, a man-about-town who claimed descent from John of Gaunt; Viscount Soveral and his brother, nephews of Edward VII's great friend who had been Portuguese Minister in London; the Baron Almeida Santos, his sister Alda and his American wife Barbara; the Finance Minister, Lumbrales; Nuno Brito e Cunha, a noted sportsman; and Tomás Pinto Basto, the jovial young director of a famous shipping company. Led by Ricardo and Mary, members of this group would descend on Cascais for lunch at the *Boca do Inferno* – a buffet affair served on the swimming-pool terrace – where they were delighted to find the former King of England and his wife leading a very simple existence. They ate practically nothing, made agreeable small talk, and seemed glad of company. The visitors were charmed by the Duke, who asked numerous questions about Portugal. They were prepared to dislike the Duchess, but on the whole found her lively and amusing. Politics, the war and the future were never mentioned; but it was noticed that the Duke quietly consumed a fair amount of whisky, and he seemed to harbour some deep unhappiness and frustration.[8]

---

* He appears to have kept the secret perfectly: apart from the few people such as Eccles who knew about it already, none of those who came into contact with him before 10 July seem to have been aware of the appointment until they read about it in the newspapers. On this matter at least he knew how to be entirely discreet.

After lunch the Duchess usually played bridge with the visitors, while the Duke went to the Estoril Golf Club for a daily round with Ricardo, Soveral and Brito e Cunha. The course occupied a hilly site above the town with splendid views of the sea, but was difficult to play in summer as only the greens were watered and the fairways became brown and parched. The Duke was judged a fair player; he had a handicap of twelve. The party was shadowed on every occasion by a vanload of secret policemen, who swarmed over the course.[9]

Apart from these golfing parties, and the Duke's frequent business visits to the British Embassy, excursions outside the confines of the *Boca do Inferno* were few, carefully managed, and always shadowed by a force of vigilant protectors. They included occasional hours at the Estoril Casino, a visit to the British hospital in Lisbon,[10] and an afternoon at a Portuguese bullfight, at which they were recognized and given an ovation by the crowd.[11] They also paid an informal call on General Carmona, the President of Portugal, who lived at Cascais in the former Royal Palace; the conversation was about Portugal's African colonies, from which the President had recently returned and which the Duke had once visited.[12]

In the evening, they usually had three or four guests to dinner at the *Boca do Inferno*. Their own hosts, the Ricardo Espírito Santos, were often there. So was David Eccles, who wrote jocularly to his wife of being

> seduced by the Windsors who have made a dead set at me, and by heaven when they turn their united charm on it is hard to resist. She is incredible, she changes so when dressed up, her figure exquisite in a black evening top to a pear-green skirt with magnificent jewels. And he has a confiding manner of talking which is dangerous to a degree. Anyway I dine twice a week. They are the arch-beachcombers of the world. Wallis is a very vulgar woman in gesture, she sticks her beautifully scented face to within two inches and just asks to be kissed, only of course you don't do it. It is so deceitful to take advantage of the fact you can't smack her.[13]

Other dinner guests included two men who were to be much involved with the affairs of the Duke and Duchess that month: the United States Minister Herbert Claiborne Pell, a rich and cosmopolitan New Englander (fifty-six in July 1940) who owed his post to an intimate personal and political friendship with President Roosevelt; and the Secretary-General of the Portuguese Foreign Ministry, Dr Luis Teixeira de Sampaio, an eccentric and benign bureaucrat (sixty-five in July 1940) who was Salazar's closest adviser and one of the leading monarchists in Portugal. We shall hear more of these two men. A number of Paris friends of the Duke and Duchess who turned up as refugees in Portugal – all of whom had horrific experiences to relate – also found their way to the dinner table at the *Boca do Inferno*.

In the course of after-dinner conversation, the Duke and Duchess touched upon their current preoccupations and sometimes let fall careless remarks. Teixeira de Sampaio told the Italian Minister that the Duke, 'though normally extremely reserved', had once described his brother the King 'as having given proof of much feebleness'.[14] Pell wrote in a private letter to President Roosevelt that the Duchess was, 'at least in her private conversation, by no means enthusiastic about Great Britain's prospects'.[15] The Duchess once remarked to Eccles (who reported the remark to London) that she saw England's crisis as a kind of judgment for the treatment of her husband.[16] Such casual indiscretions were prone to become magnified by repetition and eventually to find their way to the German and Italian Legations. Moreover, the Duke had a number of private conversations with his host in which he spoke fairly freely of his personal frustrations and his view of the war; and Ricardo gave his own version of these talks to his friend the German Minister. All of which was to constitute another important factor in the events which were to develop.

While the Duke and Duchess were in Portugal, the British Embassy did everything to keep them at a distance, to avoid any suggestion that their visit had an official significance, and to play down the fact of their presence in the country. The Press Attaché, Marcus Cheke, a somewhat precious aesthete who was thirty-four in July 1940 and was later to become British Minister to the Vatican, saw to it that they had no contact with the local British community and that as little as possible was written about them in the local press. (It was also his job to ensure that the Duchess was never curtsied to; a British woman journalist found herself sharply reprimanded by him for committing this sin.[17]) Inevitably this attitude attracted the very comment it was designed to avoid. It could hardly escape general notice that not a word had been written about them in the *Anglo–Portuguese News*, a weekly which dealt with matters of British interest in Portugal and was subsidized by the British Ministry of Information.[18] On 8 July the recently appointed Italian Minister to Lisbon, Renato Bova Scoppa, reported to Rome that their arrival had been

> fully covered in the Portuguese press. But the next day the censor forbade publication of an interview – entirely devoid of political content – given by the Prince to the editor of the *Diario de Noticias*, and since then comment about him

has been confined to a few lines in obscure corners of the papers. This is attributed to the desire expressed by the British Embassy that the sojourn of the former sovereign should not in any way lessen the impact of the Duke of Kent's official visit.[19]

The Duke called regularly at the Embassy to consult Selby and Eccles about his affairs and send telegrams to London, but it was not until 16 July – two weeks after their arrival – that they were entertained there. The Selbys then gave a small dinner for them; apart from members of the Embassy, the other guests were people of whom they had already seen a great deal in Lisbon – the Ricardo Espírito Santos, the Herbert Pells, and Dr Teixeira de Sampaio.[20] The Ambassador was in a state of high jitters and the evening began in a far from relaxed atmosphere; but the situation was saved by the Duchess, who insisted that they all play charades after dinner.[21] This solitary act of hospitality, however, could not efface the impression that the Embassy was cold-shouldering the Duke. On 22 July Bova Scoppa was still reporting that 'the British Embassy affects the most complete indifference as to his existence and his movements in Portugal'.[22]

This policy on the part of British officialdom was extremely dangerous. It encouraged Axis observers in the view that the Duke was in disgrace, that there was some great and unbridgeable political gulf between him and the British Government. This danger had been wisely recognized by Sir Samuel Hoare, who while the Duke had been in Madrid had 'felt the only possible course was to take him as much as possible under my wing and to make it as clear as I could to the whole world that he was in friendly relations with all of us and merely stopping in Madrid on his way to England',[23] and who had accordingly 'had him constantly in and out of the Embassy and to luncheon and dinner'.[24] Hoare's sensible policy had defeated the German propaganda surrounding the Duke in Spain. The Lisbon Embassy, by adopting the opposite policy, aroused German suspicions and hopes to a strong degree. This was to be yet another factor in the events which were to develop.

Owing to a leak in Whitehall, the announcement of the Duke's Governorship – which finally enabled him and the Duchess to occupy themselves with practical preparations – took place half a day ahead of time: it was broadcast by the BBC at 8.45 pm on Tuesday 9 July.[25] In a somewhat transparent effort to bolster his morale, the Duke was showered with messages of congratulation and encouragement from British official

a family continuing a feud when
the very Empire is ~~there~~ threatened and
not putting every available man in a
spot where he would most useful
call anything be small and hideous
What will happen to a country that allows
such behavior? We will leave here
when we can get on something and
may have to go to N.Y. if so you will hear
it all on the radio—

all my love

Wallis

The Duchess's letter to her aunt

quarters. Churchill assured him that the news had been greeted 'with general satisfaction here and delight in the Bahamas';[26] while the Duke's new chief, the Colonial Secretary, Lord Lloyd, wrote wishing him 'both interest and enjoyment in your time in the Bahamas'.[27] *The Times* devoted a leading article to the post, describing it fulsomely as 'one of the oldest and most honourable of appointments under the Crown. Others no doubt rank higher in formal dignity and in the extent of the jurisdiction. Even if that measure be applied, the greater the honour now done to a historic colony and the greater the credit due to the Duke himself.'[28]

What was the attitude of the Duke himself towards his post? Upon accepting it on 4 July he seems at first to have experienced a mild sense of euphoria. He had made his decision; his short-term future seemed settled. But had this mood survived a week of brooding? And how did his wife feel about the Bahamas?

The papers of the Duke and Duchess in Paris contain the originals of two revealing confidential letters written by them to regular correspondents in the week following the announcement. One is from the Duke to his trusted solicitor in London, George Allen; the other is from the Duchess to her beloved aunt in Washington, Bessie Merryman. These letters – both of which give the impression of having been dashed out spontaneously in a state of great haste and confusion – constitute the best available direct evidence of what their authors were thinking and feeling before they were engulfed by conspiracy. The Duchess's letter to her aunt,* scribbled on blue air-mail paper from Cascais in a forthright hand with erratic punctuation, bears the postmark 15 July:

> Dearest Aunt B – I simply can't concentrate enough to write a decent or clear letter as one's time is spent trying to communicate with France to make some arrangements for one's houses. Young† is not an intellectual giant and a slow mover – we must do everything through a neutral as England seems to have arranged to wage war against most of Europe. We have nothing but a few suitcases containing strange garments packed in a hurry – a fine looking pair to arrive in Nassau. The St Helena of 1940 I hear is a nice spot. At least the British have got the Duke as far as possible. We refused to return to England except under our own terms, as the Duke is quite useless to the country if he was to receive the same treatment as when he returned to offer his services wholeheartedly in Sept only to suffer one humiliation after another. Once burnt twice shy, and they would guarantee him no different treatment – so he asked for something out of England and he got it! Naturally it is the family who are scared of him‡ – and I hope the press have seen through this one. All the foreigners have including the Germans, who will use it as propaganda I imagine. I shall be interested to hear what the US press said cracks and all. However it's not the Duke's fault and he is the only one of his country I find who makes any sense of this whole European muddle. Everyone is here and in a confused state about their possessions. I think the world is mad – or the

---

* Seventy-five in July 1940 and the only sister of the Duchess's mother (who had died in 1929), the widowed Aunt Bessie (Mrs D.B. Merryman) received regular letters from her niece, who looked upon her as a confidante. A large number of such letters written during the war are quoted in *The Duke of Windsor's War*.

† Backley Young, United States Consul in Lisbon.

‡ What the Duchess is suggesting is that the Royal Family regard her husband as a threat on account of his charisma.

politicians are – and we still stick to the Verdun speech.* Can you fancy a family continuing a feud when the very Empire is threatened and not putting every available man in a spot where he would be most useful? Could anything be [so] small and hideous? What will happen to a country which allows such behaviour? We will leave here when we can get on something and may have to go to N Y – if so you will hear it all on the radio.

All my love,
WALLIS[29]

The Duke's letter to his solicitor† – typed (inexpertly by himself) on the writing paper of the British Embassy in Lisbon – is dated 17 July. It consists of two pages, the second of which concerns purely his private business affairs, the first of which reads as follows:

My dear Allen,

It is a very long time since I have written, and we are all sinking deeper and deeper into the mire of this infernal war. What a wretched mess it all is, and I see no outcome except disaster to the whole of civilization unless it ends soon.

The Government wanted the Duchess and I [sic] to return to England, but I refused to do so except on my own terms, which were that the King and Queen should behave normally towards us and make it publicly known that the petty family feud was over once and for all. Those were the only conditions on which I could accept an appointment in England at the present time as I was not going to have a repetition of the humiliating job I was given last September and which I endured for seven months by putting my pride in my pocket.

However, as the Court still hold out against us, the Prime Minister has had to compromise with this futile appointment to the Bahamas which cant [sic] fool anyone except possibly some readers of the London Times, vide their editorial, as being other [than] St Helena 1940!

The climate I understand is pleasant and it will while away some dreary months of war, but we are experiencing incredible difficulty in getting a few of our personal effects sent here from La Cröe. The shortage of petrol in France seems to be our biggest obstacle, but we hope eventually to get our things as we were not able to bring away any more than any of the rest of the refugees. We expect to sail from here for New York on 1st August in a small ship of the American Export Line, unless the US Lines send another refugee ship over, in which case we would wait for the larger vessel. But we have had a belly full of

---

* The broadcast delivered by the Duke from Verdun in May 1939 appealing to Europe's leaders not to go to war.

† Fifty-two in July 1940, A.G. Allen of Allen & Overy had served the Duke with great loyalty before, during and especially after his reign, and was an intimate friend of the Duke's other adviser Sir Walter Monckton.

H.R.H. DUKE OF WINDSOR.   _for Allen._

RECEIVED
22 JUL 1940
Ansd. 26.7.40.

BRITISH EMBASSY,
LISBON.

17th. July, 1940.

My dear Allen,

It is a very long time since I have written,
and we are all sinking deeper and deeper into the mire of
this infernal war. What a wretched mess it all is, and I see
no outcome except disaster to the whole of civilisation unless
it ends soon.

The Government wanted the Duchess and I to
return to England, but I refused to do so except on my own
terms, which were that the King and Queen should behave normally
towards us and make it publicly known that the petty family
feud was over once and for all. Those were the only conditions
on which I could accept an appointment in England at the
present time as I was not going to have a repetition of the
humiliating job I was given last September and which I endured
for seven months by putting my pride in my pocket.

However, as the Court still hold out against us,
the Prime Minister has had to compromise with this futile
appointment to the Bahamas which cant fool anyone except
possibly some of the readers of the London Times, vide their
editorial, as being other St, Helena 1940!

The climate I understand is pleasant and it
will while away some dreary months of war, but we are
experiencing incredible difficulty in getting a few of our
personal effects sent here from La Croe. The shortage of
petrol in France seems to be our biggest obstacle, but we hope
eventually to get our things as we were not able to bring
away more than any of the rest of the refugees. We expect to
sail from here for New York on 1st. August in a small ship of
the American Export Line, unless the U.S. Lines send another
refugee ship over, in which case we would wait for the larger
vessel. But we have had a belly full of Portugal, and as we
cannot get back to La Croe, are anxious to get away from here.

The Duke's letter to his solicitor

Portugal, and as we cannot get back to La Cröe, are anxious to get away from
here.[30]

These two letters – with their highly significant revelations as to what
was most occupying the minds of their authors, and their bitter reflections

on fate and the war – show that euphoria had evaporated, giving way to a mood of weary (and in the Duchess's case angry) resignation. Unlike certain indirect accounts which will be quoted in the pages which follow, they do not carry any suggestion that the Duke was changing his mind about going to the Bahamas. But they do indicate a deepening disillusion – and this was to be a critical factor in the events which were to develop.

5
The Plot
10–13 July

The news that the Duke had accepted the appointment in the Bahamas, which filled the world's newspapers on the morning of Wednesday 10 July, provoked widespread comment in the despatches of Axis diplomatists. Renato Bova Scoppa wrote to Rome that it 'really and truly gives the impression that he is a banished man [*un confino*] and illustrates the grave discord said to exist between the Duke, the Court and the British Government.'[1] From Washington, the German *Chargé d'Affaires*, Hans Thomsen, wrote in similar vein to Berlin that the post represented 'a kind of banishment [*Verbannung*] whereby the Duke will henceforth be hindered from exercising or acquiring any influence over English policy', as well as 'a cunning move on the part of English propaganda designed to prevent the occupation of the West Indies by the United States and to bind the pro-English Americans who visit the famous West Indian health resorts still further to the English Royal House'.[2] Such a theory no doubt made an impression on Ribbentrop. What impressed him most of all, however, was the report of the German Minister in Portugal, Hoyningen-Huene.

Oswald Baron von Hoyningen-Huene was fifty-five in July 1940 and had been *en poste* for six years in Lisbon, where he was renowned for his distinguished looks, his aristocratic reserve and his beautiful manners. He was not a Nazi; some, indeed, have credited him (perhaps a little too readily) with having been an active secret oppositionist to Hitler. He was probably too cautious and lethargic an individual to involve himself directly against the régime, but he certainly had little love for it, and his diplomatic career was to fizzle out three-and-a-half years later when he was brought back to Germany and put under arrest. His background was cosmopolitan. He was born in Switzerland of an English mother and a Baltic German father whose family (ennobled in the sixteenth century) had long traditions in Imperial Russian service. After legal studies at Swiss and German universities, he had made a good career in the German judicial service; and after the First World War (in which he served with the German Red Cross) he transferred to the legal department of the German Foreign Office. Then, in 1928, he had become principal legal adviser to President Hindenburg – and so had been consulted over the numerous constitutional crises which marked the unhappy last years of the German Republic, culminating in the granting of power to Hitler. Hoyningen-Huene may therefore be seen as a key (if shadowy) member of that conservative German establishment which played its cards so badly in the early 1930s – imagining it could control and use Hitler only to discover itself totally outwitted by him. In October 1934, only a few weeks after Hindenburg's death and Hitler's self-declaration as his successor, he found himself appointed to Lisbon, a post probably designed to get him out of the way.[3]

With his half-shut eyes, charming manners, and policy of doing as little as possible in any situation, Hoyningen-Huene got through the next five years quite happily in Portugal in spite of whatever qualms he may have felt about what was happening in Germany. His nightmare began with the outbreak of the Second World War, an occasion which he marked by ringing up his many English and pro-British friends to say goodbye.[4] Lisbon was now a key neutral capital and espionage centre, and to the Baron's horror his sleepy legation was suddenly flooded with secret agents and party men of every description, a rabble which seemed to be constantly intriguing against him and over which he had no control. They built a tower on top of his chancery to spy on the ships in the harbour; they even excavated secret passages connecting his private residence with 'safe houses' in the town.[5] Worse was to come. In the late spring and summer of 1940 there arrived the great influx of refugees into Portugal. The surveillance – and not infrequently the harassment and expulsion, leading eventually to torture and execution – of large numbers of these refugees became the main business of the mission over which the wretched Minister presided. Among the new arrivals who claimed the attention of the Legation spies were the Duke of Windsor and his party.

Hoyningen-Huene was well aware of the interest of his masters in the Duke. He remarked to Teixeira de Sampaio ('admittedly with a laugh', as the Secretary-General noted) that the Duke would be 'our first President of the Great British Republic'.[6] Hoyningen-Huene was also in an ideal position to obtain information about the Duke through his friendship with

Ricardo Espírito Santo. However, while his Italian colleague had bombarded Rome with details concerning the arrival of the Duke and Duchess in Portugal, Hoyningen-Huene appears to have waited until 10 July before sending a despatch to Berlin on the subject of the ex-King. It was startling enough, and read as follows:

> As Spaniards from the entourage of the Duke of Windsor have reported in strictest confidence during a visit to the Legation, the appointment of the Duke as Governor of the Bahamas is for the purpose of keeping him away from England since his return would greatly strengthen the position of English friends of peace whereupon his arrest at the instigation of his enemies could be counted upon. The Duke intends to postpone his journey to the Bahamas for as long as possible, and at least until the beginning of August, in the hope of an early change in his favour. He is convinced that had he remained on the throne war could have been avoided and describes himself as a firm supporter of a peaceful compromise with Germany. The Duke believes with certainty that continued heavy bombing will make England ready for peace.[7]

When shown this document in 1953, the Duke wrote 'NO' beside it in capital letters. Was it a wholly inaccurate account of what he had been saying? It has been seen that he was prone to rather loose, indiscreet talk across the dinner table at the *Boca do Inferno*. One can hear him remarking, in a careless sort of way, that the war was a mistake, that it ought never to have started, that perhaps he might have been able to stop it, that it ought to stop now. Melancholy and heavy-drinking major-generals in flight from military disaster are inclined to talk in such a way. But the content of Hoyningen-Huene's telegram (the source of which is not at all clear) seems to go far beyond this. It is not easy to hear the Duke expressing himself in so categorical and far-reaching a way. Indeed, there are good reasons for regarding the whole report as a fake. It is curiously reminiscent of the campaign of German propaganda lies which had accompanied the Duke's arrival in the Peninsula three weeks earlier: that too spoke of arrest if he returned to England. On the other hand it is curiously different from another, well-authenticated Spanish report of him at this time, in which he appears to accept his destiny as Governor of the Bahamas.* But what is important about Hoyningen-Huene's telegram is not the source of its information or the accuracy of its information, but the effect it had on Ribbentrop.

The German Foreign Minister received the despatch on the morning of

* See below, pp. 113–14.

11 July at his stolen castle at Fuschl in Austria, where – within a short drive from Hitler's retreat at Berchtesgaden – he increasingly isolated himself from reality and from the official world which held him in such contempt. It roused him to instant action. For three weeks his foreign service had been listening for a sign of willingness on England's part to come to terms. None had come. The preparations were already beginning for an operation across the Channel – an operation which Hitler, for various sentimental and practical reasons, did not want to have to launch. Now came the news that the Duke of Windsor would not be returning to England – that he would be tarrying for some weeks more in the Peninsula before going on to the Bahamas. Indeed, according to Hoyningen-Huene's telegram it was far from clear that he would be going to the Bahamas at all. For that telegram seems to suggest that the Duke has a following in England as the champion of a negotiated settlement; that on account of this there is an active political conspiracy against him, condemning him to exile; that he means to resist that conspiracy and return home to lead his 'party'; and that he believes Anglo–German peace to be tied up with his own tenure of the English throne. This view of things appears to have become instantly accepted in Berlin. As General Kurt von Tippelskirch, the head of German Army Intelligence (*O.Q.IV*), scribbled in his pencil diary on 11 July: 'Windsor is to be sent away [*entfernt*] because he is seen as a rival for the throne. . . .'[8]

The Hoyningen-Huene telegram immediately reactivated Ribbentrop designs on the Duke of Windsor, which had been temporarily interrupted by the Duke's departure from Spain one week earlier. Indeed, according to the memoirs of Erich Kordt, ever since the Duke had arrived in Portugal Ribbentrop had been trying to think of some way 'to frighten him into returning to Spain'.[9] Here now was what he evidently regarded as a heaven-sent opportunity to put in motion a full-scale plot to bring the Duke under German power and use him for German purposes. Late on the night of 11 July Ribbentrop despatched from Fuschl one of the most notorious telegrams to emerge from the archival morass of the Second World War. It was addressed to Stohrer in Madrid, and marked: '*Top Secret. Special Confidential Handling.*' There is an interesting indication of just how secret it was. In accordance with practice, the original copy was stamped in the bottom left-hand corner of the first page with a list of senior officials and heads of departments: as State Secretary, Weizsäcker had to indicate to which of these mandarins further copies were to be distributed. The entire list is crossed out.

By way of preamble, the Fuschl telegram opened with the full text of the despatch which Ribbentrop had received some twelve hours earlier from Hoynigen-Huene. It then continued:

We are especially interested in having the Duke of Windsor return to Spain at all events. In our view it is of decisive importance for the success of such a plan that our interest should in no way become known. Therefore it seems best that the Spanish should undertake the affair. Certainly according to the telegram from Lisbon the Duke wishes to postpone his journey to the Bahamas until August. We are however convinced that he is surrounded by British agents who will try to get him out of Lisbon as soon as possible, if necessary even by force. In our opinion speed is therefore called for. We cannot for the moment see by what means the Spanish, particularly in the light of the relations currently existing between the Spanish Foreign Minister and the Duke of Windsor, may be able to get him back into Spanish territory without further trouble. From here it would seem best if close Spanish friends of the Duke were privately to invite him – and of course his wife also – for a short visit to Spain for a week or two on some pretext which would appear plausible to him, to the Portuguese, and to the English agents. In other words, the Duke and Duchess, as well as the English and Portuguese authorities, must all believe that Windsor will be returning there whatever happens. If things do not happen that way there is a danger, according to our information regarding the Duke's entourage, of the real reason for the Duke's return to Spain becoming known to England and of England accordingly preventing it by every possible method. What follows is for your strictly personal information.

After their return to Spain the Duke and Duchess must be persuaded or compelled to remain on Spanish soil. For the latter eventuality we would have to secure the agreement of the Spanish Government to the internment of the Duke under the neutrality regulations for as a British officer and a member of the British Expeditionary Force the Duke could be arrested as a deserting military refugee. Please let me know what you think the reaction and underlying reasoning of the Spanish Government would be in connection with this possibility.

At any rate, at a suitable occasion in Spain the Duke is to be informed that Germany wants peace with the English people, that the Churchill clique stands in the way of that peace, and that it would be a good thing if the Duke were to hold himself in readiness for further developments. Germany is determined to force England to peace by every means of power, and upon this happening would be prepared to pave the way for the granting of any wish expressed by the Duke, especially with a view to the assumption of the English throne by the Duke and Duchess. Should the Duke have other plans, but still be prepared to co-operate in the restoration of good relations between England and Germany,

Telegramm (Geh.Ch.V.)

Sonderzug Fuschl, den 11. Juli 1940
Ankunft den "   "   "   23.55 Uhr

Nr. 2 vom 11.7.   Citissime

Vermerk
Telegramm wurde nach Madrid
unter Nr. 1023(Geh.Ch.V.)   Für Behördenleiter.   Verschluss-Sache.
am 12.7. 2.20 weiterge-   Strengst geheim!
leitet.

    Ihr Telegramm 2298 betr.Herzog von Windsor soeben er-
halten. Ebenfalls erhielten wir ein Telegramm vom Gesand-
ten in Lissabon folgenden Inhalts: "Lissabon Nr.661 vom
11. Juli. Geheim.

    Wie Spanier aus Umgebung des Herzogs von Windsor streng
vertraulich bei Besuch auf der Gesandtschaft mitteilten,
bezwecke Ernennung des Herzogs zum Gouverneur von Bahama -
Inseln,ihn von England fernzuhalten, da seine Rückkehr
stärkste Förderung englischer Friedensfreunde mit sich
bringen würde, sodass auf Betreiben seiner Gegner bestimmt
mit seiner Verhaftung zu rechnen wäre. Herzog beabsichtige,
in Hoffnung auf baldige für ihn günstige Änderung,Abreise
Bahama-Inseln soweit wie möglich, mindestens bis Anfang
August hinauszuschieben. Er ist davon überzeugt, dass bei
seinem Verbleiben auf Thron Krieg vermieden worden wäre
und bezeichnet sich als unentwegten Anhänger Friedensaus-
gleichs mit Deutschland. Herzog glaubt mit Bestimmtheit,
dass fortgesetzte starke Bombardierungen England friedens-
bereit machen würden,Huehne",Schluss des Telegramms aus
Lissabon.

    Wir haben besonderes Interesse, dass Herzog unter
allen Umständen Spanien zurückkehrt. Entscheidend für Ge-
lingen eines solchen Plans ist nach unserer Auffassung ,
dass unser Interesse hieran keinenfalls bekannt wird. Es
scheint daher am günstigsten, wenn Spanier diese Sache
übernehmen. Herzog will zwar laut Telegramm Lissabon
Abreise nach Bahama- Inseln bis August verschieben. Wir
sind aber überzeugt, dass er umgeben ist von englischen

B 002549

The Fuschl Telegram (first page)

we would likewise be prepared to assure him and his wife an existence which
would enable him, either as a private citizen or in some other position, to lead a
life suitable for a king. When the time comes you will receive more detailed
instructions in this matter.

    The following is also for your personal information. (1) It is reported from

Lisbon that the Duke is at present staying with a reputedly pro-German Portuguese banker. (2) Information has reached us today from a Swiss agent who for years has been in close touch with the English Secret Service according to which the English Secret Service intends, by sending the Duke to the Bahamas, to get him into English power in order to do away with him at the first opportunity. There is no objection to your mentioning this to the Spaniards – in strictest confidence.

As soon as you receive this telegram would you please let me know in detail what possibilities you see of getting the Duke and Duchess back to Spain as quickly as possible. Also I ask you to be extremely cautious in what you tell the Spanish, except for those persons of whose discretion you can be absolutely sure from personal experience. Even in those cases, however, I request that you say only what is necessary.

Will you please place this telegram personally under lock and key.[10]

Thus was the plot launched. As outlined in Ribbentrop's telegram, it was in three stages: the Duke was to be brought to Spain; he was to be kept there; he was to be approached with a German message. The telegram must now be carefully analysed, not with a view to pronouncing on the realism of Ribbentrop's project – as to that the reader may judge for himself – but rather to discovering what was in the German Foreign Minister's mind.

The first thing to note is that, although Ribbentrop obviously hopes that the Duke will prove co-operative in the end, his plan is not in the least dependent on the Duke's knowledge or consent. The whole idea is to lure him into a trap. He must be brought back to Spain under false pretences, without in any way suspecting German interest in him; and if he subsequently tries to get away from Spain he must be held there by force, the Spanish Government being persuaded to imprison him at the German request. The absurd story that the British Secret Service mean to assassinate him (which Stohrer can reveal 'confidentially' as something of which he has been notified by his Government) is evidently no more than a ruse for the consumption of the Spanish authorities and the Duke himself – part of the design, recalled by Erich Kordt, to 'frighten him into returning to Spain'.

But though his plan is based on deceit and the possible use of force, Ribbentrop nevertheless harbours two great hopes with regard to the Duke of Windsor. The first is that the ex-King will jump at the prospect of being restored to the throne (or given similar privileged treatment) by the Germans at the end of the war. The second is that, until that time, the

Duke – having been assured a royal future – will be happy to 'co-operate' with the Germans with a view to 'the restoration of good relations between Germany and England'. It would seem that Ribbentrop, his fantasies tempered by a spark of realism, was never absolutely certain the Duke would react in this way, and realized that persuasion or coercion might be needed to make him play the German game: hence the insurance policy of getting the Spanish to agree to lock him up if necessary. Nevertheless, the prospect of a collaborating Duke mesmerized by restoration was regarded seriously by Ribbentrop; and this was no doubt the prospect he had held out to Hitler.

However, the telegram tells us little about Ribbentrop's own motives or intentions with regard to the Duke. It only mentions, and in very general terms, what the Duke is eventually to be told – what bait he is to be offered – to get him to co-operate (if indeed he will voluntarily co-operate) in the German Foreign Minister's plans. But what are those plans? How does Ribbentrop mean to use the Duke once he has landed his fish? As a peace negotiator? A hostage? A Quisling? Is the idea to keep him in Spain, or some other neutral country under German pressure, where he can pose as an independent champion of peace, and keep himself 'in reserve' for his future destiny? Or is it to bring him to Germany, be it as a prisoner or a collaborator? Does the Duke's main importance lie, in Ribbentrop's mind, in his immediate use as a device to weaken England's will to resist, or in his future use, once the war is over, as England's pro-German ruler? And if he is to be restored, is it to be as an independent sovereign or a mere German puppet?

The probable answer to these questions is that Ribbentrop did not know himself. A man of misty hunches with little sense of logic, inclined to take hold of an idea (particularly an idea which appealed to Hitler) and elaborate it into some fantastic theory, he had convinced himself (and the Führer) that the Duke held the key both to the end of the war and to the future of Anglo–German relations. He could not yet see precisely how the Duke might be exploited in Germany's short-term and long-term interest – that would depend on the Duke's attitude and the course of events – but he felt that the mere fact of the Duke being in German hands (or simply out of British hands) would be an advantage (possibly a decisive advantage) to Germany and a blow (possibly a disastrous blow) to the morale of Churchill's England. He was like a chess player who cannot see many moves ahead and only dimly perceives the strategy of his opponent, but believes that the capture of one particular piece will completely transform his position on the board. It is interesting that a number of those who were involved in the plot use playing-card metaphors to explain why Ribbentrop wanted the Duke of Windsor. To Nicolás Franco, Spanish Ambassador to Portugal, the Duke represented 'a trump for peace'. Alcázar de Velasco, the Spanish Abwehr agent whose role will occupy the later chapters of this book, recalls that Canaris told him 'that Ribbentrop thought it would be an important card to have the Duke in Germany'. Stohrer, in his unpublished memoirs, wrote that 'Ribbentrop evidently believed that he could play the Duke off [*ausspielen zu können*] against the new King and the existing British Government'. Exactly how this valuable card would be played was a matter for the future; the immediate task for Ribbentrop was to get it into his hand, by fair means or foul.

Ribbentrop's determination to get hold of the Duke was also dictated by another motive: his constant desire to please and flatter Hitler. It is unfortunate that no notes appear to have survived of the conferences which took place on the subject between the Führer and his Foreign Minister; but Ribbentrop's technique is well known. As Weizsäcker put it: 'He had a special gift for getting hold of some political idea of Hitler's and then, when the idea seemed fixed in Hitler's mind, bringing his own ideas into line with it, and then outbidding him in the same direction.'[11] Though the plot appears to have been Ribbentrop's own, it was tailor-made to fit in with Hitler's known views and hopes of the Duke; and there can be no doubt that Hitler personally sanctioned it and set great store by it, that he read the telegrams (which were specially typed out for him in large print which would not tire his weak eyes[12]) and was consulted at every stage. (Though it will later be seen that the cynical Ribbentrop may have meant to go much further in sanctioning the use of force than Hitler, who genuinely admired the Duke and saw in him a possible future executant of his plans for Anglo–German brotherhood.)

Once Hitler had ranged himself behind the plot, it acquired for Party and State an almost holy significance. It became a component of the sacred mythology of Nazi policy. It could not be abandoned. Its success could not be doubted. Its underlying premises could not be called into question. To dare to consider it ill-advised, to carry it out with anything less than tremendous zeal, would be treasonable behaviour in a German public servant. This was the problem which faced Dr Eberhard von Stohrer, whose enormous bulk bent over the telegram at the Madrid Embassy on the morning of Friday 12 July.

* * *

For Stohrer, the receipt of these instructions highlighted a dilemma which by this time haunted not a few servants of the Third Reich. He had been trained to serve the state, irrespective of which government was in power; he had served the Empire, the socialist Republic of Ebert and the conservative Republic of Hindenburg with equal fidelity. Much as he disliked many aspects of the new régime, he continued the habits of loyal service under Hitler, and duly paid lip service (he had little choice) to the tenets of National Socialism (though he incurred much suspicion for his efforts to help Jews, his reluctance to accept party membership, and his expulsion from Spain of party fanatics meddling in Spanish affairs). But what was he to do when asked to put into effect the mad and damaging policies of Ribbentrop, the *eiskalter Schuft*? The latest instructions were both stupid and dangerous. Stupid, because they showed a total ignorance of the mentality of the English in general and a man like the Duke in particular; dangerous, because they might lead to an act of force which could do no good to Germany's standing in the world. To his wife (who was also his confidante) he described the scheme as 'idiotic'.[13] In later years he often spoke of it to his young son Berthold, who recalls that 'he never believed in the soundness or even the political advisability of this venture, which in his mind was just another crazy project of Ribbentrop whose judgment on persons and subjects my father strongly contested'.[14] Stohrer knew that it would be both useless and personally disastrous for him to try to reason with Ribbentrop, or to give any impression of lukewarmness in pursuing his wishes. But during thirty years in diplomacy he had acquired certain skills in humouring his masters, in carrying out orders in his own way, in turning things to his advantage.

Ribbentrop demanded an immediate report, so Stohrer could not delay in making the requested approach to the Spanish authorities. Since Beigbeder was beginning to show the pro-British attitude which would soon lead to German pressure for his removal, Stohrer did not make for the Spanish Foreign Ministry. Instead he went to see the Spanish Interior Minister, Don Ramón Serrano Suñer, who was General Franco's brother-in-law and the Ambassador's closest friend within the Spanish Government.

Ten days earlier, on 2 July, Stohrer had written to Ribbentrop about a possible visit to Germany by Serrano Suñer. The Minister, he wrote, was

without doubt the most important and influential Spanish politician today. But
he is just as surely the man with the most enemies in Spain. . . . His attitude to
us has always been friendly. His friendship for Germany, however, has come
about by way of the Axis, that is to say Italy, which he knew in his youth and
admired very greatly. . . . In his inmost heart Serrano Suñer, who is a strict not
to say intolerant Catholic, may still have certain reservations with regard to
the Third Reich. That he nevertheless believes in and hopes for our victory I
have stressed at various times. His hatred of England is our absolute guarantee of this. . . .[15]

The complex and controversial character depicted in these lines was
thirty-eight in July 1940. Hailing from a middle-class Aragonese background, he had been a brilliant law student in the 1920s and had won a
scholarship to continue his studies in Rome, where he had become a
fervent admirer of Mussolini who had then just taken power. To him
fascism seemed to offer the two things that his own country most needed
– order and social equality. Back in Spain he began a successful law practice in his home town of Saragossa, where he was elected to the *Cortés* as
a right-wing deputy and befriended the head of the local military
academy, General Francisco Franco. He married Zita Polo, sister of
Franco's young wife Carmen. Imprisoned in Madrid on the outbreak of
the Civil War, he succeeded in escaping to the Nationalist zone; but his
two brothers were shot after apparently appealing in vain for refuge in
the British Embassy. This reinforced Serrano Suñer's strong antagonism
towards England, which had come about through his study of Spanish
history and his conviction that Great Britain had thwarted Spain in her
great imperial destiny. Soon after arriving in the Nationalist capital of
Burgos Serrano Suñer was appointed Interior Minister in Franco's
Government, a post which gave him control of the police, the press, and
all political life in Nationalist Spain. His first task was to consolidate the
various political factions fighting on the Nationalist side, and in particular to reconcile the *Falange*, Spain's radical national movement, with
the Church, the monarchists and the army. In accomplishing this task he
made himself widely unpopular. Nicknamed the *cuñadisimo* (brother-in-
law-in-chief), he became regarded as Franco's *eminence grise*; Franco
certainly needed him and relied on him, while mistrusting his brilliance
and ambition. His sinister reputation was reinforced by an unusual
appearance: pale, thin and handsome, with prematurely white hair,
transparent skin and slightly fanatical blue eyes.

Over the past forty years there has been much historical debate over

Serrano Suñer's attitude towards Nazi Germany during the Second World War. After the war (in the course of which he had eventually been disgraced by Franco) there was a tendency both inside and outside Spain to portray him as the arch-germanophile who had worked to bring Spain into the conflict on the German side. This view was especially encouraged by Sir Samuel Hoare's best-selling memoirs *Ambassador on Special Mission*. That work, however, has now been discredited,* and modern historical scholarship tends to support the view that Serrano Suñer was a patriot who, while admiring and favouring the Axis dictator-ships and wanting them to win, was above all concerned with the inter-ests and independence of Spain and the need to keep her out of a long war for which she was disastrously unprepared. There can certainly be no doubt that the German political and military leaders, who began by regarding him as their principal friend in Spain, became bitterly disillu-sioned with Serrano Suñer ('that Jesuit', as Hitler called him) when they realized that he was consistently hindering the moves towards a Ger-man–Spanish alliance behind a screen of flattery and promises.

In his efforts to maintain both friendship with Germany and Spanish neutrality, Serrano Suñer's greatest ally was Stohrer, who loved Spain and did not wish to see her ruined. 'He spoke the language and knew the people,' wrote Serrano Suñer in 1945. 'He always thought of Spain as well as Germany. Even when it seemed that Germany was about to win the war, Stohrer remained modest and courteous and full of understanding for Spain's position.'[16] The Ambassador and the Minister met constantly that summer to discuss how Spain might help German interests while staying out of the war; and it was in this context that Stohrer went to see Serrano Suñer on 12 July about the matter of the Duke of Windsor.† That evening he sent Ribbentrop the following 'top secret' account of their discussion:

> Since the required strict discretion cannot be guaranteed in the Spanish Foreign Ministry owing to connections leading to the English Embassy and other English circles, I have spoken of the Duke of Windsor matter strictly per-sonally and confidentially with the Spanish Interior Minister (brother-in-law of the Generalissimo) and requested his and Franco's personal support. In this

---

* See for example Eccles, *By Safe hand*, pp. 103–4; and Hugh Thomas's preface to Heleno Sana, *El franquismo sin mitos* (Madrid, 1982). To my great shame, I relied on Hoare's mendacious account in *The Duke of Windsor's War* (pp. 76–90); I owe an apology here to Don Ramón.

† Serrano Suñer had not hitherto been in any way concerned with the Duke of Windsor, whom he had neither met nor wished to meet on his visit to Madrid. All questions regarding the Duke's entry into Spain, his sojourn there – and German interest in him there – had been for the Foreign Ministry.

connection I did not make use of the ideas for the future contained in your telegraphic instructions, but used instead the report about the Intelligence Service threat to the Duke.

The Minister showed complete understanding. He will report to the Generalissimo today and upon receiving his consent, which will probably be given tomorrow, will send to Lisbon under a suitable pretext an absolutely reliable Spanish confidential emissary [*Vertrauensmann*]* who has been a friend of the Duke for a long time.† The confidential emissary will request the Duke to return with the Duchess to Spain for a short time 'before his departure for the Bahamas' since the Interior Minister would like to discuss with him certain questions regarding Spanish–English relations and give him a very important message concerning the person of the Duke. The pretext for the journey would be a hunting invitation. The Duke will be requested, because of the watch kept on him, to conceal his destination.

Should this plan succeed, the Interior Minister, after discussing, for instance, the Gibraltar question, will inform the Duke of a thoroughly reliable report (communicated to me in your telegraphic instructions) supposedly received by the Spanish Security Service concerning a threat to the life of the Duke. The Minister will then invite the Duke and Duchess to accept Spanish hospitality and possibly financial assistance as well. It may also be possible to prevent the Duke's departure in some other way. In this whole plan we remain completely in the background.[17]

This was just the reply Ribbentrop would have been hoping for. It cast not a cloud of doubt over his cherished scheme. The Spanish Interior Minister seemed to be entering into the whole spirit of the plot, and had spontaneously agreed to send a suitable agent (chosen, one would say, by himself) to 'fetch' the Duke. But Stohrer had said nothing to the Minister about 'the ideas for the future', and had so arranged things that 'we remain completely in the background'. A hunting invitation, a suggested discussion of Anglo–Spanish relations, the communication of 'a very important message' concerning his safety – such would be the baits to draw the Duke back to Spain. The Germans would not be mentioned at all. Only on one point does Stohrer not appear to deliver the goods – on the

---

* *Vertrauensmann* – or *V-mann* or *Vertrauensperson* – is a key and constantly recurring term in the German telegrams. Literally 'a man of our confidence', it has no precise equivalent in English, but must be variously translated as 'confidant', 'agent', 'trusted agent', 'secret agent', 'confidential agent', 'emissary' or 'confidential emissary'. I have followed the practice of the translators of *Documents on German Foreign Policy* in using the last-mentioned of these equivalents save where obviously inappropriate; but 'secret agent' might be a more accurate rendering, since *Vertrauensmann* is a term of art which of itself conjures up images of adventure stories and secret service operations.

† In 1953 the Duke underlined this passage and wrote 'Miguel' beside it.

question of the Spanish Government's willingness to intern the Duke. But even on that front there are 'possibilities'.

This, at any rate, was the picture Stohrer gave Ribbentrop. Well may one wonder whether it was a strictly accurate picture of what had transpired between the Ambassador and the Spanish Minister. Don Ramón Serrano Suñer's recollections of that interview are certainly very different.* His version is as follows.[18]

One morning in the summer of 1940, Stohrer, who was Don Ramón's personal as well as political friend and who came to see him daily, announced to him that he had a complicated request to make on behalf of Germany. Don Ramón feared that he was about to be faced with a demand that Spain declare war on Great Britain. What Stohrer had to tell him, however, was that Ribbentrop wanted a Spanish agent to be sent to the Duke of Windsor in Portugal to persuade him to return to Spain. Stohrer frankly added that what Ribbentrop had in mind was to offer to put the Duke back on the throne, which he imagined represented the ex-King's wishes, and that he wanted the Duke to be in Spain to discuss the matter. Stohrer did not seem to be at all happy about the project, but hoped Don Ramón would go along with it in order to appease Ribbentrop and to relieve the pressure on Spain to enter the war.

Don Ramón 'did not doubt that behind this request lay every kind of intrigue', but he considered the whole idea to be 'puerile'. He had not met the Duke of Windsor and did not think very highly of a man who had given up great public responsibilities for personal reasons, but he thought it 'absurd' to imagine that the Duke would deal openly with his country's enemies or agree to become 'a Quisling king'. His main feeling, however, was of relief that he was not being asked – not yet at any rate – to waive Spain's neutral status; and he realized that, by granting Ribbentrop this favour, which might well result in nothing, he could be staving off the asking of other favours to which he could not so easily consent. There was moreover no reason in his view why the Spanish Government should not invite the Duke of Windsor to come to Spain.† Don Ramón therefore

---

* See Prologue, pp. 14–15 above. Making all allowance for passage of time and distortion of memory, I believe Don Ramón to be an honest and reliable witness, and the circumstantial evidence in favour of his account to be heavy. He had not read the German telegrams at the time I first met him.

† Don Ramón wrote to me on 9 March 1983:

We would have been glad to give the Duke of Windsor the necessary facilities to return to Spain if that had seemed to him more safe and suitable than remaining anywhere else. I am of course well aware that from the English point of view – as much for the Government in London as for the Ambassador in Madrid – such a course would seem undesirable; but from our point of view there was no reason why we should not invite him to Spain and give him every facility for crossing the frontier.

replied to Stohrer that he would be glad to co-operate, provided Franco agreed. However, he remembers that it was clearly understood that the Duke, *while still in Portugal*, should be sounded out by the Spanish agent about his willingness to be restored to the throne in the event of a German victory. Before taking the plan any further, the Minister and the Ambassador wanted to know exactly what his intentions were.

Stohrer then suggested that Don Miguel Primo de Rivera be selected as the Spanish envoy to the Duke of Windsor. At the mention of this name, Don Ramón's eyebrows rose.

Don Miguel Primo de Rivera y Saenz de Heredia, third Marquis of Estella, later first Duke of Primo de Rivera (his name was the most significant thing about him), was thirty-six in July 1940. His father, a general, had been dictator of Spain in the 1920s, and had died in 1930 leaving three sons. The eldest of these, the brilliant and charismatic José Antonio, had been the founder (in 1933) of the *Falange*, while the youngest, Fernando, had been a lawyer of talent. Both had been shot by the Reds in the Civil War. There remained only Miguel, who possessed neither brilliance nor talent but the most famous surname in Nationalist Spain. It is generally agreed that he also possessed in full measure the expansive charm of his native Andalusia; but that was about all. He is chiefly remembered for his frivolity, his irresponsibility, his propensity for landing himself in scandal, and his obsessive interest in women and wine. To Don Angel Alcázar de Velasco, his colleague in the *Falange*, he was 'a spoilt youth who went through life with a bottle in each hand and a girl under each arm'.[19] To the Duque de Baena, his colleague in diplomacy, he was 'a great silly lovable irresponsible child'.[20] To Maria-Ursula von Stohrer he was 'a joke' who 'always drank too much and always wanted to see me alone'. To the historian Agustin Figueroa (now the Marquis of Santo Floro) he was 'a well-meaning, light-hearted good companion. Intelligence was not the most noticeable thing about him'.[21] These witnesses were friends of his who were fond of him (as many were); but Serrano Suñer had no time for him at all. He regarded him as '*un golfo*' (a twit), a man disgracefully different from his outstanding father and brother, 'a frivolous and irresponsible buffoon who sought posts and honours but never did a stroke of work in his life'.[22]

Don Miguel presented an embarrassing problem for the régime. As a founder-member of the *Falange* and the only surviving brother of the great falangist martyr and folk hero José Antonio, he had to be seen to be given some significant position in the state; but he was quite unsuited to any kind of public office. Not only was he incompetent ('even as mayor of a provincial town a disaster,' recalls Baena), but he was vain and meddling, always looking for something to do and totally lacking in political sense. High-sounding jobs had to be found for him which would keep him happy but in which he could do relatively little harm. Later on, Miguel was to become Minister of Agriculture at a time when Spanish agriculture had almost ceased to exist, and Spanish Ambassador to London when Anglo–Spanish relations were at a low ebb and unlikely to improve. In 1940 he held the appointment (which had been specially created for him) of Civil Governor of Madrid (Madrid being under purely military government), in which he was responsible to an exasperated Serrano Suñer.

When Stohrer proposed Don Miguel as the Spanish Government's emissary to the Duke of Windsor, Don Ramón was therefore at first a little surprised. But he rapidly overcame his surprise and readily agreed to the choice, realizing that it possessed several advantages. First, any idea was welcome which got the inconvenient Miguel out of the way for a while and satisfied his enormous vanity. Secondly, Miguel was an appropriate envoy in the sense that he was something of a friend of the Duke of Windsor: he had been the Duke's guide and boon companion on his visit to Spain as Prince of Wales in 1927, and had lavishly entertained the Duke and Duchess during their recent stay in Madrid. Thirdly, the involvement of so notorious a bungler made it all the more improbable that the whole unlikely scheme would come to anything. Indeed, there seems to have been something of a twinkle in Stohrer's eye when he suggested the name of Miguel; and Don Ramón had the impression that the suggestion had been thought up not by the Ambassador himself (who shared his own uncomplimentary view of Miguel) but by the voluptuous Baroness von Stohrer, whom Miguel much admired and whose *salon* he frequented.*[23]

It remained for Franco to be consulted. Don Ramón remembers his interview (which appears to have taken place on the following day, 13 July) with the *caudillo*, who reacted to the whole story in much the same way as himself. He thought the plot absurd, and did not believe Don Miguel (whom he regarded with contempt and called 'the drunkard') would be capable of accomplishing such a mission. But it would be a useful favour to the Germans and might buy time for Spain. Rather typically, he left the matter in his brother-in-law's hands to deal with as he saw fit,

---

* The Baroness can now recall no details, but thinks this 'quite likely. Miguel would have done anything for me. And if he had had anything to do with a plot like that it would have been bound to fail.'

thus making him responsible. He concluded: 'If you think it a good idea, go ahead.'[24]

Don Ramón then summoned and instructed Don Miguel, whose reactions were exactly as anticipated and comic to witness. He was childishly excited to be asked to visit the Duke as a secret envoy, and looked forward to his trip both as a rip-roaring pleasure jaunt and a task of the highest international significance. 'A historic mission' was what he called it.[25]

That evening, Stohrer sent a further telegram to Ribbentrop: 'Following an interview with Franco, the Interior Minister tells me that the confidential emissary will be leaving for Lisbon tomorrow.'[26]

6
Preparations for Exile
10–25 July

———

Back in Cascais, at the *Boca do Inferno*, the Duke and Duchess remained wholly unaware of the plot to keep them in Europe and bring them under German power. Since the announcement of the governorship, they had been absorbed in preparations for their Bahamas exile. For the Duke, this meant endless efforts to secure passages for himself and his party (they were hoping to sail for New York on 1 August by the American packet steamer *Excalibur*), and endless correspondence with Gray Phillips in London about various practical arrangements. For the Duchess, it meant an extraordinary campaign.

The main interest in life of the Duchess of Windsor was household management. Many people have paid tribute to her remarkable talent for entertaining, interior decorating and creating an agreeable atmosphere.[1] Learning that she was to become Governor's lady in the Bahamas, her overwhelming concern was that Government House, Nassau, should be a model establishment of its kind. Her husband might only be the King's representative in a third-class British colony, but at least his surroundings would befit his former rank. While still in Portugal, the Duchess devoted all of her very considerable powers of organization to this end. There can be no doubt that, in her mind, the war took second place. There can equally be no doubt of her belief that July that she and her husband would be leaving Europe and installing themselves in their colonial post, such as it was.

The Duchess had spent the last eighteen months of peace moving into her two houses in France – La Cröe at Cap d'Antibes and the Paris residence in the Boulevard Suchet; and she could not bear the thought that their contents – all the silver and porcelain and linen and pictures and furniture, as well as the Duke's memorabilia – should now be lost. Her priority, therefore, was to rescue as many as possible of these

treasures for shipment to the Bahamas. La Cröe was now in the Unoccupied Zone, and the Duchess – amazing though it may seem – conceived
the idea of briefly returning there with the Duke to collect their things.*
The Duke went so far as to ask the British Embassy to obtain the necessary French and Spanish visas for this journey, before being persuaded of
its utter impracticability. Meanwhile, the Duchess had managed to get in
touch with her former chef, Pinaudier, who was living in unoccupied
France. This famous *maître cuisinier* and his wife were happy at the
prospect of leaving Europe and spending the rest of the war in the service
of the Governor of the Bahamas, and the Duchess wanted to arrange for
them to come to Portugal with a vanload of trunks from La Cröe – for
which it would be desirable to have the co-operation of the Spanish
authorities, as well as the assistance of United States consuls.

Paris, on the other hand, was occupied by the Germans. However,
while in Madrid, the Duke had managed, through Tiger and the Spanish
Foreign Ministry, to obtain an unofficial assurance from the Germans as
to the protection of the house in the Boulevard Suchet; and the Duchess
now wondered whether, again through Spanish offices, it might not be
possible to get the Germans to acquiesce in a visit to Paris by her French
maid, Mademoiselle Moulichon, for the purpose of packing up those
household belongings needed for the Bahamas. A more prudent woman
might have hesitated before having this favour (albeit an indirect and
purely domestic favour) asked of Great Britain's enemies. It did not look
well by the standards of the time, it might result in mischief, and it would
certainly mean much trouble for many people. All one can say is that the
Duchess was in the grip of an obsession, and no plan was too bold, no
disturbance too great, in the furtherance of her fixed design. Nor was her
husband (who left to himself might have been indifferent to material
considerations) likely to stand in the way of her intentions.

Since the key to the rescue operations both at Paris and Antibes was
Spanish assistance, the Duke, soon after accepting the Bahamas post,
had got in touch with Beigbeder through the Spanish Embassy in Lisbon
to enlist his help. He could not yet explain the kind of help he had in mind,
since the appointment remained secret until its announcement; but he
asked if a Spanish agent might come out to see him in Portugal. On 9 July
Stohrer informed Berlin: 'The Spanish Foreign Minister told me today

---

* It will be remembered (p. 23 above) that they had left Antibes with a vanload of possessions, but
that the van and its driver had been turned back at the Spanish frontier.

that the Duke of Windsor has requested that a confidential emissary [*Vertrauensmann*] be sent to Lisbon to whom he might give a communication for the Foreign Minister. The Foreign Minister will immediately fulfil this request.'[2] To the delight of the Duke and Duchess, the emissary turned out to be their old friend Tiger Bermejillo, from whom they had been parted in Madrid less than a week before.

The Duke's visitors' book shows that Tiger arrived at the *Boca do Inferno* on 8 July and stayed there five days.[3] His jolly company helped revive their spirits, and enlivened the lunch parties by the swimming-pool.[4] But he was there for a purpose. He discussed at length with the Duchess the tactics and strategy for retrieving their possessions (the whole affair was beginning to take on the appearance of a military operation), and promised to do his utmost to secure both Mademoiselle Moulichon's trip to Paris and the Pinaudiers' journey from La Cröe. Indeed, he was almost desperate to be of service to two people to whom he felt he owed his life. He did not anticipate any serious difficulties. He was sure that the German Ambassador in Madrid (whom he would go to see personally) would arrange the necessary permit for the maid, and that Beigbeder would put the resources of his Ministry at the disposal of the enterprise. Did Tiger also have a message for the Duke from Beigbeder? Stohrer informed Berlin that, through his emissary, the Spanish Foreign Minister had 'warned the Duke against taking up the Bahamas post, which would not only be degrading but would also spell danger. Furthermore the Foreign Minister offered him once again the most lavish Spanish hospitality.'[5] This, at any rate, was what Beigbeder had told Stohrer, and it was what the Germans wanted to hear.

Tiger left Cascais for Madrid on 13 July. Having presented a bill for expenses of 3,000 escudos,[6] he reported to Beigbeder and also to Stohrer, explaining the Duke's general position as well as his desire to send Mademoiselle Moulichon to Paris. This news was communicated by Stohrer to Ribbentrop in two personal telegrams of 16 July. The first was marked 'very confidential' and read as follows:

.... The appointment as Governor of the Bahamas was communicated to W. in a very cool and categorical letter from Churchill, with instructions under all circumstances to go and take up the post immediately. Churchill had threatened to court martial W. had he not accepted the post. (This appears to have been communicated to the Duke only verbally.) Through the Colonial Secretary the Duke had then received one and a half months' grace (apparently because the Duke had declared that he would need to get certain effects for the move from his Paris house).

The confidential emissary also reports that the Duke has resigned all his military appointments and has declared that he is now only a Governor.* The Duke sees in the appointment recognition of the equal rights of his wife. The attitude of the British Embassy in Lisbon on instructions from London is very reserved towards the Duke.[7]

Against this, the Duke wrote in 1953: 'Correct'. (In fact it is not entirely correct.†) Nothing here suggests that the Duke did not mean to go to the Bahamas, or that Beigbeder's message through Tiger had had any effect. But Stohrer concluded the telegram with the news that the Spanish Foreign Minister had 'instructed Nicolás Franco, the Spanish Ambassador to Lisbon, who is at present here for a short visit, to warn the Duke once more urgently against taking up post'.[8] We shall see in what manner these instructions were fulfilled by Nicolás Franco.

The second telegram was marked 'top secret' – and until recent years it remained secret. It read as follows:

The Duke of Windsor through the confidential emissary of the *Foreign* Minister has again expressed thanks for co-operation in the matter of his house in Paris and has requested that a maid of the Duchess be allowed to travel to Paris in order to pack up various objects there and transport them by van to Lisbon, as they are required by him and the Duchess for the Bahamas.

Without committing myself I at once replied that the maid could present herself at the Madrid Embassy; meanwhile I would consult Berlin. I recommend that the wish of the Duke and Duchess be fulfilled since if necessary the maid's journey to Paris and above all the return journey to Lisbon could be held up by us as required in order to postpone further their departure should the confidential emissary of the *Interior* Minister, who is expected back in Madrid at the end of the week, not succeed in bringing about a complete change of mind on the Duke's part. I request telegraphic guidance.[9]

So here was a new plot – apparently Stohrer's brainchild – to detain the Duke and Duchess in Europe by effectuating the disappearance of their luggage and their maid. It must be said that the Ambassador, whatever

---

* By reporting this, Stohrer was indicating that it was no longer possible for the Duke to be arrested in Spain as an Allied officer, as Ribbentrop had proposed in his telegram of 11 July.

† The Bahamas offer had been made to the Duke by telegram and had given him the choice of acceptance or refusal. The court martial threat – also by telegram – had been in relation to Churchill's earlier insistence that he return to England. The Duke had only asked for four weeks' grace, and had *not* informed the British authorities of the plan to send the maid to Paris.

his private feelings about the Windsor affair, was showing considerable zeal. Perhaps the idea was that, though the attempt to lay hands on the Duke and Duchess might come to nothing, it would look good if there were at least a successful kidnapping of one of the ducal servants. But Berlin seemed in no hurry to reply to Stohrer's suggestion.

Meanwhile Tiger had informed the Duchess that all seemed in order for Mademoiselle Moulichon to come to Madrid to get her German permit. On 17 July the Duchess wrote to him from the *Boca do Inferno*:

Dear Tiger,

I am overcome with gratitude over all you have done and can never tell you how much we appreciate it. I feel I can never repay you for all your trouble. I am also very touched by the effort from other quarters. Here are a few points which I think should be quite definite before she starts.

(1) That she has the *re-entry* permit into *Spain* and into *Portugal*.

(2) That the *contents* of the camion pass the *customs* in Spain and Portugal. (Peireira* in Madrid I should think would do that for us.)

(3) Is she to return to Madrid in the camion or Lisbon? The latter would involve passport to Portugal for driver of camion – otherwise things could be put on train with her in Madrid with necessary papers should she return in camion to Madrid.

(4) She has signed cheque from the Duke so that you may fill out in pounds for amount needed in pesetas – camion, tickets etc. She has 30,000 francs with her. It should be arranged that she is allowed to bring back with her any remaining francs.

(5) I think it should be seriously considered the method of return with a Spanish camion coming all the way to Lisbon – whereas going from St Sebastian to Madrid is so to speak home territory and you are there to receive her and put the luggage and her on the train with the necessary papers to get off at this end. I leave it to your judgment and you will give instructions accordingly.

(6) ... I think we must allow from 2 to 3 days in Paris and I don't know how clear the roads are but ordinarily it is only a day Biarritz–Paris and I imagine a day San Sebastian–Madrid.

(7) An honest driver and *sufficient petrol* are essential whatever the cost.

That is all I can think of for the moment that might cause difficulties and delays – we can't afford the latter if our ship sails August first – and then you must be here for the great farewell to Europe.† The Duke is going to add a few lines. All the best Tiger dear –

WALLIS[10]

* The Portuguese Ambassador in Spain.

† It seems that the Duke and Duchess were already planning a *diner d'adieu* for their friends. This took place at the Hotel Aviz on 31 July – see below, p. 197.

The Duchess would have made a good general. She had planned her operation (such as it was) with meticulous thoroughness, and had thought of every possible complication – except the possibility of Mademoiselle Moulichon being detained by the Germans for sinister purposes. In a postscript, the Duke added his 'sincere thanks and appreciation ... for all the trouble you have taken' and also informed Bermejillo: 'We were delighted to see the Estellas here for dinner this evening, who brought us news from Madrid.' Don Miguel had arrived with his wife on the 14th, just missing Tiger (who was an old boon companion of his) by a day. We shall return later to the 'news' he brought, which the Duke mentioned so lightly.

Bearing this letter, Mademoiselle Moulichon arrived in Madrid by air around noon the following day, 18 July.[11] Aged forty and unmarried, she had been in domestic service since the age of thirteen. She was an excellent servant, cheerful, hard working and intelligent, and possessed a deep religious faith which would sustain her through her coming trials. She had entered the ducal service at the end of 1938 as *lingère* (linen-room keeper) at La Cröe, but her quality had been quickly recognized by the Duchess, who had promoted her to be her personal maid. She was devoted to her employers, and considered her mission to Paris to be of the highest importance. She remembers that she was particularly instructed to fetch the contents of a locked safe and all the Windsor linen. As a former *lingère*, she considered this a very sensible priority: nothing mattered more to civilized life than linen.[12]

In Madrid, Madmoiselle Moulichon was looked after by Tiger, whom she regarded as a sort of saint. She had expected to spend only a night there before journeying on to Paris – but her permit to enter the Occupied Zone turned out not yet to have been granted. Every day she went with Tiger to the German Consulate (a terrifying forest of stretched-arm salutes), only to be told to try again later.[13] After four days of this, Tiger wrote to the Duke in his colourful English explaining the situation:

Sir – I am most depressed and desolated for my failure in succeeding the transport of Your Royal Highness's trunks, and also for having deprived the Duchess of her maid during these days but, although the promise given to me by the Embassy that they would grant the permit as soon as Marguerite had presented her passport, it happens that today is the 22nd and they are still awaiting a telegraphic reply from 'headquarters'. It is my opinion that the cause of not authorizing the entry into France is the closing of the frontier, prelude to an attack [!].

Even if the permission was given today, I don't think it possible that the lorry would be in time at Lisbon, according to Your Royal Highness's instructions, so I'll send the maid by rail to Cascais. . . .

Tomorrow the Ambassador has asked me to lunch so if I hear anything of importance I'll let you know Sir.[14]

That day Stohrer – who had heard nothing from Berlin – telegraphed again asking for 'instructions . . . concerning journey of Duchess of Windsor's maid to Paris'.[15] Mademoiselle Moulichon continued to await her permit – and her mistress, news of her departure for Paris.

Meanwhile, the Antibes rescue operation – for which the Duchess had enlisted the reluctant support of Herbert Pell and the United States consular authorities – was meeting with no greater success. As the Duke wrote in his letter of 17 July to George Allen, they were 'experiencing incredible difficulty in getting a few of our personal effects sent here from La Cröe. The shortage of petrol in France seems to be the biggest obstacle, but we hope eventually to get our things as we were not able to bring away more than the rest of the refugees.'[16] He did not mention to Allen the plan to recover personal effects from German-occupied Paris, nor did he tell the British Embassy of this plan, to which they would almost certainly have objected. The first the Foreign Office heard of Mademoiselle Moulichon was some weeks later, by which time she had been effectively abducted by the Germans and was being sought all over Europe by her anxious and puzzled employers.[17]

The curious affair of Tiger, the maid, the chef and the trunks was far from being the Duke's only preoccupation in the second and third weeks of July. He had also spent much time with the Lisbon agents of the American shipping lines, trying to arrange a passage, and had been in regular communication with Gray Phillips about this, and about the perennial questions of luggage, uniforms and servants. The following were the principal telegrams of this very royal correspondence. Piper Fletcher and Corporal Webster of the Scots Guards had been the Duke's soldier servants during his nine months as a British major-general in France; they had left him in Antibes in the middle of June to return to England by sea.

The Duke to Major Phillips, 7 July: If transportation is difficult to arrange at your end I think I can fix up with United States Line but I

117

must know quickly. I understand that you can send staff and luggage here by plane. Try for secretary recommended by Clive Burn.... Send for Fletcher as soon as possible after a short leave. What personnel in House and are chauffeurs available? Is white uniform needed?[18]

The Duke to Major Phillips, 9 July: Essential we go via New York for Duchess to see specialist. If this complicates any arrangements you are making repeat suggestion that I contact United States or American Export Line regarding voyage....[19]

Sir Walford Selby to Lord Halifax, 11 July: Duke of Windsor has as yet heard nothing ... as regards arrangements for his journey. I think it important in present circumstances that decision should be taken as soon as possible and arrangements made.[20]

The Duke to the Prime Minister, 12 July: Phillips reports having seen you, now writes advising I should arrange transportation from here. I had already contacted European agents of United States and American Export Lines, who point out how neutrality laws complicate passage for ourselves and staff in American ship. I feel this obstacle would be overcome if our voyage to America be officially arranged between His Majesty's Government and the United States Government....[21]

The Duke to Major Phillips, 12 July: Your letter and wire received. You will see the copy of the message to the Prime Minister regarding our transport in the American vessel. Approve your sending luggage direct to New York. Glad aide-de-camp and Fletcher arranged, but latter to join me here as soon as he comes off leave. Tell Scots Guards I want to take Webster as well. Do not engage secretary as I have found one in New York. ... Will deal with bedroom when we get there. George Wood flying to England tomorrow with instructions and answers to your other questions. Please send off my cigarettes and tobacco by next flying boat.[22]

The Duke to Major Phillips, 16 July: Have made tentative reservations small ship of American Export Line sailing on August 1st. ... Important that the Government ask State Department for adequate police protection in America. Gurney [appointed] aide-de-camp and think useful if he sails with us from here as well as Fletcher and maid if one found. Webster and butler must accompany luggage direct from England to Waldorf Towers, New York.... Bag brought by Fletcher [from Antibes to England] contained uniform and to be sent direct to New York. Have no intention of buying new Garter insignia. . . . Hope George arrived safely. Please send cigarettes and tobacco.[23]

Sir Walford Selby to Lord Halifax, 17 July: Duke of Windsor has ascertained that ship of American Export Line is leaving here for New York on August 1st. Agent here has informed His Royal Highness that at present ship is fully booked, but that if [requested] through State Department, Head Office of the line in New York will instruct him to give priority to His Royal Highness's passages being arranged. Prompt intervention is most desirable in view of the great difficulty of securing passages from here at present.[24]

Three things are apparent from these telegrams. First there is the remarkable fact that the Duke was originally left to make his own travel arrangements to the Bahamas. Secondly, there is his eagerness to stop in America – no doubt a reflection of the desires of his wife, who had not seen her native land for seven years. Thirdly, there is his royal concern that he should be correctly dressed in his new post: hence his insistence on uniforms, and on the re-engagement of his valet.

By 17 July it seemed all would be well. The Duke would have his servants; he would be travelling to Nassau via New York (which was in fact the normal route); and the passages impossible to obtain in Lisbon would be arranged diplomatically in London and Washington. It is worth recalling that he wrote to Allen that day that they expected to sail 'on 1st August in a small ship of the American Export Line, unless the United States Line send another refugee ship over, in which case we would wait for the larger vessel. But we have had a belly full of Portugal, and as we cannot get back to La Cröe, are anxious to get away from here.'[25]

The next day, however, this comfortable assurance was shattered. A letter and a telegram from Gray Phillips broke the news that the Duke would be allowed neither to retain his military servants nor travel to America.[26]

The undesirability of the Duke of Windsor visiting America had occurred both to the British and the American Governments. The presidential election campaign was about to start in earnest, with Roosevelt's re-nomination at the Democratic Convention in Chicago on 17 July; and the arrival in New York of the glamorous ex-King of England, who was everywhere rumoured to be out of sorts with his family and disenchanted with the war, would have been a potential godsend to the President's isolationist opponents, however discreetly he behaved. (And an indiscretion

119

might spell disaster.) 'The more I think of it', wrote Lord Lothian, the British Ambassador to Washington, 'the more I am convinced that it is very undesirable that His Royal Highness should come to the United States at all en route to the Bahamas. . . . If he visits New York there will inevitably be a great deal of publicity, much of which will be of an icy character and which will have a most unfortunate effect at the present juncture.'[27] In Lisbon, Herbert Pell had much the same thoughts. He wrote in a personal letter to Roosevelt that the American plans of the Duke and Duchess, of which they had spoken to him, he considered 'manifestly unwise. The couple will be met by all the reporters in America ready to make a first-class sob story on the combined themes of King Cophetua, Cinderella and Napoleon at St Helena. The whole story of four years ago will be raked up and used by those who have a wish to discredit Great Britain, whether the wish is inspired by affection for Hitler or dislike of you.'[28] The President agreed with his old friend;[29] and Washington acceded to London's request that the *Excalibur* be diverted to Bermuda.[30]

The Prime Minister to the Duke, 18 July: A ship of the American Export Line leaves Lisbon on August 1, and we are asking the United States Government to arrange for this vessel to make a special call at Bermuda, the additional expense being borne by us.* This would bring Your Royal Highness to Bermuda on the 11th, and there is a Canadian National steamship of 8,000 tons, *the lady somers*, due to call at Bermuda on August 13. We consider that this would be the most convenient arrangement.[31]

But would the Duke accept it? Churchill's Private Secretary Eric Seal thought it 'silly to start off by crabbing him in this way'; but Halifax and Lloyd were adamant that he should avoid America, and Churchill shared their view.[32] The result was a short but serious row between the Duke and the British Government. The Duke found it hard to understand the sudden interdict, which he at first interpreted as a calculated slight. The matter of the army servant seemed to add insult to injury.

The Duke to the Prime Minister, 18 July (crossing with the above telegram): Understand from Phillips that Colonial Office have raised some

---

* The cost was 7,500 dollars, together with a war risk insurance charge of '10,000 dollars or more' as the diverted liner might be a 'sweet morsel' for seizure by enemy submarines (File in National Archives, Washington).

objections to my sailing in American ship to New York on technical grounds of my being Commander-in-Chief as well as Governor of Bahamas. . . . Have been messed about quite long enough and detect in Colonial Office attitude very same hands at work as in my last job. Strongly urge you to support arrangements I have made as otherwise will have to reconsider my position.[33]

The Duke to the Prime Minister, 18 July (sent five hours after preceding telegram): Feel sure you do not know red tape we are up against as regards new appointment. Feel diffident in asking you but it would help enormously if you could see Phillips again who can explain details.[34]

The Duke to Major Phillips, 18 July: Serious handicap starting with new valet. . . . Fletcher essential, Webster less important. . . .[35]

Lord Lloyd to the Duke, 18 July: Phillips informs me that Your Royal Highness wishes to obtain the services of two Guardsmen as chauffeur and valet. I venture to hope that I may try and send you for this purpose men over military age or otherwise unsuitable for military service. War Office represent that to take fit and efficient soldiers out of Army at this juncture would set an unfortunate precedent. Lord Athlone, who made similar request, has acquiesced in War Office view.[36]

The Duke to Lord Lloyd, 19 July: Your message just received. Piper Alastair Fletcher, Scots Guards, has been my servant since my appointment as Major-General last September. As change of servant at this time would constitute serious handicap to me in my new appointment strongly urge War Office make an exception in Fletcher's case and he be made available to rejoin me not later than July 27th.[37]

The Prime Minister to the Duke, 19 July: Your message of 18 July has crossed mine of same date. The Colonial Office had nothing to do with any difficulty about your sailing in American ship. It was necessary to consider American Neutrality Legislation. Indeed it was on suggestion of Colonial Office that we are in communication with Lord Lothian to remove any such difficulty by pointing out that, although you will technically be Commander-in-Chief, appointment of Governor is of purely civil nature. I am therefore very glad to consider the last sentences of Your Royal Highness's telegram as non-existent. I gather from your latest telegram that this is what you would wish.[38]

The Duke to the Prime Minister, 19 July: While appreciating the arrangements you are making with United States Government to transport myself and my party direct to Nassau via Bermuda, feel that in view of the fact that it is anyway essential that I take the Duchess to New York as soon as possible for medical reasons, additional expense to the Government and myself hardly justified. It would therefore seem far more practical and convenient to waive Colonial Office technicalities and go direct to New York, as I had originally arranged, as once I have arrived in my post, it would normally be some time before I should wish to take leave in America. . . .[39]

The Prime Minister to the Duke, 20 July: I regret that there can be no question of releasing men from the Army to act as servants to Your Royal Highness. Such a step would be viewed with general disapprobation in times like these, and I should ill serve Your Royal Highness by countenancing it.[40]

Minute of J.H.Peck to the Prime Minister, 20 July: I have just spoken to Lord Lloyd on the telephone. He asked me to let you know as soon as possible that he entirely agreed that we should remain adamant on the subject of his going to New York. On the point of the servants he wanted you to appreciate that ... HRH had to be treated as a petulant baby, and that there was a by no means remote possibility that he was prepared to face a break on this subject, and that he was unable to appreciate how ludicrous the affair would appear when made public. Consequently Lord Lloyd suggested that you should relent on this point.[41]

The Duke to Major Phillips, 22 July: Prime Minister wires Fletcher cannot be released but as I pointed out to Lord Lloyd he is, as far as I know, still my soldier servant. However, on account of the appointment involving public appearances cannot leave without a valet and you must not come here until you have found one.[42]

The Prime Minister to the Duke, 24 July: Arrangements have been made for Your Royal Highness to leave by American Export vessel on August 1 for Bermuda, and proceed thence by Canadian National Steamship 'Lady Somers' on the 13th direct to Nassau. His Majesty's Government cannot agree to Your Royal Highness landing in the United States at this juncture. This decision must be accepted. . . . Sir, I have now succeeded in overcoming War Office objection to the departure of Fletcher, who will be sent forthwith to join you.[43]

The Duke to the Prime Minister, 25 July: I agree to arrangements you have made for journey to Nassau via Bermuda. Regarding not landing in United States at this juncture I take it to mean that this only applied until after the events of November [i.e. the presidential election]. May I therefore have confirmation that it is not to be the policy of Her Majesty's Government that I should not set foot on American soil during my terms of office in the Bahamas?... I appreciate your successful efforts regarding my soldier servant.[44]

The Prime Minister to the Duke, 27 July: I am happy that Your Royal Highness is able to agree to arrangements made for journey via Bermuda.... As regards your visiting the United States, we should naturally wish to fall in with Your Royal Highness's wishes. It is difficult to see far ahead these days, but ... we should naturally do our best to suit Your Royal Highness's convenience.[45]

It is easy to regard this correspondence as painfully absurd, belonging more to the age of Lord Raglan and Lord Cardigan than to the Second World War. For the whole of a week critical to Great Britain's fortunes, the Duke – having been thwarted in two matters affecting his immediate personal convenience – engaged in a serious and time-consuming quarrel with the powers that be, even hinting at one moment that he might decline to leave for his post. It is all somewhat reminiscent of his efforts to recover his belongings which were then in progress, and his attempt to lay down conditions for his return to England only a few weeks before. In each case he appears to show a lack of sense of proportion, a royal indifference to the rest of the world, a preoccupation with his own (and the Duchess's) interests and future. But this is not how the Duke would have seen things. To him, he had made the grand patriotic gesture of accepting a petty governorship; he was entitled to special consideration; he had been asked to make his own arrangements – and now those arrangments were being frustrated by a mixture of red tape and ill-will.

Though it exasperated Whitehall and wasted the precious time of a number of important people (notably the Premier himself), the dispute in itself was trivial and fleeting. By the end of the week it seemed to be over, the Duke agreeing to give America a miss, Churchill agreeing to let him have his soldier servant. Its importance lies not in its direct effect upon events, which was negligible, but in its psychological effect upon the Duke, which proved to be fateful. At the height of the quarrel, he became intensely bitter and depressed. The mood passed; but while it was on him, it was suggested to him from two separate quarters that he should not depart for the Bahamas but retire instead to Spain. Don Miguel Primo de Rivera made the suggestion on behalf of the Spanish Interior Minister, and Don Nicolás Franco made it on behalf of the Spanish Foreign Minister. A week earlier the Duke had seemed intent on setting out for the Bahamas; a week later he would appear to have abandoned any intention he may have had of going to Spain. But between 18 and 24 July, filled as he was with anguish and uncertainty, he was impressionable to the Spanish suggestions. He may not categorically have accepted them, but he did not reject them – and, without knowing it, he greatly encouraged the Germans in their plans to bring him under their power.

The Duke frankly described his state of mind in a letter to George Allen of 20 July:

> We are encountering every conceivable form of governmental obstruction and red tape in the making of our arrangements for the voyage and the taking up of this wretched appointment. Any keeness [sic] that I had at first been able to evoke has been completely knocked out of me, and both the Duchess and I view the prospect of an indefinite period of exile on those islands with profound gloom and despondency. However, as I refuse to accept an appointment in England under the conditions which prevail, I suppose there is no alternative but to go, although I am at times sorely tempted to chuck the whole project and retire entirely from the contest. . . .[46]

7

Persuasions

17–26 July

Accompanied by his wife (a long-suffering woman), Don Miguel arrived in Portugal around 14 July and returned to Madrid on the 22nd. He appears to have been in no hurry to accomplish his mission. He and his *marquesa* dined with the Duke and Duchess at Cascais on the 17th and again on the 20th. On the second of these evenings Ricardo Espírito Santo was present too, and the Duke's visitors' book shows that Ricardo stayed the night at Cascais instead of returning to Lisbon – an indication, possibly, that the conversation continued late. The following morning the Duke rang Tiger at the Spanish Foreign Ministry, partly to ask about Mademoiselle Moulichon's progress but also to seek his views on some curious news of Don Miguel. Tiger – who knew Miguel and his wife all too well, but knew nothing of the plot to keep the Duke in the Peninsula – pooh-poohed the idea that the Duke might be in any danger. 'In view of the lack of serious-ness of my friends', he wrote to the Duke, 'I would not give too much importance about the fear they had about Your Royal Highness's personal security, probably founded upon your appointment.'[1]

Neither the Duke nor Don Miguel left any direct account of what passed between them in Portugal. There is nothing about the mission in Don Miguel's surviving papers, nor in the accessible Spanish archives.[2] After the war the Duke occasionally referred to it, treating it as a kind of joke. Writing in August 1958 to Lord Templewood (as Sir Samuel Hoare had become), he remarked that Don Miguel (who had just been recalled in disgrace from his post of Spanish Ambassador to London after a series of amorous scandals) had gone to see him in Cascais in 1940 'to entice me back to Spain, although in due fairness to him his efforts were distinctly half-hearted . . .'.[3]

Meanwhile, back in Madrid, Serrano Suñer and Stohrer awaited Don Miguel's return. The days passed. He seemed to be taking his time. This came as no great surprise to Don Ramón, who had never expected much from the mission of a frivolous fool like Don Miguel. He suspected Don Miguel of making a thorough holiday of his visit to Portugal and to have given but scant attention to its original purpose – and when the tardy emissary finally materialized, this indeed appeared to have been the case. He had clearly enjoyed himself, and said so. He told Don Ramón how delightful the society had been, how charming the climate, how excellent the golf, how delicious the food and drink. As for the Duke and Duchess – they had been wonderful hosts, they were in fine form, it had been so good to see them again. Don Ramón cut short this fatuous gush, and asked Don Miguel to come to the point. How had the Duke reacted to the suggestion that he come to Spain? And above all, how had he reacted to the idea that he might be restored to the throne in the event of a German victory?[4]

Don Miguel's report was conveyed to Berlin by Stohrer in two despatches, dated 23 and 25 July. These documents became famous when they were published in 1957; but they must be regarded with caution as historical sources. They are third-hand accounts. The Duke had spoken to Don Miguel, Don Miguel had reported to Serrano Suñer, Serrano Suñer had reported to Stohrer, and Stohrer was now reporting to Ribbentrop. Any of the four protagonists may have distorted the record in order to put themselves in a better light, or tell their interlocutor what he wanted to hear. The relevant part of the 23 July despatch read as follows:

> The confidential emissary of the Interior Minister returned from Lisbon only yesterday. He had two long interviews with the Duke of Windsor; at the second the Duchess was also present.
>
> The Duke expressed himself most freely. He felt almost a prisoner in Portugal, surrounded by spies etc. Politically the Duke has moved further and further away from the King and from the present English Government. The Duke and Duchess do not fear the King, who is utterly stupid, as much as the clever Queen, who is said to intrigue constantly against the Duke and particularly against the Duchess.
>
> The Duke is toying with the idea of disassociating himself from the present tendency of British policy by a public declaration and breaking with his brother.
>
> The Duke and Duchess were extraordinarily interested in the secret communication promised to the Duke by the Interior Minister. When asked what it might concern, the confidential emissary declared that he himself had no information on the subject but that the news was no doubt of a serious character. The Duke and Duchess said that they very much desired to return to

Spain and expressed thanks for the offer of hospitality. The Duke's fear that he would be treated as a prisoner in Spain was dispelled by the confidential emissary, who in answer to a question stated that the Spanish Government would certainly agree to the Duke and Duchess taking up residence in southern Spain (which the Duke seems to prefer), perhaps in Granada, Malaga, etc.*

The Duke said that he had some time ago handed over his passports to the English Legation with the request that they should get him Spanish and French visas (for a possible personal visit to his Paris house†). The English Legation however was clearly unwilling. Under these circumstances he must ask the Spanish Interior Minister how he might re-cross the Spanish frontier and perhaps to assist him in the border crossing.[5]

When the Duke was first shown this telegram at Downing Street in 1953, he made a number of marginal comments which are of interest.[6] Against the first paragraph he wrote nothing. Against the second paragraph he wrote: 'Correct'. Against the third paragraph he wrote: 'No'. Against the fourth paragraph he wrote nothing. Against the fifth paragraph he wrote: 'No'.

The despatch of 25 July read as follows:

The confidential emissary of the Interior Ministry had the following to add about his interview with the Duke and Duchess: when he advised the Duke not to go to the Bahamas but to return to Spain, as the Duke might yet be destined to play a large part in English politics and even to ascend the English throne, both the Duke and Duchess seemed astonished. Both seemed completely enmeshed in conventional ways of thinking, for they replied that under the English constitution this would not be possible after the Abdication. When the confidential emissary then expressed the expectation that the course of the war might produce changes even in the English constitution, the Duchess in particular became very thoughtful.

I would emphasize that, as already reported, I told the Minister nothing about the considerations for the future contained in your telegraphic instructions No. 1023 of 11 July, and it therefore follows that the confidential emissary, who in any case knows nothing of my own or any German interest in the matter, in fact broached the subject of the throne on his own account as an old friend of the Duke.[7]

---

* It must be remembered that Don Miguel was a native of Andalusia, which was also the Spanish province furthest from the German armies now standing on the Pyrenees. And it was here that Beigbeder – another Andalusian – had suggested a refuge, at Ronda.

† In fact for a visit to La Crӧe. See above, p. 112.

The Duke had no written comment to make on this telegram when he was shown it in 1953. However, when Serrano Suñer was shown it thirty years later, he insisted that the last paragraph was a lie. 'It is not true', he wrote to me on 9 March 1983, 'that Miguel was acting without authority in mentioning to the Duke the possibility of restoration to the throne, and that he merely said something which had come into his own head. He had been specifically told to refer to the matter.'

For it was this above all that Serrano Suñer and Stohrer had been waiting for – news of the Duke's political intentions, and in particular of how he reacted to the prospect of ruling England under the aegis of the Germans. And here the news was clear: as they had both expected, the Duke was not willing to contemplate any such prospect. The fact (of which Don Miguel had tried to make as much as possible) that he was a disappointed man out of harmony with British policy could not disguise this fundamental truth. That is Serrano Suñer's principal recollection of Don Miguel's report. His other recollection is that the Duke, for all the interest he may have expressed, never actually committed himself to coming to Spain. ('Though we would have been glad to give the Duke of Windsor the necessary facilities to return here', adds Don Ramón, 'if that had seemed to him more safe and suitable than remaining anywhere else. . . .')

However, Don Ramón was not the only person to whom Don Miguel reported on his return to Madrid. He also gave an account of his meetings with the Duke – and a rather different account – to one of his oldest friends, the Conde de Montarco, who was then Political Secretary to Don Ramón. Don Eduardo de Rojas y Ordoñes, Conde de Montarco, was thirty in July 1940. He was a puckish-looking and quixotic character: a passionate *falangista* in the 1930s, he was to become a passionate royalist in the 1940s and a passionate pan-European in the 1950s. He and Don Miguel had been founder-members of the *Falange* and comrades during the Civil War, and Miguel now confided to him that he had tried to persuade the Duke to flee from Portugal and his British entourage, plant himself in Spain under German eyes, and there issue a peace manifesto behind the back of his own Government – 'a kind of Rudolf Hess in reverse', as the Conde neatly describes it:

> It would have looked pretty like treason, but I never thought the Duke would give much serious attention to the idea, which would have been contrary to his patriotic instincts. I thought, from what Miguel told me, that the Duchess might have been quite keen on it, though, and might try to talk him into it. But that was just a guess: we never knew for certain.[8]

There is nothing about this plan in the documents. But perhaps it provides a clue to those statements in Stohrer's telegram of 23 July which the Duke contested: that he was thinking of denouncing British policy, and that he had asked how he might make a clandestine journey to Spain. From what Montarco says, these courses represented not what the Duke himself originally had in mind but what Don Miguel had tried to talk him into. (With what success remained to be seen.) All this appears to have been a private initiative of Don Miguel; its significance, and the role the Conde de Montarco was intended to play in it, will become apparent in a later chapter. It may merely be noted here that Don Miguel had involved himself in not one plot but four. There was the effort to get the Duke to retire in Andalusia (which had originated with Beigbeder); the 'secret communication' ruse to persuade him that he would only be safe in Spain (behind which lay Ribbentrop); the attempt to discover (for the benefit of Serrano Suñer and Stohrer) which way the ducal cat was going to jump, given the chance of restoration; and now the peace manifesto variant, the personal plot of Don Miguel.

What, then, is the truth of Don Miguel's encounters with the Duke of Windsor? What picture emerges from this jumble of evidence? One must bear in mind the personality of Don Miguel. He was an old friend of the Duke, but in no sense was he a serious character. 'Miguel was a jolly, expansive, pleasure-loving person,' recalls Montarco, 'a lover of women and wine and tremendous fun to be with, but quite without depth or political sense or any persuasive talents. He was really not the man to persuade the Duke of Windsor to do anything.'[9] This is the general view of those who knew him. His friends saw him as a light-hearted good companion; others as a half-witted debauchee; no one credited him with much intellect or strength of character. Don Miguel had spent a week in Portugal, in the course of which he had seen much of the Duke socially but (by his own account) had had only two conversations with him about the future. What form did these conversations take? Were they historic interviews conducted in hushed rooms, each word carefully weighed? Far more likely that they consisted of loose chatter across a good dinner table, with the wine flowing freely. Don Miguel was all his life a devotee of the bottle, and the Duke himself was hitting it fairly hard at this time in the face of tension and gloom. Don Miguel was a gusher, and it is not hard to envisage him – after a great deal of liquid fortification – letting it all out in a great gush. Did not the Duke look forward to being restored to the throne by the Germans? In the meantime, surely he would be going back to Spain rather than suffer the indignity of colonial banishment? And would he not issue a peace manifesto while he was there, and so change the course of history? (Don Miguel was a great believer in destiny.) By the way, there was an important message from Serrano Suñer. What was it? Something about a secret communication. . . .

What can one tell of the Duke's reactions to these propositions? It would appear that he rejected the idea of restoration; that he asked for further particulars of the secret communication; and that he committed himself to nothing. On the other hand, he evidently expressed no little interest in going to Spain; and he also poured out his sorrows to his old boon companion. He felt 'almost a prisoner', 'surrounded by spies', 'further and further away from the King and from the present English Government', fearful of 'the clever and constantly intriguing Queen'. This was the part of Stohrer's first despatch against which the Duke wrote 'correct' – so we may assume it is. It sounds suspiciously like the litany of a man who has been having one too many.

Above all, one must remember the Duke's mood when he saw Don Miguel on 20 July. He was in the slough of despond, asking himself whether he could face going to the Bahamas. Two days earlier, the quarrel had broken out with the British Government over his travel arrangements. He had written to Churchill that he had been 'messed about long enough' and might 'have to reconsider my position'. He had written to Allen that he regarded the prospect of Bahamian exile 'with profound gloom and despondency', that there were times when he was 'sorely tempted to chuck the whole project and retire entirely from the contest'. He had always kept the Spanish Government's offer of hospitality up his sleeve in case other plans went wrong; and did it not now seem that they might well go wrong? Any suggestions of Don Miguel, of course, were not to be taken too seriously. But there was someone else present at the dinner party on the 20th who was far more plausible than Don Miguel, and who might well have taken up his points and expressed them with far greater conviction and lucidity – Ricardo Espírito Santo. And Ricardo would not have failed to report that evening's conversation to his friend the German Minister.

And so the Duke, in the course of a possibly convivial discussion, expressed an interest in going to Spain, and no doubt let fly a number of ill-advised remarks about his position and the war which he did not expect to be repeated. But can he have expressed a very definite interest? For throughout those days, he continued to forge ahead with preparations for his governorship. He engaged another maid and ADC through Gray

Phillips and settled the terms of their employment;[10] he arranged for his furniture stored in England to be shipped to the Bahamas;[11] he transferred £26,000 from his and the Duchess's London bank accounts to the Royal Bank of Canada in Nassau;[12] and he continued to press for the recovery of his belongings from La Cröe, and Mademoiselle Moulichon's journey to Paris. There appears to have been no moment when he actually abandoned the idea of going to the Bahamas. 'I'll think about it' appears to have been the limit of his committment to Don Miguel's propositions. Indeed, being non-committal was part of his royal training; he had a lifetime's experience in giving the impression that he sympathized with the person he was talking to, in stringing people along, in keeping his options open, in the art of wait-and-see.

This is not, however, the impression given by Stohrer's despatch of 23 July. There everything is expressed very categorically – the extent of the Duke's rupture with the British authorities ('toying with the idea ... of breaking with his brother'), the impression upon him of Serrano Suñer's mysterious message ('extraordinarily interested'), the degree of his intention to go to live in Spain (a course 'very much desired' by him and the Duchess). The bad news – that he appeared unwilling to play the German game of restoration – was held back for two further days, and even then served up in a somewhat hopeful form. And in neither telegram is there any hint that the emissary of the Spanish Interior Minister was none other than the notorious frivolous lightweight and fatuous intriguer Don Miguel; he is merely described as an old friend of the Duke. At best, the despatch of 23 July was an exaggerated and incomplete account, designed to keep Ribbentrop happy, show how well Stohrer had fulfilled his instructions, and illustrate Serrano Suñer's zeal in accommodating the Germans. It was intended to give Berlin the idea that all was going to plan – and it was to succeed all too well in that intention.

However, Don Miguel was not the only Spaniard who encouraged the Duke to return to Spain around that time. It will be recalled that, on 16 July, Stohrer had reported to Ribbentrop that the Spanish Foreign Minister had instructed his Ambassador in Lisbon 'to warn the Duke once more urgently against taking up post.'* This Ambassador was Don Nicolás, the corpulent elder brother of General Franco. On 24 July – two days after Don Miguel's return to Madrid – Stohrer was able to report:

* See above, p. 114.

'The Spanish Foreign Minister has just informed me that the Spanish Ambassador in Lisbon has made the *démarche* to the Duke of Windsor as instructed and that the Duke and Duchess are ready to return to Spain.'*[13]

Don Nicolás Franco y Bahamonde – who plays one of the most mysterious parts in this story – was forty-nine in July 1940, two years older than his brother Francisco. He is remembered by numerous people in Lisbon, but it is not easy to get a good overall view of him, because he remained Ambassador there almost into the 1960s by which time he had become a loathsome individual – the very caricature of a fat, greedy, indolent, corrupt, lecherous ambassador. The photograph of him reproduced in this volume tells its own tale. But the man of 1960 was not the man of 1940, and during the Second World War he played a key role in keeping the Peninsula neutral. He possessed no particular talent, and little personal allure; before the Civil War he had made a very ordinary career in the navy, ending up on the staff of a naval engineering college. But he did have three qualities: he was (according to his lights) a patriot, he possessed all the shrewdness of his native Galicia, and he was completely devoted to his brother Francisco. He appears to have been one of the very few men Francisco Franco ever really trusted. At first he served as Francisco's private secretary; in April 1938, when Salazar officially recognized the Spanish Nationalists, he was sent to Lisbon. It was a tense moment, for Hitler had just grabbed Austria, and Salazar was disturbed by reports that ultra-nationalist Spaniards wanted to follow suit by grabbing Portugal in a peninsular *Anschluss*. Don Nicolás managed to dispel these fears, and brought about an agreement known as the Iberian Pact (March 1939) by which Spain and Portugal recognized the 'indissoluble duality' of the Peninsula and agreed never to support each other's enemies.

In July 1940 Don Nicolás was busy negotiating a protocol to the Iberian Pact in the light of the new European situation. This reaffirmed existing treaties (including the Anglo–Portuguese alliance) and provided for consultation on matters affecting common security. (Curiously, this vague and ambiguous declaration – which was published on 29 July – was regarded with satisfaction by both the British and the German Governments.) It was while Don Nicolás was in Madrid in the middle of the month discussing the protocol that Beigbeder had asked him to urge the

* That same morning Don Nicolás had told Teixeira de Sampaio at the Portuguese Foreign Ministry that 'the Duke and Duchess of Windsor would now be going to Spain'. (*Dez anos de política externa*, Vol. VII, Lisbon, 1971, p. 295, doc. no. 1047.)

Duke of Windsor not to leave for the Bahamas. By 19 July Don Nicolás was back in Lisbon; and by 24 July he had seen the Duke (possibly more than once) and raised the matter of return to Spain.

Don Nicolás had already been in touch with the Duke over his efforts to rescue his possessions (with German permission) from France, and took a dim view of that proceeding. As he told Teixeira de Sampaio on a visit to the Portuguese Foreign Ministry: 'A prince does not ask favours of his country's enemies. To request the handing over of things he could replace or dispense with *no está bien* [is not correct].' Yet Don Nicolás went on to tell the Secretary-General that it was of the utmost importance that the Duke remain in Europe. As he put it:

> In spite of his wayward character, which made him a problem for his ministers (and which was one of the reasons for the Abdication), the Prince still represents a last resort, one final hope, in the event of an internal upheaval in the British Empire. If as a result of the war the Empire were to experience an upheaval, it would not suit the rest of the world for an organism of that nature to fall into anarchy. The Duke of Windsor, free from responsibility for the war, in disagreement with the English politicians, would be the man to take charge of that Empire.[14]

But *would* the Duke remain on the continent to fulfil this destiny? On the evening of 24 July Don Nicolás raised this question when he and Teixeira de Sampaio dined with the Italian Minister to Lisbon, Renato Bova Scoppa. He mentioned that the Duke had asked for a visa to go to Spain 'for a few days',* and wondered whether this would affect his decision to leave for the Bahamas. Teixeira de Sampaio expressed the view 'that the Duke, notwithstanding the bitterness he feels over his appointment, will leave obediently for his new post . . . on the first of August next'.[15]

It appears from this that the Duke, whatever indications he may have given of his desires and intentions, had not committed himself to Don Nicolás on the subject of return to Spain any more than he had to Don Miguel. And Don Nicolás for his part was certainly not making much secret of the fact that the Spanish Government were trying to get the Duke to remain in the Peninsula, and that he seemed to be responding to their influence. Not only had the Germans been informed, but he had lost no time in telling the Portuguese and the Italians about it. And – amazing though it may seem – he also appears to have let the British know about it, through David Eccles.[16]

---

* This was originally in connection with the Duke's proposed visit to La Cröe, which he appears by this time to have abandoned.

Eccles had been seeing Don Nicolás about a proposed tripartite economic agreement whereby the British Government would give credits and navicerts to the Spanish to enable them to purchase Portuguese colonial products. This treaty (which had great political as well as economic implications, since it was a tacit admission on the part of the Spanish Government that they did not anticipate the immediate defeat of Great Britain) was signed on 24 July, the same day that Don Nicolás spoke to various persons of the Duke's Spanish intentions. Eccles was due to go to London the following day, to report on the agreement to the Ministry of Economic Warfare,[17] but before he left Don Nicolás let him know of the pressure being put on the Duke of Windsor to go to Spain and stay there. 'Nicolás Franco was a great blabber,' Lord Eccles explains. 'He was the sort of self-made person who always seemed to be saying "Look at me! I'm an ambassador!", and would illustrate the fact by repeating all kinds of things he had got to know recently. We relied upon him for much of our political information. Not only was he indiscreet, but we always felt he was on our side.'[18] It is indeed the case that Don Nicolás was widely credited with pro-British sympathies; some people in fact believed him to be a paid agent of British intelligence.* Whatever the motive, Don Nicolás made Eccles aware of what was being planned for the Duke, even hinting at German connections; and on Thursday 25 July Eccles was on his way back to London, where he would place the news immediately before the relevant authorities.

That same Thursday, as Eccles was speeding homeward with this disquieting information, a large luncheon was given for the Duke and Duchess at the British Embassy – the second and last time they were to be entertained there. Apart from members of the Embassy and of the Portuguese Government, the guest list included the Spanish Ambassador and Madame Franco, possibly in return for hospitality the Duke and Duchess had received at the Spanish Embassy.[19] The lunch over, the Duke retired with Sir Walford Selby for 'a lengthy discussion'.

After a week of dispute with the British authorities, the Duke was

---

* In an extraordinary interview published in the *Guardian* on 15 January 1983, Lord Eccles described himself as 'an apostle of bribery' during the war and explained that one of his tasks in the Peninsula had been to 'buy' eminent neutrals. Asked whether General Franco had been approached in this way, he replied: 'Not by us.' Asked whether he had bribed Don Nicolás he replied: 'Well, the brother was a jolly man.' Eccles wrote to his wife on 13 February 1942: 'Spain has a remarkable ambassador in Don Nicolás Franco, from whom we can derive many advantages, but he won't open his heart to anyone but me' (*By Safe Hand*, p. 336).

awaiting Churchill's verdict on his travel arrangements and the matter of his soldier servant. This had now arrived: Selby handed him the Prime Minister's telegram of 24 July informing him that the deviation of the *Excalibur* had been arranged, that the Government could not agree to his going to America at that moment, but that Piper Fletcher would be released and sent to join him. After conferring with Selby, the Duke replied accepting these arrangements. His row with the Government seemed to be at an end. Selby added in a separate telegram that the Duke 'perfectly appreciated' why Churchill wanted him to avoid America just then, though he hoped he might go there later on 'provided political conditions permit'.[20]

However, there was another telegram the Duke sent to London that day, subsequent to his reply to Churchill. It was addressed to Phillips, to whom the Duke wrote that, although he had agreed 'in principle' to the new sea voyage arrangements, the agents of the American shipping company were 'insistent' that it was 'far preferable we sail August 8th instead August 1st' as it would be 'easier to displace American reservations with less inconvenience and bad feeling for later voyage'. The Duke thought it 'more diplomatic sail August 8th besides giving us extra week for the chance of getting some of our things from La Cröe', and asked Phillips to 'urge same arrangements be made for sailing August 8th and we can wait at Bermuda for the next available Canadian or other ship to Nassau'.[21] Perhaps there was something a trifle over-anxious in the Duke's explanations for wishing to delay his departure. But Selby backed him up, telegraphing to Halifax: 'In the absence of any sudden development in the situation I see no objection to the postponement.'[22]

These telegrams were received at the Foreign Office at breakfast time on Friday 26 July. The powers that be had just received Eccles' alarming intelligence about the Duke, and the government decoders had cracked some even more alarming intercepts. Now came the news that the Duke was trying to delay his departure. That day, there was something akin to panic in London on the subject of the Duke of Windsor.

8
In Berlin
13–25 July

Having put in motion the plot to lure the Duke of Windsor back to Spain, Ribbentrop and the *Auswärtiges Amt* seem to have dismissed him temporarily from their minds. There was nothing to do but await the result of the Spanish emissary's mission; and meanwhile there were other things to think of. The Soviet Union had just annexed the Baltic States with their large German populations; Hungary and Romania were being pressed to settle their differences and become allies of Germany; there were new diplomatic efforts to encourage isolationism in the Americas; and there was the tiresome business of liquidating the sovereignty of defeated nations. So the intrigue in the Peninsula was left to look after itself, and no new instructions concerning the Duke were sent to Stohrer or Hoynigen-Huene. Until Don Ramón's unidentified *Vertrauensmann* returned and reported, the ball was in the Spanish court.

In the meantime, other relevant developments were taking place elsewhere on the German stage. For Hitler was at last having to decide how to deal with England. He hoped, as always, that invasion would be unnecessary. But the Churchill Government remained unaccountably uninterested in peace negotiations. At a staff conference at the Berghof. on 13 July Hitler confessed that he was perplexed as to 'why England does not yet want to take the road to peace'. He could only imagine that she was holding on in the hope of support from Russia or America. If that were the case he supposed he would have to 'compel her to make peace by force', though he 'did not like to have to do such a thing'.[1] Three days later he issued his Directive No. 16, which began:

> Since England, despite her militarily hopeless situation, still shows no sign of willingness to come to terms, I have decided to prepare a landing operation against England, and if necessary to carry it out.
> The aim of the operation is to eliminate the English homeland as a base for

carrying on the war against Germany, and if it should become necessary, to occupy it completely.

To this end I issue the following instructions. . . .[2]

If it should become necessary. . . . Even now, Hitler did not despair of a peaceful solution with England. It was on 19 July, three days after signing the directive, that he delivered his Reichstag speech calling upon England to come to terms with Germany.

It is far from clear whom this speech was designed to impress or what it was meant to achieve. The original idea had been to announce the actual peace terms which Germany was offering England.* However, at the last moment Hitler changed his mind. Perhaps he feared that his terms would be rejected and that he would then look a fool. So instead he delivered a long, aggressive, hectoring address, containing no definite proposals and no ideas of substance. It was not so much an appeal as an accusation, and addressed not so much to the British Government and people as to 'history' and domestic and neutral opinion:

> From Britain I now hear only a single cry – not of the people but the politicians – that the war must go on! I do not know whether these politicians have a correct idea yet of what the continuation of this struggle will be like. They do, it is true, declare that . . . even if Great Britain should perish, they would carry on from Canada. I can hardly believe that they mean by this that the people of Britain are to go to Canada. Presumably only those gentlemen interested in the continuation of the war will go there. . . . Mr Churchill . . . no doubt will already be in Canada, where the money and children of those principally interested in the war have already been sent. For millions of other people, however, great suffering will begin. Mr Churchill ought perhaps, for once, to believe me when I prophesy that a great Empire will be destroyed – an Empire which it was never my intention to destroy or even to harm. . . .
>
> In this hour I feel it to be my duty before my own conscience to appeal once more to reason and common sense in Great Britain as much as elsewhere. I consider myself in a position to make this appeal since I am not the vanquished begging for favours but the victor speaking in the name of reason.
>
> *I see no reason why this war must go on.*[3]

---

* It is quite well known what these terms were to have been. England was to recognize Germany as master of the continent; there was to be a non-aggression pact; and the German colonies were to be restored. These conditions may sound generous for a near-defeated nation; but Hitler would not deal with the existing British Government, only with politicians of his own choosing, and thus it was clear that the post-peace Britain would be far from independent.

Although it is difficult to see what could seriously have been expected from this speech, it gave rise to massive publicity internationally and a burst of optimism inside Germany. On the 21st Hitler told Brauchitsch, the army Commander-in-Chief, that while he still wanted the invasion preparations to go ahead at full speed, he nevertheless saw some signs that peace might be in sight. The English press had first attacked his speech but then become 'milder'. The Führer claimed that Lord Lothian, Lloyd George and the Duke of Windsor had all urged a positive response (the last two in letters to the King*), and that there was an idea of a 'peace cabinet' consisting of Lloyd George, Halifax and Chamberlain.[4] But such hopes were soon to be dashed. On the 22nd the British Government gave its unofficial reply in the form of a wireless broadcast by Halifax.† This was uncompromising:

> Many of you will have read two days ago the speech in which Herr Hitler summoned Great Britain to capitulate to his will. I will not waste your time by dealing with the distortions of almost every main event since the war began. He says he has no desire to destroy the British Empire, but there was in his speech no suggestion that peace should be based on justice, no recognition that the other states of Europe have any right to self-determination, the principle he has so often invoked for Germans. His only appeal was to the base instinct of fear, and his only arguments were threats. . . .[5]

In Berlin, even those who had not been over-sanguine were surprised by the finality of this response. Weizsäcker wrote in his diary on the 23rd

---

* On 22 July, the *Gazeta de Popolo* of Turin reported that the Duke of Windsor had sent a telegram to the King urging that 'serious consideration' should be given to the idea of a Lloyd George–Halifax––Chamberlain peace Cabinet. This story was taken up the next day by the *New York Times*, which commented (on p. 3) that the Duke was 'reported to favour peace negotiations if an honourable basis can be found' and that he might 'elaborate' his views if he came to the United States. No trace of the alleged telegram is to be found either in the Public Record Office or in the Duke's papers in Paris. While the Duke certainly privately favoured negotiations, one wonders whether he would have recommended to his brother the dismissal of a government which still had the support of Parliament, or whether he believed that Lloyd George and Chamberlain, who hated each other, would be willing to serve together in the same Cabinet.

† The War Cabinet that morning had decided that the Reichstag speech 'was intended for home consumption. It did not contain any specific offer . . . but made an appeal which did not call for any definite reply' (CAB 65/8; War Cabinet 209). Is this to say that some of those present might have been in favour of responding to a suitable specific offer? The possibility of a House of Commons debate seems to have been raised but turned down – and all other British records on the subject (including part of these same Cabinet minutes) remain secret.

that the door to peace had been closed.[6] But before that day was out, another door appeared to have opened. For at 9.50 that evening there arrived Stohrer's telegram giving the report (or as it turned out, part of the report) of the Spanish emissary to the Duke of Windsor. For once Ribbentrop was in Berlin, instead of following Hitler around in a special train or conducting diplomacy at long distance from Fuschl.[7] He saw the despatch immediately – and he wasted no time in acting upon it.

Coming as it did as he was smarting from the Halifax speech, the telegram could hardly have delighted him more. Everything seemed to be going to plan. The Duke, according to the report, was ready to go to Spain. But he would be going there without any suspicion that he would be putting himself in German hands. He appeared to have swallowed the story about his imperilled security. On the other hand, his remarks to the *Vertrauensmann* – that he was increasingly distant from the British Government, and even considering a public statement disavowing their policy – gave every reason to suppose that he would eventually lend himself to German purposes.* Perhaps if Ribbentrop had seen Stohrer's second report – that the Duke had discounted the possibility of restoration – he might have been more cautious; but that (perhaps intentionally) was only sent two days later.

Obviously the next move was to send a German agent to the Peninsula. His duties would be to see to it that the Duke and Duchess were brought safely over to Spain, to frustrate the anticipated counter-moves of the British secret service, and finally to approach the ex-King on behalf of the German Government. He would have to be a trained secret serviceman with experience of Spain and Portugal; he would have to be skilled in the art of improvisation; and he would have to be a man of tact and resource and proven persuasive ability. On the night of 23 July Ribbentrop discussed the matter with Hitler;[8] and the choice fell on Walter Schellenberg.

Schellenberg was only thirty in July 1940, and already held the rank of *Brigadeführer* (major-general) in the SS as well as the cover of *Regierungsrat* (government counsellor) in the German civil service. The son of a Saarland piano maker who had been ruined in the great depression, he had found himself short of money as a law student in 1933, and joined

---

* According to Erich Kordt, Ribbentrop was particularly impressed by the news that the Duke 'was apparently ready to break with his brother, who was entirely under the influence of the Queen, who was not well-disposed towards the Windsors' (*Nicht aus den Akten*, p. 399).

the Nazis (or so he later claimed) in order to increase his chances of getting a government grant. 'Although it was my own financial difficulties which decided me to join the Party', he wrote in his memoirs, 'I cannot say that I reached this decision with any great reluctance or difficulty.'[9] There is no evidence that he was an ideologically committed Nazi: he regarded party policy with cynicism and the party leaders with critical disdain. But he was clever and ambitious. He joined the SS, then an elite formation, and was quickly drafted into the SD, the secret service within the SS which exercised 'all the powers of spying and intelligence, interrogation and arrest, torture and execution on which dictatorship ultimately depends'. The leader of the SD, the brilliant and sadistic Reinhardt Heydrich, singled him out as a rising man. Soon he was immersed in the world of Nazi espionage – a world, as Alan Bullock writes, 'in which nothing was too fantastic to happen, in which normality of behaviour and simplicity of motive were curiosities and nothing was taken at face value, in which lies, bribes, blackmail and false papers, treachery and violence were part of the daily routine'.[10] He set up 'Salon Kitty', the Berlin brothel designed to entrap foreign diplomats. He was involved in the Tuchachevsky affair, in which Hitler helped Stalin foil an army plot. His greatest coup came in November 1939, when two British secret service agents, with whom Schellenberg had been 'negotiating' after persuading them that he was one of the leaders of a secret opposition to Hitler, were kidnapped on the Dutch frontier and brought to Berlin. For his role in his operation (which created an international scandal) Schellenberg was promoted to general rank, and put in charge of the foreign counter-espionage section (*Amt IVE*) of Heydrich's new organization the RSHA, which absorbed both the Gestapo and the SD.

Hugh Trevor-Roper has left a well-known and withering portrait of him:

> Among the parochial minds of the SS, Schellenberg, its youngest general, enjoyed an undeserved reputation. He was credited with understanding foreign affairs. ... A North German, he was also exempt from the ideological gibberish of the Austrian and Bavarian Nazis. He believed not in force, nor in nonsense, but in subtlety; and he believed that he was subtle. This was perhaps his greatest mistake, for he was in fact a very trivial character.... Like so many Germans, he was an admirer, a despairing admirer, of the British Intelligence Service – an organization of which he knew very little, but of which he had evidently read much in those amazing novelettes which filled the reference library of the Gestapo.[11]

It is true that he had some curious notions; and many of his doings now appear comically naïve. But he was no fool. He was a sharp-witted and ruthlessly ambitious young man who recognized how far his masters were immersed in fantasy and knew how to humour them and play up to them.* He was a shrewd player in a great game – a game of power and intrigue played out not so much in the theatre of war as within the faction-ridden Nazi machine. In many ways he was appropriate for the task which Ribbentrop had in mind – a seasoned professional skilled in the art of deception. But his main concern would be to emerge with credit from the affair, to use it to further his own ambition, and above all to ensure that, if there was going to be trouble, he would not be on the receiving end.

In his memoirs, Schellenberg gave the following account of his original interview with Ribbentrop – an interview which took place, according to contemporary evidence, on the morning of 24 July, the day after the arrival in Berlin of Stohrer's telegram.†

One morning in July 1940, I received a call from one of my friends at the Foreign Office, warning me to expect a call from the 'old man' – meaning Ribbentrop – as soon as he was 'ready for action'. My friend did not know what it was all about, but it seemed to be something terribly urgent.

At noon Ribbentrop's sonorous voice came over the telephone: 'Tell me, my dear fellow, could you come over to my office at once? You have time, haven't you?' 'Certainly,' I replied, 'but could you tell me what it's about?

---

* In his memoirs, Erich Kordt wrote that one of the reasons Ribbentrop's plans for the Duke of Windsor came to nothing was that 'the agent Ribbentrop selected – who must have cost him dear – was particularly astute and knew how to give wings to his master's fantasies' (*Nicht aus den Akten*, p. 400).

† Schellenberg's role in this story is revealed by three sources. First, there are his telegraphic reports to Ribbentrop and Heydrich from the Peninsula, a number (but not apparently all) of which are among the captured German documents. These culminate in his final report of 2 August, which is reproduced below pp. 202–6. Secondly, the surviving papers of the RSHA contain a log he kept of the operation, listing his principal movements and encounters; the text of this valuable and hitherto unpublished source is given in Appendix III below, pp. 234–6. Finally there are the memoirs which Schellenberg wrote after the war and which were first published in London in 1956, four years after his death. These contain a chapter about the affair, which prompted the Duke of Windsor to issue a public statement to say that he had never previously heard of Schellenberg. The accuracy and authenticity of these memoirs has been questioned by some historians – a matter discussed below in Appendix II, pp. 233–5. Suffice it to say here that, while they are weak on chronology (they describe as having taken place over many weeks events which in fact took less than ten days), there is no good reason to mistrust them where they are not inconsistent with other sources.

There may be some material that I should bring along.' 'No, no,' said Ribbentrop, 'come at once. It's not a matter I can discuss over the telephone.'

I called Heydrich immediately and reported the conversation, for I knew his pathological jealousy. Heydrich said at once, 'I see; the gentleman no longer wishes to consult me – old idiot! Well, go over there and give him my best regards.' I promised Heydrich that I would give him a detailed report of what Ribbentrop wanted.

As usual Ribbentrop received me standing behind his desk with folded arms and a serious expression on his face. He asked me to be seated and, after a few polite remarks, came to the point. He had heard that I had various connections in Spain and Portugal and had even achieved a measure of co-operation with the police of these countries. I did not know where these remarks were leading, and answered very cautiously. Dissatisfied with my evasive replies, he shook his head. 'Mmm,' he said, then he was silent. Suddenly he said, 'You remember the Duke of Windsor, of course? Were you introduced to him during his last visit?' I said that I had not been. 'Have you any material on him?' Ribbentrop asked. 'I really cannot say at the moment,' I replied. 'Well, what do you think of him personally? How do you evaluate him as a political figure, for instance?' I admitted honestly that these questions had taken me by surprise and that at the moment my knowledge was not sufficient to give a proper answer. I had seen the Duke at the time of his last visit to Germany and, of course, knew what was generally known about the reasons for his abdication. It seemed that the English had handled the whole problem very sensibly; that in the end tradition and responsibility had had to take precedence over human feelings and personal emotions. It seemed difficult to decide whether the matter should be adjudged a sign of weakness or of strength in the English Royal Family. It seemed that in the lengthy conferences on the subject the members of the Government had shown understanding of the human and political problems involved. When I had finished I thought that Ribbentrop's eyes would pop out of his head, so astonished was he at the uninhibited manner in which I expressed these opinions. He lost no time in putting me right.

The Duke of Windsor was one of the most socially aware and right-thinking Englishmen he had ever met. It was this which had displeased the governing clique; the marriage issue had been a welcome pretext to remove this honest and faithful friend of Germany. All the questions of tradition and ceremonial that were raised were completely secondary.

Here I tried to object, but was silenced by an abrupt gesture. 'My dear Schellenberg, you have a completely wrong view of these things – also of the real reasons behind the Duke's abdication. The Führer and I already recognized the facts of the situation in 1936. The crux of the matter is that, since his abdication, the Duke has been under strict surveillance by the British Secret Service. We know what his feelings are: it's almost as if he were their prisoner.

Every attempt that he's made to free himself, however discreet he may have been, has failed. And we know from our reports that he still entertains the same sympathetic feelings towards Germany, and that given the right circumstances he wouldn't be averse to escaping from his present environment – the whole thing's getting on his nerves. We've had word that he has even spoken about living in Spain and that if he did go there he'd be ready to be friends with Germany again as he was before. The Führer thinks this attitude is extremely important, and we thought that you with your Western outlook might be the most suitable person to make some sort of exploratory contact with the Duke – as the representative, of course, of the Head of the German State. The Führer feels that if the atmosphere seemed propitious you might perhaps make the Duke some material offer. Now, we should be prepared to deposit in Switzerland for his own use a sum of fifty million Swiss francs – if he were ready to make some official gesture dissociating himself from the manoeuvres of the British Royal Family. The Führer would, of course, prefer him to live in Switzerland, though any other neutral country would do so long as it's not outside the economic or the political or military influence of the German Reich.

'If the British Secret Service should try to frustrate the Duke in some such arrangement, then the Führer orders that you are to circumvent the British plans, even at the risk of your life, and, if need be, by the use of force. Whatever happens, the Duke of Windsor must be brought safely to the country of his choice. Hitler attaches the greatest importance to this operation, and he has come to the conclusion after serious consideration that if the Duke should prove hesitant, he himself would have no objection to your helping the Duke to reach the right decision by coercion – even by threats or force if the circumstances make it advisable. But it will also be your responsibility to make sure at the same time that the Duke and his wife are not exposed to any personal danger.

'Now, in the near future the Duke expects to have an invitation to hunt with some Spanish friends. This hunt should offer an excellent opportunity for you to establish contact with him. From that point he can immediately be brought into another country. All the necessary means for you to carry out this assignment will be at your disposal. Last night I discussed the whole matter again thoroughly with the Führer and we have agreed to give you a completely free hand. But he demands that you let him see daily reports on the progress of the affair. Herewith, in the name of the Führer, I give you the order to carry out this assignment at once. You are ready, of course, to carry it out?'

For a moment I sat stunned. I really couldn't grasp the whole thing so quickly. So to gain time I said, 'Herr Reichsminister, may I ask a few questions – to clarify my understanding of the matter?' 'Be quick about it,' Ribbentrop answered. 'You spoke of the Duke's sympathy for Germany,' I said. 'Is it sympathy for the German way of life, for the German people, or does it also include the present form of government?' I saw at once that I had gone too far.

Brusquely he said, 'When we speak of Germany today, it is the Germany in which you also live.' 'May I ask', I went on, 'just how reliable is this secret information of yours?' 'It comes', he said, 'from the most reliable circles of Spanish society. The details of these reports need not concern you now. Any details which are of importance you can discuss with our Ambassador in Madrid.' I asked one further question: 'Do I understand that if the Duke of Windsor should resist, I am to bring him into this "other country" that you speak of by force? It seems to me there's a contradiction in that. Surely the whole action must depend on the voluntary co-operation of the Duke?' 'Well,' answered Ribbentrop, 'the Führer feels that force should be used primarily against the British Secret Service – against the Duke only insofar as his hesitation might be based on a fear-psychosis which forceful action on our part would help him to overcome. Once he's a free man again and able to move about without surveillance by British Intelligence he'll be grateful to us. As far as the money to be placed at his disposal is concerned, fifty million Swiss francs by no means represents the absolute maximum. The Führer is quite ready to go to a higher figure. For the rest – well, don't worry too much. Have confidence in yourself and do your best. I will report to the Führer that you have accepted the assignment.'

I nodded, rose, and was about to say goodbye, when Ribbentrop said, 'One moment – ', and taking up the telephone, asked for Hitler. He handed me the second earpiece, so that I could listen in, and when Hitler's peculiar hollow voice came on the line Ribbentrop briefly reported our conversation. I could tell from Hitler's voice that he was not too happy about the whole thing. His replies were curt: 'Yes – certainly – agreed.' Finally he said, 'Schellenberg should particularly bear in mind the importance of the Duchess's attitude and try as hard as possible to get her support. She has great influence over the Duke.' 'Very well then,' said Ribbentrop, 'Schellenberg will fly by special plane to Madrid as quickly as possible.' 'Good,' Hitler answered. 'He has all the authorization he needs. Tell him from me that I am relying on him.' Ribbentrop rose, made a bow towards the telephone and said, 'Thank you, my Führer, that is all.'

I asked Ribbentrop about the transmission of my reports, which were to be sent through diplomatic channels, and our conversation ended with a brief discussion of technical questions about currency, passports and so forth.

I went at once to Heydrich, who received me somewhat coolly. 'Ribbentrop always wants to use our people when he gets ideas like this. You are really much too valuable to me to waste on this affair. I don't like the whole plan. Still, once the Führer gets hold of such a notion it's very difficult to talk him out of it, and Ribbentrop is the worst possible adviser. You have to realize that you will be making front-line contact with our opponents, so I don't want you to travel alone. Take two reliable and experienced men with you who can speak the

IN BERLIN

language. At least you will have some protection. Certainly if I were head of
the British Secret Service, I would settle your hash for you.'

Soon afterwards Ribbentrop called me again and said curtly, 'Please come over
to my office right away.' When I arrived there all he wanted was to ask whether
I was satisfied with my preparations and if I had enough money. He also asked
whether I had worked out a plan. I said not yet. He then said that of course
everything concerning the affair had to be kept entirely secret and that the
Führer would personally punish the slightest violation of secrecy – the Führer had wanted him to tell me that. It was typical of Ribbentrop's methods that
he mentioned this only now. I reassured him, and finally was able to take my
leave.[12]

According to this plausible account, Schellenberg had received two warning signals which boded ill for the affair. He sensed that Hitler had
reservations about the plan but had been talked into it by Ribbentrop –
and that his own boss Heydrich, out of jealousy of Ribbentrop, was not
anxious that the plan should succeed.

Accompanied by his two SD escorts Heineke and Böcker, Schellenberg
set out for Madrid by air at ten o'clock on the morning of Thursday
25 July.[13] He had been instructed to report daily; and the code-name
selected for the Duke was *Willi*.

9
New Schemes in Madrid
23–26 July

While the Schellenberg mission was being prepared in Berlin, the plot was being carried a stage further in Madrid. Stohrer had concluded his despatch of 23 July by recounting 'a long conversation' he had had with Serrano Suñer. The Interior Minister was 'unusually interested and active in this case' and now proposed sending a second Spanish *Vertrauensmann* to Portugal to bring to fruition the work begun by the first. (For it would arouse too much suspicion to send Don Miguel a second time.) 'This new confidential emissary', wrote Stohrer, 'is to persuade the Duke to leave Lisbon as if for a long motoring excursion and then to cross the border at a prearranged place, where the Spanish secret police will see to it that he comes over safely.'[1] It is interesting to note that the Duke would need to be 'persuaded'; in spite of his supposed keenness to go to Spain of which Stohrer had written a few lines earlier, it could not be assumed that he would fall in with this plan.

Once again, Serrano Suñer has a rather different recollection of this conversation.[2] He denies that he was 'unusually interested and active' in the matter. In fact he recalls that, once Don Miguel returned with the news that the Duke was not willing to contemplate restoration, he was all for bringing the affair to an end. But Stohrer assured him that Ribbentrop would not be content to leave things there, and suggested that they make at least a pretence of continuing the plot, playing on the theme that the Duke ought to flee to Spain for his own safety. Don Ramón agreed: but from this moment he ceased to have any real interest in the affair. It was just a game to keep the Germans happy, a game in which he was certainly glad to co-operate but in which the Ambassador (with possible assistance from his ingenious wife) planned all the moves.

By the evening of 24 July Stohrer was able to report to Berlin the details of a new scheme which had been worked out. The second emissary (who was not identified) had been chosen and was ready to go to Portugal to take to the Duke a letter from his old friend the first emissary. 'In this letter the first confidential emissary says that he has not yet heard what the important message is which the Interior Minister wants to give the Duke, but he has the impression that it has to do with a great danger which threatens the Duke and Duchess.' The letter would also propose to the Duke a delightful plan whereby he might slip into Spain without arousing the suspicions of the British or the Portuguese authorities. He and the Duchess were to visit 'a well-known resort in the mountains near the Spanish frontier' where 'by chance' (Stohrer uses ironical inverted commas in the despatch) they would run into their friend the first confidential emissary together with 'one of the secretaries of the Interior Minister', who happened to own an estate in the adjacent part of Spain. It would be casually suggested to the Duke and Duchess that they pay a brief social visit to the Spanish estate. 'In this way it is to be hoped that the ducal couple will come unmolested over the border.'[3] This scheme had the merit of sounding splendidly conspiratorial; how much real prospect of success it had remained to be seen.

The Minister's secretary referred to was Don Eduardo, the Conde de Montarco, the young landowner-politician who has already been encountered as the recipient of the post-Lisbon confidences of Don Miguel. He owned a fifteenth-century castle at Ciudad Rodrigo, that fine mediaeval town in the west of Spain where Wellington had won his great victory in 1812, lying some twenty-five miles from the frontier and some fifty miles from the equally historic Portuguese mountain stronghold of Guarda. He had been following the affair both as the political secretary of Don Ramón and the friend and confidant of Don Miguel (he does not think he ever discussed it with both of them together); and it was Miguel who had invited him to join the conspiracy and make his property available as the destination of the Duke and Duchess.[4] For however sceptical Stohrer and Serrano Suñer may now have been about the plot, Don Miguel was getting more and more excited about it. In Portugal he may have taken his time and given himself over to pleasure; but back in Spain he appears to have been struck as never before by the historic nature of what he was up to. He was convinced that the Duke would fall in with his plans and take to flight; the cunning letter he was writing the ex-King would see to that! (We shall see in due course the text of this document.) He impressed upon Don Eduardo the great destiny which had been chosen for his castle; for it was there that the portentous peace manifesto would be issued!

147

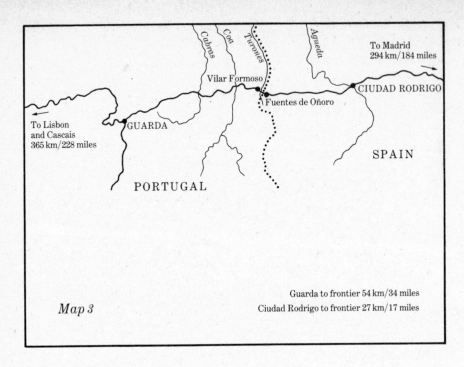

Map 3

Guarda to frontier 54 km/34 miles
Ciudad Rodrigo to frontier 27 km/17 miles

There that Europe's history would be changed! It is easy for imagination to run riot at this point. We may visualize Don Miguel and Don Eduardo dashing off to prepare the house for the ducal arrival. We may picture the swarms of secret policemen and the ceremonial guard of honour, the state apartments deftly transformed to suit the Duchess's standards of comfort, the draft peace manifesto lying on the table with the gold-encrusted fountain pen beside it, the broadcasting equipment. . . . But none of this came to pass in fact. Montarco, though tremendously amused by Don Miguel's enthusiasms, was realistic enough to remain in Madrid until definite news arrived of the Duke's impending flight. The castle waited.

Meanwhile, in the Spanish frontier town of Fuentes de Oñoro (through which it was necessary to pass in order to cross from Guarda to Ciudad Rodrigo), the Portuguese Consul, Dr Zacarias Berenguel Vivas, heard from some Spanish friends that he ought soon to expect a very high English personage to be arriving from Portugal to stay in the locality – strange news which Dr Vivas communicated to his masters in Lisbon.[5]

The second emissary (as to whose identity there is virtually no clue in the German telegrams except that, unlike the first emissary, he was a person unknown to the Duke of Windsor) was now about to leave for Portugal with Don Miguel's letter when a telegram arrived from Berlin asking that his departure be held up.[6] For Schellenberg was now due to arrive in Madrid. His log shows that he reached there by air at six o'clock on the afternoon of Thursday 25 July. The sudden appearance of 'the SS man who had distinguished himself in the kidnapping on the Dutch border' (as Stohrer later and presumably ironically described him) must have been an uncomfortable moment for the Minister and the Ambassador. Up till then they had been free to play their own game, stringing Ribbentrop along with glowing reports. Now everything changed. A piece of amateur Spanish play-acting was being transformed into a professional German secret service operation. Would the charade turn into deadly melodrama? It remained for Stohrer to find out about his man.

In his published memoirs, Schellenberg gives a detailed account of his stay in Madrid. It contains one serious error (possibly as a result of imaginative editing of the original manuscript): it describes his experiences there as if they took place over the course of several days, whereas his log shows that he spent a little under twenty-four hours in the Spanish capital. Apart from this, his account would seem to be a fairly accurate description of the situation he found there and of his various encounters. In good secret service tradition he registered at a hotel on arrival, went on to a private house where he was actually to stay, and then drove by a circuitous route to the German Embassy, where he was at once received by Stohrer:

> I told him briefly about my assignment. It seemed that he had not been given a very clear picture of it. It also transpired that the information upon which the authorities in Berlin had based their decision had come in the first place from him. He had social connections which led, through several members of the Spanish aristocracy, to the Duke of Windsor. Several Spanish and Portuguese nobles were very close friends of the Duke, and one evening he had told them at a party how annoying the continual surveillance of his movements had become and had expressed dissatisfaction with his whole situation. He also seemed to be unhappy about his appointment as Governor of Bermuda [sic]. During various conversations he had often said that he would be pleased to pay a long visit to Spain so that he could get away from it all and live undisturbed with his wife.*

---

* This is a fairly accurate summary of Don Miguel's report, as conveyed to Ribbentrop in the telegram of 23 July. Schellenberg shows quite a good memory for such details, writing about them eight years later without papers.

Thereupon an invitation to hunt had been sent to him and he had accepted it. The date had not yet been settled. . . . The place the Duke was to visit was near the Spanish-Portuguese border. To allay British suspicions of a planned flight into Spain it might be best to name a locality on the border itself, then during one of the hunting excursions a removal 'by mistake' into the Spanish interior would be possible.[7]

Following this discussion, Stohrer (according to Schellenberg's log) called Serrano Suñer – presumably to give him the go-ahead for the despatch of the second emissary.

Schellenberg next consulted the Police Attaché at the Embassy.[8] This was *Kriminalkommissar* and SS *Sturmbannführer* Paul Winzer, who was thirty-two in July 1940; he had helped train Franco's police during the Civil War, and his function now was to 'maintain a liaison' between the Spanish police and the Gestapo. Schellenberg describes him as 'a very able and experienced man' who besides his 'regular' work 'carried out secret service missions'. (He also had experience of kidnapping, since he was responsible for bringing back to Germany any German in Spain who was thought to have become 'unreliable'.) They discussed the details of the plan and the contacts they might use. Winzer recommended an agent he had been cultivating among the senior ranks of the Portuguese police, and thought they could also rely on the full co-operation of the Spanish police (which was under Serrano Suñer's control) – though it would be wiser not to tell them everything about the final object of the mission.

Schellenberg then dined with the Ambassador, and they talked late into the night about the European situation. The conversation was significant. Stohrer begged the young man to tell Ribbentrop how ill-advised it would be to drag Spain into the war. Much as they liked and wanted to help Germany, the Spanish establishment did not want to have to fight and were not physically capable of doing so. The post-Civil War state was too weak and impoverished. While impressed by German victories, well-informed people were far from certain that the war would soon be over. Great Britain remained undefeated. . . .[9] Stohrer concluded with the reflection that, while the Third Reich had achieved great feats by force of arms, there had been few diplomatic victories. Germany was not loved and respected, but feared and hated. Her position in Europe rested solely on the point of bayonets. No doubt this line of thought was intended to make Schellenberg reflect on the purpose of his mission. Was it going to produce a desperately needed diplomatic triumph for Germany, by inducing one of the most distinguished of Englishmen to move voluntarily into the Axis camp? Or could its only success be one of brute force in the form of the abduction of that personage, an act which would scandalize many people and lower still further the general esteem in which Germany was held by the rest of the world?

According to his memoirs, Schellenberg had already made up his mind about these issues. As he wrote: 'I had decided to let the whole thing depend on the Duke of Windsor's attitude. I was against the use of force except to counteract any movements the British Secret Service might make.' And Schellenberg (as he later claimed) was far from sure that the Duke would be willing to play. There had been no more news from Portugal. 'It seemed that the Duke of Windsor was in no great hurry about the hunting excursion. The more I thought about it, the more likely it seemed to me that the whole thing was based merely on an impulsive remark, the result of a passing mood perhaps, and that the seriousness which had been attributed to it was entirely due to wishful thinking.' He resolved to push on to Lisbon without delay, where he could form his own estimate of the situation.[10]

It remained for Schellenberg to report to Berlin on the plan which had been worked out. This he did the next morning. The report (addressed to Ribbentrop, but with a request that it also be communicated to Heydrich) is the first of his several despatches among the German telegrams and is worth quoting in full. The terse, impersonal, cumbersome language, the use of special terms and of the passive voice, the author's habit of referring to himself in the third person, is all typical of the Nazi police style.

> The influence upon the Duke and Duchess exerted by the confidential emissaries is already so effective that a firm intention by the Duke and Duchess to return to Spain can be assumed as in the highest degree probable.
>
> In order to strengthen this intention, the second confidential emissary, who was detained yesterday in line with instructions, was sent off today, 26 July, with a letter to the Duke very skilfully composed psychologically by the first confidential emissary; as an enclosure to it was attached the very precisely prepared plan for carrying out the crossing of the frontier. According to this plan the Duke and his wife should set out officially for a summer vacation in the mountains at a place (providing opportunity for hunting) near the Spanish frontier, in order to cross the frontier at a precisely designated place at a particular time in the course of a hunting trip. Since the Duke is without passports,* the Portuguese frontier official in charge there (a captain who is

---

* The passports had been given to the British Embassy two weeks earlier so that visas might be obtained for the visit the Duke and Duchess were then hoping to make to La Cröe (see above, p. 112). In a

personally obligated to the Spanish Minister) will be won over. At the time set according to plan, the first confidential emissary of the Minister is to be staying at the frontier with Spanish forces suitably placed in order to guarantee safety.

Schellenberg with his group is operating out of Lisbon in closest working relation to the same purpose.

For this purpose the journey to the place of summer vacation, as well as the vacation itself, will be shadowed with the help of a trustworthy Portuguese police chief who is an acquaintance of *Kriminalkommissar* Winzer, attached to the Embassy. There is also the closest working relationship here with the Schellenberg group.

At the exact moment of the crossing of the frontier as scheduled the Schellenberg group is to take over the security arrangements on the Portuguese side of the frontier and continue this into Spain as a direct escort, which is to be unobtrusively changed from time to time.

For the security of the entire plan the Minister has selected another confidential emissary, a woman [*eine weibliche Vertrauensperson*], who can make contact if necessary with the second confidential emissary, who was sent off today, that is the 26th, and can also if necessary get information to the Schellenberg group.

In case there should be an emergency as a result of action by the English Intelligence Service, preparations are being made whereby the Duke and Duchess can reach Spain by air. In this case, as in the execution of the first plan, the chief requisite is to obtain willingness to leave by psychologically adroit influence upon the pronouncedly English mentality of the Duke, without giving the impression of flight, through exploiting anxiety about the I.S. and the prospect of free political activity from Spanish soil.

In addition to the protection in Lisbon, it is being considered whether willingness to leave might not also be induced if necessary by suitable scare-manoeuvres to be attributed to the I.S.

Should the entire plan succeed, security in Spain will be regulated by the Schellenberg group after agreement with the Spanish Minister.[11]

What is interesting here is the speculation as to the Duke's likely reactions. It was 'in the highest degree probable' that Don Miguel had instilled in the Duke 'a firm intention' to return to Spain. Don Miguel's letter, 'very skilfully composed psychologically' (we shall see how much so), could only 'strengthen that intention'. Nevertheless, it was recognized that the Duke's 'pronouncedly English mentality' might hold him

later telegram of 26 July (AA-B15/B002595) Stohrer reported that the Duke had now in fact received the passports back, endorsed with the originally requested Spanish visas, but that 'the plan elaborated in the previous telegram will in all events be followed through anyway, since a counteraction by the I.S. is possible even now that the visa has been granted'.

back; in this case 'willingness to leave' might be 'induced' through 'scare-manoeuvres' [*Schreckmanöver*], alarming staged incidents to be laid at the door of the British Secret Service. We shall hear a great deal about these scare-manoeuvres. In this report we also learn of yet another unidentified agent – female this time – who may be acting as the liaison officer between Schellenberg and the second emissary.

Having sent a telegram to Hoyningen-Huene to announce his arrival, Schellenberg set out for Portugal by air that same afternoon, Friday 26 July. His two SD escorts, Heineke and Böcker, followed him by road, in a fast car which might be needed in the operation.[12] The second Spanish emissary, bearing Don Miguel's letter, had also left by car that morning. But how far was the second emissary aware of Schellenberg's parallel mission? How far was he aware of what he himself was doing? And – above all – who *was* the second emissary?

This was the question which obsessed me for over a year. Curiously, neither Serrano Suñer nor Montarco could tell me who he was – although Don Ramón had sent him out in the first place and Don Eduardo was the man at the other end, so to speak, liable to become the Duke's host (or gaoler?) as a result of the second emissary's efforts. For that matter, the Duke himself had forgotten his identity by 1953, if he ever knew it.* However, in the early autumn of 1983, quite by chance, I came across a man who *might* have been the second emissary. I asked him, and, indeed, he *claimed* to be the second emissary. After twice interviewing him in Madrid, I was satisfied beyond reasonable doubt that he *was* the second emissary – though some of the things he told me were so extraordinary that I felt obliged to regard them at first with a great deal of caution.

Don Angel Alcázar de Velasco y Velasco (for such was the individual's name) was thirty in July 1940, and the keynotes of his career up to that time had been conspiracy, intrigue and romantic adventure. Of humble origins in the provinces, he had gone to Madrid to seek his fortune at the age of nine, beginning life as a waiter and later training as a bullfighter. By 1932 (in which year a serious injury put an end to his bullfighting career) he had become a nationally famous matador, and fame had

---

* When asked by his lawyers who the agent might have been, the Duke could only hazard the guess that it could have been Tiger. This was, of course, entirely mistaken. Tiger's had been the earlier and quite different mission on behalf of Beigbeder; he had nothing to do with the plots carried out through Serrano Suñer; and his correspondence with the Duke shows that he spent all of the second half of July in Madrid.

brought him many friends – including Miguel Primo de Rivera, with whose support he studied and became a journalist. Like Don Miguel and the Conde de Montarco (another friend and himself an amateur bullfighter), he was one of the founders of the *Falange* in the autumn of 1933; indeed, he was a fanatical *falangista* and an ardent admirer of Nazi Germany in all its aspects. On the outbreak of the Civil War he was imprisoned by the Republicans, but escaped to join Franco's Nationalists. However, within a year the Nationalists had put him in prison too. It is important to understand why this happened – for therein lies the key both to the motives of Don Angel and the part he claims to have played in the Duke of Windsor saga.

There was an important difference between the Franco régime and the régimes of Hitler and Mussolini. In Nazi Germany and Fascist Italy a single political movement, with well-defined political aims, had gained power by constitutional means and then suppressed all opposition. In Spain, however, the Nationalists gained power through civil war and not through politics, and their side consisted of a whole variety of political groups with widely differing aims, only united by their common detestation of the socialistic republic. There was the Church; there were the monarchists; there were the reactionary Carlists; there was the army; and, last but not least, there was the *Falange*. Franco was the great juggler who managed to keep this uneasy coalition together – and his greatest problem was how to reconcile the Spanish conservatives and the 'revolutionary' *Falange*, who were at daggers drawn. Moreover, the power of the *Falange* was becoming a threat to his own authority. In the spring of 1937, therefore, Franco began to unify the *Falange* and all other political organizations on the Nationalist side into a new National Movement under his own supreme control. In the interests of unity, most *falangistas* (taking their cue from Serrano Suñer) accepted the new position; but for 'old shirts' like Alcázar de Velasco, for whom Spain's future belonged to the *Falange* and the *Falange* alone, what was happening was nothing less than treason and heresy. They resolved to bring down Franco and to replace him with their own leader, Hedilla, and in April staged an uprising in the Nationalist capital of Salamanca.[13] This was soon put down and the ringleaders sentenced to death, Don Angel among them. His sentence, however, was reduced to life imprisonment, and a year later he was released on account of his role in helping to foil a mass break-out of communists from the prison in which he had been incarcerated. At the end of the Civil War he obtained through his friends the post of press officer to the new Institute of Political Studies set up by Serrano Suñer in Madrid, which occupied the former buildings of the Cortés, the now defunct Spanish parliament.

This, however, was merely a cover for the real activities of Alcázar de Velasco. Since 1935, he had been a secret agent of the *Abwehr*, the legendary Germany military intelligence organization run by the mysterious Admiral Canaris. By the summer of 1940 he was being groomed for the most spectacular of his many espionage roles – that of chief *Abwehr* agent in wartime England. Under the guise of Press Secretary at the Spanish Embassy, he arrived in London in the autumn of that year, and for some months posed, with remarkable success, as an admirer of England striving to bring about closer Anglo–Spanish relations. Sir Samuel Hoare and Anthony Eden were among the many people he took in. Glowing tributes to him appeared in the English press,[14] and a lunch was given for him in the House of Commons, before he was finally 'rumbled' by MI5 in the spring of 1941.* But we must return to July 1940, when Don Angel was still in Madrid – and about to undertake a mission of a rather different sort.

Don Angel struck an impressive and rather exotic figure at that time. Not exactly handsome, his appearance would best be described as gnarled. The experience of bullfighting, imprisonment and civil war, as well as half a decade in the nether world of professional espionage, had left their mark both on his body and on his mind, and he looked older than his thirty years. But the impression he gave was fiery and robust, and he had charm. His reactions were quick and his observations keen. His face might at one moment have a Mephistophelean air, at the next melt into a disarming innocence. He was a man of fanatical principles and beliefs, which he was perfectly able to conceal.

I think the best thing here is simply to publish the text† of my first interview with Don Angel,[15] concerning the circumstances under which he was sent out to see the Duke that July.

---

* There is some controversy as to how valuable an agent Alcázar de Velasco was to the Germans in England. According to the American author Ladislas Farago, he managed to set up an effective British spy network and discover a number of important secrets before being found out (*The Game of the Foxes*, pp. 515–16). However, the British secret service historian Nigel West claims that, when MI5 burgled Don Angel's safe in Madrid, they discovered a series of bogus reports which he had apparently concocted in order to conceal his lack of success (MI6, p. 184). To this, Don Angel replies that he was tipped off about the burglary and planted the false reports.

† Edited so as to remove a certain amount of irrelevant rambling.

Q: At what moment did you become aware that there was a plot to bring the Duke and Duchess back to Spain from Portugal?

A: I can't remember precisely. But there was a meeting in my office at the Institute in Madrid. Apart from myself there were Montarco, Miguel Primo de Rivera and a sculptor called Aladré, and in the course of the conversation Miguel said: 'The Duke of Windsor has got to be brought back from Portugal.'

Q: How did the sculptor come to be there?

A: We four were all of us old, genuine *falangistas*. There were not many of us: most of the true *falangistas* were killed in the Civil War, and the majority of those who called themselves *falangistas* were just Franco men whom we despised. Another member of our group was Dionisio Ridruejo,* and he may have been at that meeting too. Anyway, we met quite often and at one of our meetings Miguel said, referring to the Duke: 'We really must get him out of Portugal and into Spain and we have to find somewhere to put him.' And Miguel suggested that I might be the man to bring him back to Spain.

Q: In other words, the first time you ever heard about the matter was on that occasion from Miguel?

A: At any rate, the subject came up at that meeting. I think I first heard about it from Miguel.

Q: Was this after Miguel himself had returned from his mission to the Duke in Portugal?

A: Well, I'm not sure. I don't think the mission was mentioned, but that may have been discretion on Miguel's part. The thing was that the conversation was very general, and the subject of the Duke just came up in the course of general conversation, not in connection with any mission. But a few days later Miguel called to say: 'There is a mission to be carried out. . . .'

Q: By whom?

A: By me. He said: 'You're off to Lisbon, to take a letter to the Duke of Windsor. I'm not sure whether or not he will give you an answer. Try to take a route to Lisbon which will not arouse the suspicions of the authorities, and when you get there don't say anything about this to Nicolás Franco.' I got the letter that same afternoon, and so as not to arouse suspicions I first went to Sevilla and from there went to Portugal by way of Huelva.

Q: Did you read the letter?

A: Yes, I read it and I made a copy of it. But I don't remember exactly what it said. It was all to arrange the Duke's trip to Spain, and where he was to put up when he got there. That was where Montarco came in, with his castle at Ciudad Rodrigo.

---

* A romantically handsome and ultra-radical *falangista* and co-author of the Nationalist marching song *Cara al Sol*, Ridruejo was twenty-seven in July 1940 and in charge of Spanish Government propaganda. He was soon to become a bitter right-wing opponent of Franco and eventually to go into exile.

Q: We have a copy of the letter. Do you remember it saying anything about a British plot against the Duke and Duchess?

A: Oh yes, I remember discussing all that with Miguel. The idea was to persuade him that he would only be safe if he came to Spain.

Q: Because the British secret service wanted to do him in?

A: Yes, that was the idea.

Q: Did you really believe that, or did you just regard it as a ruse to get him to Spain?

A: Oh, I was a professional secret agent, you know. I would have regarded it as a ruse.

Q: So you realized that there was no truth in it?

A: That's right. We had a good ruse and we used it. As a matter of fact, if the Duke had come to Spain and stayed there – which is what we were proposing to him at the time – he wouldn't have been safe at all.* He would only have been safe under German protection in Germany – or under British protection in the Bahamas.

Q: And did Miguel believe that the Duke's life would be in danger unless he came to Spain, as he wrote in the letter?

A: No, never.

Q: What impression did you have of the letter? Was it well written? It was in English, wasn't it?

A: Yes, in English. It was written rather ... *a la falangista*. Not really a suitable letter for the Duke of Windsor or for any English gentleman. It was the sort of letter one friend might send to another. I'm afraid the English wasn't very good: none of us knew very good English, though Miguel spoke it fluently. . . . Yes, the letter was to say that everything had been prepared for the Duke to go to Spain.

Q: Did you realize that the plan had been worked out by the Germans? That Ribbentrop was behind it?

A: Oh yes! Yes, yes. I was quite sure that it was all concocted by Ribbentrop. Ribbentrop and Hitler.

Q: How did you know? Did Miguel tell you?

A: I heard about it from Canaris.† Canaris told me that Ribbentrop thought it would be an important card to have the Duke in Germany. At the time I very much doubted whether the thing would come off.

Q: What did Canaris think of the plan?

A: Well, since it had been sanctioned by Hitler, he would have pretended to be in favour of it whether he was or not.

Q: And why were you so sceptical? Others seem to have been quite optimistic.

A: There were several reasons. To begin with, I was convinced (and still am) that

---

* Presumably because the British and German secret services would have fought to gain control of him.

† Canaris had in fact been in Madrid on 23–24 July, on his way to inspect the defences around Gibraltar (Heinz Höhne, *Canaris*, London, 1979, pp. 423–31).

the Duchess was a secret agent of American intelligence. I once told Canaris this and he said he had never heard such rubbish, but I had my reasons for believing it.* And then, by the time I got involved there were four or five non-professionals who knew about it all, and I was sure they would be talking about it to their mistresses and that the whole thing would soon leak out. So I didn't have much confidence in the plan. The people who were confident had convinced themselves in advance that the Duke would be willing to put himself in German hands, and so they thought they could bring it off. Ribbentrop, of course, was very confident.

Q: What was Miguel's attitude? What did he imagine he was doing?

A: He imagined that the war would be won [by the Germans]; that the Duke would become national leader of England; and that he, Miguel, would be the Duke's friend in Spain and would eventually take over from Franco. And that's the truth of it!

Q: Did you encourage Miguel in this idea of replacing Franco?

A: Yes. We true *falangistas* all hated Franco.

Q: And Miguel thought that the Duke, as ex-King, would want to be restored to the English throne?

A: Yes ... well, not quite. Miguel and I talked about this on several occasions, and my impression was that what Miguel had in mind was a rather different role for the Duke. . . .

Q: Do you mean that the Duke might want to be a dictator in England?

A: Yes, we thought he had the instincts of a dictator.†

Q: So when Miguel returned from Portugal, he was optimistic?

A: Yes. He came to my office – it was the safest place for us to meet – and Dionisio Ridruejo was there, just the three of us – and Miguel was optimistic. Though not about the Duchess. He was suspicious of her.

Q: On whose authority were you sent to Lisbon?

A: It was on Miguel's own authority.

Q: So Miguel had the authority to arrange all these things just by himself?

A: Oh no, he didn't put it like that. What he said was that we were organizing the Spanish side of the operation to bring the Duke of Windsor to Germany. The idea was that he should be in Germany at the time that England was invaded.

Q: Well, we have seen the German documents about this, and it appears from them that the proposal that you should be sent out on this mission was made either by Don Ramón Serrano Suñer or the German Ambassador, von Stohrer.

---

* Don Angel's evidence for this rather unlikely proposition is that he once saw a 'report' written by the Duchess of her visit to Germany in 1937.

† On 29 July Renato Bova Scoppa reported that 'a Spaniard of *falangist* tendencies' – presumably Don Angel – had told a member of the Italian Legation in Lisbon: 'The Prince thinks like us' (telegram in the possession of David Irving).

The two of them had decided that there would have to be a second mission to the Duke, but that it would be a mistake to send out the first emissary again.

A: Yes, that's correct.

Q: Did you know Serrano Suñer?

A: Very well! Better than he knew himself. If you ask anyone who knows about the politics of that time, they will tell you that I was closer to Serrano Sūner than anyone. He never took a step without consulting me.

Q: And did you know Stohrer?

A: Less well. He was the man who informed Ribbentrop, and I communicated directly with the *Abwehr*.

Q: Did Stohrer know you were working for the *Abwehr*?

A: Not officially, but he would have known. He had his own very good intelligence service which would have told him.

Q: According to the documents, it was either Serrano Suñer or Stohrer who proposed your name.

A: It was the Ambassador. Stohrer proposed it and Serrano Suñer accepted it. Be careful now, and make sure that the tape recorder gets this loud and clear. Stohrer said 'What about Alcázar de Velasco?', because he knew full well that Serrano Suñer would reply: 'Why yes, that's the best man we can send.' But that's not what Serrano Suñer says now! Now he claims to have forgotten the whole thing and says he had nothing to do with it!

Q: Well, you know, it isn't quite like that, because we have seen Serrano Suñer and he told us that he didn't take the affair too seriously and did it mainly as a favour to the Germans.... Can you remember exactly what happened when Miguel asked you to take the letter?

A: It all happened at my office. Only Miguel and myself were there, no one else. And he told me what I have already told you – that I had been chosen to take the letter, being the friend and subordinate of Serrano Suñer.

Q: So this was after Stohrer had proposed your name and Serrano Suñer had accepted it?

A: Yes, after.

Q: And then you made a copy of the letter?

A: Oh no, it was the German Embassy which did that. They kept one copy for the Ambassador and gave me another to send to Canaris.

Q: And you had no direct contact with Serrano Suñer at all over this matter?

A: Yes, now I come to think of it Serrano Suñer did ring me to say that Miguel would be giving me a letter to take to a place he would tell me about personally. That was the day before, I think.

Q: Why did Miguel tell you not to confide in Nicolás Franco?

A: Because we knew he was an agent of the British secret service. Also it was important to keep from him the details of the plot, seeing that the ultimate aim was to bring down Francisco Franco and replace him with Miguel.

Q: Did you know that Schellenberg was involved in the plot?

A: Schellenberg! Why yes, I knew him well – especially after the fall of Canaris, when he became my last German spymaster. I was in Germany when they shot Canaris, you know. . . . Yes, it is all coming back to me now. When all this was happening, Schellenberg came to see me in Madrid and said to me: 'Is there any way of keeping Canaris out of all this ? We suspect him of being disloyal, and the more he has to do with it the less likely it is to come off.' I myself had been suspicious of Canaris ever since my training days in Berlin, but I must admit it shocked me rather to be told this.*

Q: And so what did you do?

A: I sent no more reports to Canaris until the plan had failed.

Q: Did you see Schellenberg in Lisbon?

A: No, that was in Madrid.

Q: But did you see him in Lisbon too?

A: Yes, I remember we dined together.

Q: And did you know that Schellenberg was in charge of the counter-espionage side of things in Lisbon?

A: Yes.

Q: So you knew that you and he were working there for the same ends?

A: Yes, he was pleased that I was working with him.

Q: The German documents mention a female agent, who would have acted as liaison officer between Schellenberg and you in the event of the Duke deciding to go to Spain. Have you any idea who this might have been?

A: Yes: Miguel's German mistress, the Princess Ratibor.† She was one of us, working for the *Abwehr*.

What is of greatest interest here (in so far as one may rely on it) is what Don Angel tells us about the knowledge and motives of Don Miguel. According to Stohrer's telegram of 25 July Miguel knew 'nothing . . . of any Germany interest in the matter'; he was just a harmless dupe, a faithful old friend who had gone to warn the Duke of what he believed to be real dangers. But here he is portrayed as fully aware of the fact that he was taking part in a German plot – and equally of the fact that the story of a British plot was a mere ruse ('*una pura mentira*') to get the Duke to Spain. And – most extraordinary of all – Don Angel claims that Don Miguel believed (or was encouraged by his friends to believe) that the

---

* Don Angel must have been in a strange position, for the SD and the *Abwehr* were mortal rivals, and Schellenberg tried assiduously to undermine Canaris.

† The Ratibors were the most socially prominent German family in Spain, where one of their number had been Ambassador. Don Angel would appear to refer either to Agatha, the eccentric daughter of the Duke of Ratibor; or to Consuelo, wife of Prince Ernst Ratibor (now Madame Jacques Roux, who denies all knowledge of the affair).

affair might lead to the achievement of supreme power by the Duke in England – and by himself in Spain. . . .

When I first heard this, it seemed to me incredible. Everything I had been told about Don Miguel by those who had known him seemed to belie any notion of his aiming at the dictatorship of Spain. 'A frivolous and irresponsible buffoon,' said Serrano Suñer; 'a great silly lovable irresponsible child' was the verdict of Baena, 'quite without political sense' that of Montarco. Even Don Angel himself – who alone of Don Miguel's friends seems to have regarded him as quite intelligent – admitted that he was 'a spoilt child' who 'went through life with a bottle in each hand and a girl under each arm'. Was it conceivable that this character sought to replace Franco – or even that his friends could have put him up to such an idea? And yet, the whole thing becomes perfectly plausible if one takes two factors into account. The first is the childish vanity of Don Miguel. If he seriously imagined that he could change the history of Europe by persuading the Duke to make a mad dash for Ciudad Rodrigo – and if (as appears to have been the case) he imagined that he *had*, beyond a doubt, so persuaded the Duke – then there was no reason why he should not also imagine that one of the historic changes which were bound to take place was his own rise to power in Spain. The second factor was that the 'true' *falangistas* of whom Don Angel speaks had no obvious leader. Everyone of stature had been killed in the Civil War, or had gone over to the Generalissimo, or had been executed by him as a renegade. They would have liked Serrano Suñer at their head – but Don Ramón remained loyal to Franco. This being the case, the best they could hope for was to have a figurehead with a great name – and what more ideal candidate than Don Miguel, a weak, romantic character who could be relied upon to do as he was told and who possessed the outstanding credentials of being the last surviving son of the great dictator Primo de Rivera, and the last surviving brother of the founder of the *Falange*, the martyr José Antonio?

As to the logical processes by which Miguel may have thought he might become Spain's next *caudillo*, one can but guess. Perhaps he believed that, as the architect of the epoch-making declaration at Ciudad Rodrigo, his prestige would be so great that he would just be swept to power. Or perhaps the idea was that the grateful King Edward, once dictator of Britain, would send the Fleet to put him on the Spanish throne. It hardly matters. Fantasies are fantasies. Their importance lies not in their content but in their explanation of motive. And it now appears that there were at least four sets of motives among those who were seeking to bring the Duke to Spain. Hitler and Ribbentrop sought to lure him into German hands by deceit so as to use him as a pawn in a power game; Beigbeder and Don Nicolás Franco sought to appease Berlin but also to induce the Duke to remain voluntarily in the Peninsula so that he might play a role in promoting peace or in stabilizing the British Empire after its defeat; Serrano Suñer and Stohrer sought to buy time for Spain; and Don Miguel – sustained by his friends Montarco and Alcázar de Velasco – saw it all as part of his own fantastic historical design.

At any rate, the dice had been thrown. Don Angel was off to Portugal, to set in motion the wheels which were supposed to bring the Duke and Duchess over the frontier. (And Schellenberg would see to it that those wheels were well oiled.) One evening soon after his departure Don Miguel was punishing a bottle of Scotch whisky in the company of Eduardo de Montarco. 'Soon', he exclaimed to his friend with a prophetic air, 'we shall be drinking this stuff with a restored King Edward in Buckingham Palace!'[16]

10
Schellenberg in Lisbon
26–28 July

Schellenberg arrived in Lisbon at seven o'clock on the evening of Friday 26 July. His task there was clear. Assuming that 'Willi' would be willing to make for Spain in accordance with the plan which had been worked out in Madrid (and which would soon be put to him by Serrano Suñer's new emissary), he had to make the behind-the-scenes preparations for the smooth operation of that plan. This would involve 'squaring' a number of Portuguese officials to ensure that the Duke and Duchess encountered no obstacles on their journey, particularly when they tried to cross the frontier without passports. It would also involve combatting the efforts which MI5 (probably aided by the Portuguese secret police) would certainly make to keep the Duke in Portugal as soon as there was the faintest inkling of his impending flight. (For Schellenberg never underestimated the British Secret Service.) Until the moment came to put the plan into effect, Schellenberg had to keep a close eye on the Duke (who would, of course, always be totally unaware of the interest in him of a German spymaster), and also to weave an atmosphere of fear and uncertainty about him with a view to increasing his eagerness to go to Spain. To accomplish all this, Schellenberg would have to bring into existence with great speed a network of undercover agents around the Duke and Duchess – a 'protective service' (*Schutzdienst*) as he called it, in the language of secret police doublespeak.

Schellenberg at once set about getting in touch with his principal contacts in Lisbon. He was not a stranger to the Portuguese capital, which he had used as a base for an intelligence operation in French West Africa in the autumn of 1938.[1] On that occasion his main assistant had been a Japanese agent attached to his country's legation; and it was on this old colleague that he first called on 26 July. 'We had a warm and happy reunion,' noted Schellenberg in his memoirs.

I asked him to procure for me precise information about the Duke of Windsor's present residence in Estoril [*sic*], how many entrances the house had, what floors were occupied, and all possible details about the servants and the measures taken to guard the Duke. My friend showed not the slighest reaction to this request – except for his usual polite and obliging smile. Nor did he show any curiosity or ask any questions. He merely made a deep bow and said: 'For my friend no task is too much trouble.'[2]

Schellenberg next contacted Winzer's agent high in the Portuguese police. He is identified in Schellenberg's log by the initial C. In his final report Schellenberg describes him as 'the director of counter-espionage in Portugal', adding that he was able to satisfy 'almost all of our requests' in spite of the fact that his chief 'works very closely with the Intelligence Service and Scotland Yard through the British Embassy'. This chief was, of course, Lourenço, and C appears to have been Lourenço's deputy, Catela. Captain José Ernesto do Vale Teixeira Catela – who was fifty-one in July 1940 – was in fact a double agent whose links with German intelligence were well known to the Portuguese authorities;[3] if it was indeed on him that Schellenberg relied, it is not improbable that he would have tipped off his masters at some stage – which would explain a great deal of what was to happen. But when Schellenberg saw C on 26 July, he appeared thoroughly co-operative. In return for a large sum of money, he promised to remove all the obstacles the ducal couple might encounter on their way to Spain, and to recruit all the agents Schellenberg might need for his 'protective service'.[4]

Having made these preparations, Schellenberg paid a nocturnal visit to the German Legation. Hoyningen-Huene was expecting him and greeted him cordially. Schellenberg recalled in his memoirs:

He was somewhat surprised at the authority I had been given, but said repeatedly that he was completely at my disposal. I told him about my mission right away, and added that in all honesty I had come to the conclusion that it could not be carried out successfully. However, I had got to try to do the best I could, for once Hitler had made up his mind about a thing like this that was the end of any argument. I asked von Huene to help me, especially in securing information, so that I could get a clear picture of what the Duke of Windsor's attitude really was. Von Huene said that he had indeed heard that the Duke had expressed dissatisfaction about his situation, but thought that the whole thing had been grossly exaggerated by gossip-mongers.

The Minister terminated the interview by expressing relief that Schellenberg did not intend to strain German–Portuguese relations by his actions.[5]

That same night, possibly prompted by Schellenberg's arrival, Hoy-ningen-Huene sent a curiously worded report to Berlin about the Duke, the first he had sent since 10 July. It appears to have been based on informa-tion supplied by Ricardo Espírito Santo. Despite newspaper reports to the contrary, the Duke had 'no political understanding' with his brother and still regarded war with Germany as 'a crime'. (It is interesting how these German reports always seem to assume that King George VI was politically responsible for his Government's refusal to contemplate peace negotiations.) Halifax's reply to Hitler's Reichstag speech had 'in-furiated' him. However, the Duke – though delaying his departure for the Bahamas – saw 'no possibility at present of intervening in political events, as he would only come forward if he was convinced that there was overwhelming support for him to do so. Return to England at the present time could bring about civil war – if not his immediate and violent elimin-ation [sic].'[6]

The next day, 27 July, Schellenberg's system took shape. His Japanese friend provided him with a sketch-plan of the Boca do Inferno and full details of the servants and guards.[7] He had 'an exhaustive discussion with C about protective service etc. for "Willi"';[8] and that afternoon he was able to report to Berlin (via the Madrid Embassy) that 'a special agent' had already been installed in the Duke's house and that the 'pro-tective service' would start operating from that evening.[9] By the after-noon of the 28th Schellenberg had eighteen Portuguese agents working for him, 'one to three' of whom were 'constantly active in the vicinity of the Duke'[10] – so that he would soon know 'of every incident that took place in the house and every word spoken at the dinner table'.[11] According to the memoirs, he had also had stones thrown at the Duke's windows during the night, as a result of which 'an intensive search was made of the whole house by the Portuguese guard' and 'rumours were started among the servants at the villa that the British Secret Service were behind the incident'[12] – the first of the 'scare-manoeuvres'.

On the 27th Schellenberg had been joined by his two SD aides and also by Winzer, who had flown over from Madrid with the details of the Span-ish police preparations on the frontier.[13] All now seemed ready for the Duke to be whisked off to Spain. It merely remained for Don Angel to see him in order to explain the plan.

At the Boca do Inferno, the Duke and Duchess were unaware of the new intrigues that were being spun around them. But they were anything but calm and relaxed. It was now over three weeks since they had been shut up in a remote seaside villa; and their sense of unease grew by the day. The Duke had told Don Miguel a few days before that he felt 'almost a prisoner' and 'surrounded by spies'; and nothing had occurred to dispel this mood. Indeed, now he quite literally *was* surrounded by spies. The strange movements among the servants and police guards as Schellenberg set up his network, the whisperings in corners, the stones at the windows, the rumours of plots – all of this can only have intensified his steadily growing paranoia.

Is there any evidence that he was contemplating a dash for Spain the last week of July? None is readily discernible. On the 25th he had agreed to the new travel arrangements to the Bahamas. True, he had proceeded to ask for a week's grace; but his current preoccupations and those of the Duchess did not seem to indicate that they were planning to leave in an easterly rather than a westerly direction. Their attention was still focussed on the great campaign to rescue their possessions from France. ('No word from maid,' telegraphed the Duchess to Tiger on the 26th. 'Please do your best to hurry it up.'[14]) And if they had a move on their minds just then, it seems to have been a far shorter one than to the Spanish frontier. For, feeling that they had trespassed too long on the hospitality of the Espírito Santos (and possibly also feeling that the *Boca do Inferno*, for all its luxury, was something of a haunted house), they were now proposing to leave Cascais and spend the rest of their stay in Portugal at the renowned *fin de siècle* establishment, the Hotel Aviz in Lisbon.* It seemed unfair to deprive their indulgent hosts of their summer villa in the rising heat, especially as it was now proposed to delay the ducal departure from 1 to 8 August. George Wood duly booked the rooms at the Aviz. Selby duly informed the Foreign Office of the impending move.[15]

And so the news reached Schellenberg, having been reported by Ricardo to Hoynigen-Huene. For him it was bad news indeed. If the proposed change took place, Ricardo would no longer be able to report on or influence the Duke, and all Schellenberg's efforts to throw a net of spies around the *Boca do Inferno* would have been in vain. Moreover, the Aviz was a recognized fief of the British Secret Service. (The 'German' hotel was the Avenida Palace, at the other end of the Avenida da Liberdade.) Once installed there, the Duke and Duchess would be relatively safe from German attentions. Obviously the move had to be prevented. But how? It

---

* This legendary hostelry, having ruined itself through its own magnificence, was pulled down in the 1950s to make way for the Sheraton skyscraper.

would hardly do if Ricardo pleaded with his guests to prolong their stay at his house.* Schellenberg had a brainwave. He would get C to call on the Duke and Duchess, not only to persuade them to cancel their move on security grounds but also to tell them of rumours of strange dangers – another 'scare-manoeuvre'.

C (or possibly a close police colleague of C who was in on the plot) duly went to the *Boca do Inferno* on 28 July,[16] where he explained to the Duke and a terrified Duchess 'how dangerous the hotel was – unsafe personnel, drinks etc.'. He also 'cleverly alluded to intelligence reports from various countries concerning the hostile intentions of the Churchill régime towards both the Windsors'.[17] In his report to Berlin, Schellenberg summed up the effect of this visit in the following terms:

> Ducal couple will continue staying with banker, awaiting the arrival of a friend, an English minister, announced for 28 August. Departure has been postponed until 1 September. The anxiety-motive is obviously effective.[18]

And yet, in the same report, Schellenberg described the Duke as asking his police visitor for 'careful ship security for his departure for America on 1 August'. Could it therefore be that '1 September' was a slip for '1 August'? And that the 'English minister' referred to was due not on 28 August but 28 July – in other words that very day? If so, it was a remarkable error. But the date of 1 September, however erroneous, seems to have made an impression in Madrid and Berlin. 'According to the latest report from Schellenberg', Stohrer reminded the Wilhelmstrasse on 29 July, 'Windsor's journey has been postponed till 1 September.'[19] If that was indeed the case, there was plenty of time. Schellenberg concluded his report with a significant request: he asked for instructions as to what he was to do 'in the event of the Duke actually deciding to leave for America in spite of scare-manoeuvres'.[20]

The Portuguese police officer was not the only bearer of strange and alarming news who came to see the Duke on Sunday 28 July. For, that afternoon, the Duke received the Spanish agent whom it has been possible to identify as Don Angel Alcázar de Velasco. Don Angel had been in Portugal since Friday night, but had evidently delayed seeing the

---

* Interviewed years later by Geoffrey Bocca, Ricardo claimed that the *British Embassy* warned the Duke against going to the Aviz lest this make him *more* exposed to German interest (*She Might Have Been Queen*, p. 198). This is almost certainly untrue. Ricardo tends to be an unreliable and self-serving witness, and this has to be borne in mind when considering the reports of Hoynigen-Huene based on his information.

Duke until Schellenberg had completed his preparations. Now at last he was face to face with his quarry, who struck him as '*muy simpático, un gran caballero*. Of course, I was very conscious of who he was. He seemed rather sad. I got the feeling that he missed being King, and that things had not worked out as he had hoped.'[21] But Don Angel had little time for such romantic reflections. After a brief chat he performed his principal business, which was to deliver into the Duke's hands the letter of Don Miguel. This done, the Duke proceeded to read the letter in Don Angel's presence.

Here is the text of Don Miguel's letter, which has been carefully preserved among the Duke of Windsor's papers. It had been described to Ribbentrop as 'very skilfully composed psychologically'. If one wonders, reading it, that the Duke did not consign it to the waste-paper-basket and dismiss its bearer on the spot, one must remember his mood at this time, soon after a senior Portuguese police officer had warned him of unknown dangers.

ESTELLA   MADRID *July 24th 1940*

Sir:

On my return to Spain and after having reported to the Minister the conversations I had with Your Highness concerning the affair which took me to Portugal, I feel I am obliged to inform you of the following.

The Minister believes that he has fulfilled his duty in communicating to Your Highness, through me, that he had something urgent and of extreme importance to warn you of.

This is so serious that he does not dare even tell me, with whom he is so closely united, and will give all details to no one except Your Highness.

He does not wish to insist and has only acted according to his conscience in warning you.

Nevertheless I feel obliged to insist especially after my last conversation with the Minister, because in spite of his caucious [sic] words I have been able to understand that we are dealing with something of extreme gravity which directly affects the personal safety of Your Highness and that of the Duchess, should you manifest an opinion or act in someway [sic] contrary to a decision of the British Government. It is a danger which can become a reality not only in the Bahamas but also in Portugal.

I am far more preoccupied now than when last I spoke to Your Highness, because I now understand certain facts which before had not been revealed to me in all their gravity.

If considered this Your Highness and the Duchess resolve to come to Spain I have arranged a plan for you to do so without any risk, which is as follows:

Please inform the bearer, a man I trust implicitly, what date would suit your Highness to put our plan into action. I must know 24 hours before so as to be in the place assigned to meet you.

On the date chosen by Your Highness, equipped with guns or fishing apparel so as to better disguise and carry those things you may estimate the most necessary, Your Highness, the Duchess and any other person who may accompany you can leave for GUARDA, a small village located more or less 250 km North-East of Estoril. You take the road from Estoril to Coimbra, and once here do enquire which road, because there are two, is the best for Guarda.

Your Highness should try to be in Guarda at twelve o'clock noon of the day agreed upon, in order to have time to act. I will also be there at that our [sic] accompanied by a friend of mine who owns a property near Ciudad Rodrigo, a town in Spain and very near the frontier and of the Portuguese village of Guarda.*

We shall apparently meet by chance in the middle of the village. I shall then speak with the Portuguese Captain of the frontier guards, who is a man of our complete confidence. He will not oppose the slightest difficulty to my suggestion that Your Highness and party should lunch with my friend and I on the latter's property in Spain. Once in this country we will proceed normally to the place where Your Highness and the Duchess will be temporarily lodged.

In this place and in a short time, if not the same day, you will receive the Minister's call, who would then inform Your Highness with all detail of what he knows.

In advance I would like to tell Your Highness about certain points concerning your position in Spain: If Spain should enter the war, Your Highness could choose between remaining in Spain as a prisoner of honour or leaving for England or any neutral country, for instance Switzerland. If you wish to go temporarily to France the Minister can arrange matters for you to do so.

As regards your luggage it will be sent to you shortly afterwards.

With respectful regards from my wife and myself for Your Highness and the Duchess, I remain

Yours sincerely,
R. MIGUEL DE ESTELLA

A postscript dated 26 July (the day of Don Angel's departure) read: 'Recent information of the gravest nature will be explained to you verbally by my friend.'[22]

---

* See map on p. 148. Guarda (the highest town in Portugal) had a population of 7,500 in 1940, Ciudad Rodrigo of about 10,000. Both towns are the sites of Napoleonic battles; both possess a fine cathedral and well-preserved mediaeval fortifications.

Such was Don Miguel's 'very skilfully composed psychologically' letter – an uproarious document. It seems to come straight out of the pages of *Boy's Own Paper*. Yet it constitutes important evidence. According to Montarco and Alcázar de Velasco, Don Miguel was well aware of German plans for the Duke; and we know that he had raised with the ex-King (without much success) at least the matter of a German-sponsored restoration. The question therefore arises whether he might not also have let on to his old friend that it was the Germans who were behind all the suggestions that he return to Spain, and that they would be waiting for him there. But in the letter of 24 July there is no hint of this whatever; on the contrary, it is stressed that, should Spain join the Germans while the Duke was there, he would be able to escape to 'England or any neutral country'. It would therefore appear that, if indeed Miguel was aware of the German deception, he had in no way given it away; on the contrary, he was playing the German game, and his letter was an essential part of that game. It would also appear that the Duke had left him under no illusions that he might be willing to collaborate with the enemy or set foot on enemy territory.

If all went according to plan, the Duke was now supposed merely to glance at his engagement book and select a suitable date for the flight to Ciudad Rodrigo. But this did not happen. In a telegram sent two days later, Stohrer gave Berlin the emissary's report of the Duke's reactions:

> W. read the letter slowly and carefully. The impression it made, however, does not appear to have been decisive. The confidential emissary, whom the Minister described to me as very astute, also made additional statements verbally, and he very forcibly emphasized the necessity of a conference between the Duke and the Spanish Interior Minister. The Duke thereupon became very thoughtful, but finally stated only that he must think the matter over. He would give his answer in 48 hours (which would run out Tuesday evening).[23]

When shown this report in October 1983, Don Angel accepted it as true, adding some further memories. 'The Duke read the letter three times. After the first reading he looked very worried indeed. But during the subsequent readings he seemed to relax. At the end he remarked reflectively: *"Sehr gut."* (We were speaking a sort of mixture of Spanish, German and French.) Then he seemed lost in thought and kept picking the letter up, looking at bits of it, and putting it down again. Looking at his hands I somehow had the feeling that he would not be going along with us.'[24] Having received the Duke's temporizing and disappointing reply,

Don Angel withdrew to await his second interview. The news was quickly reported to Schellenberg, who noted in his log for that day: '"Viktor" saw "Willi". The latter asks for 48 hours to reflect.'*

One may picture the Duke's likely feelings after the departure of Don Angel. His state of confusion must now have bordered on torment. For weeks he had been oppressed by the war news, his personal prospects, and the confined, spy atmosphere in which he lived; he was gradually losing his sense of reality, and hardly knew what to think or believe. The past twenty-four hours had been nightmarish. There had been stones at his windows, strange rumours in the house, then warnings about his safety from a Portuguese police chief. And now this! No doubt he read the letter again and again, wondering what to make of it. No doubt he felt lonely and isolated, longing for advice from a trusted old friend. For there was no one (apart from his wife) he could discuss it with; not for weeks had he seen anything of a real friend, except for the dim and hopeless Selby.

Fortunately for the Duke, such a friend was near at hand. For the 'English minister' referred to in Schellenberg's latest report – who was not in fact a minister at all, but was indeed due on the 28th of July and not of August – was about to arrive in Portugal. That Sunday evening a flying boat from England landed on the Tagus. It was piloted by Wing-Commander Edward ('Mouse') Fielden, who had been created Captain of the King's Flight by Edward VIII four years before. Its passengers included Major Gray Phillips, Piper Alistair Fletcher – and Sir Walter Monckton.

---

* A curious journalist's book which appeared in 1983 (Peter Allen, *The Crown and the Swastika*) advanced the amusing idea that 'Viktor' may have been Rudolf Hess. But unless the Duke was telling everyone he saw on 28 July to come back in forty-eight hours, it is exceedingly unlikely that 'Viktor' could have been anyone other than Serrano Suñer's agent. ('Viktor' for Velasco, 'Willi' for Windsor.) Don Angel confirms that this was his normal German code-name.

11
The Monckton Mission
28–30 July

The new arrival was at once noticed by the Germans, who had in their pay the passport officer at the Flying-Boat landing-stage.[1] Schellenberg reported: 'Today, as announced, there arrived to stay with the Duke the English Minister who calls himself Sir Walter Turner Monckstone [*sic*], lawyer from Kent. The Portuguese confidential agent assumes, as I do, that a cover name is involved.'[2] To Schellenberg, it was inconceivable that the newcomer should not be a member of the British secret service.[3] With rather greater accuracy, Hoyningen-Huene informed Berlin that 'Sir Walter Monckstone [*sic*], who was the Duke of Windsor's legal counsellor at the time of the Abdication, has flown from London to Lisbon. This visit is in connection with the Duke's imminent departure for the Bahamas.'[4]

Sir Walter Monckton, KC, was forty-nine in July 1940. He was a jaunty, gregarious man who had made an outstanding career at the London bar; he owed his success (in the words of his biographer) to 'immensely persuasive charm' and 'an uncanny quickness in sensing the thoughts that were passing through people's minds'.[5] Since the outbreak of hostilities he had been in charge both of the interrogation of internees and of the censorship of the press in England – wide and sensitive official responsibilities which he exercised from an office at the Ministry of Information.* His friendship with the Duke of Windsor dated back to their Oxford days before the First World War. In 1932 Monckton had become the Prince of Wales's legal adviser; and in November 1936 King Edward had asked him to be his intermediary with the Government in the constitutional crisis arising out of his desire to marry Mrs Simpson. Monckton had won golden opinions from all sides for the tact with which he performed this delicate role, and

---

* Monckton's rank at the Ministry was then that of Deputy Director. He later became Director-General, but he was never Minister of Information as the Germans seemed (and as numerous contemporary authors seem) to believe.

after the Abdication he had continued to be the link between the Duke of Windsor and the powers that be. He had frequently visited the Duke in Austria and France, often as the bearer of bad news. In September 1939 he had organized the Duke's brief return to England. They had last seen each other in Paris in February 1940.

On 26 July Monckton had gone to interrogate five women in Holloway prison who were 'suspected of being Nazi agents in this country'.* When he returned to his office, there was a message from the Prime Minister asking that he call at Downing Street as soon as possible. The interview took place at a quarter to six.[6] Churchill wanted him to go out to the Duke in Portugal – to warn him of imminent peril, make sure he sailed on 1 August, and see to it that he left Europe in the right frame of mind. For on 26 July, concern over the Duke had reached a crisis in London.† That morning, his ominous telegram had arrived asking for a further week's delay.‡ Then Eccles had appeared, bearing news of the Duke's indiscretions and hesitations and above all of the Spanish efforts to keep him in the Peninsula. And by this time the Government decoders at Bletchley Park had picked up a strong whiff of the plots surrounding the Duke – and of the unwitting encouragement he was giving to those plots through careless talk. So much is clear from a letter which Churchill gave Monckton to take out to the Duke.

The letter was dated 27 July.§ The Prime Minister began by expressing his satisfaction 'to have been able to arrange for Your Royal Highness and the Duchess a suitable sphere of activity and public service during this terrible time when the whole world is lapped in danger and confusion'. Being next to the United States, the Bahamas had 'a ceaseless flow of interesting people', and except for a few months of the year it possessed 'one of the most agreeable climates'. He was sure that they

---

* Monckton Papers, Bodleian Library (*Dep. Monckton Trees 3*).

† See above, p. 135.

‡ Both Churchill and Lloyd had replied to this telegram, urging the Duke to stick to the original date (FO 371/24249/187–8). Lloyd wrote that he was 'most anxious to fall in with Your Royal Highness's wishes, but I feel that at this late hour it would be very difficult to alter all the arrangements made ...'. Having just arranged for the *Excalibur* to be diverted, the US Administration expressed dismay at the change of plan.

§ Monckton also took out a letter from King George VI dated 26 July 1940, which was mainly to express relief that the Duke had accepted the Bahamas and would not be returning to England. (See Duke's letter to Churchill of 30 June 1941 in FO 954/33.) The Duke did not reply to this letter and had no direct communication with his brother for almost three years.

would 'lend a distinction and dignity to the Governorship which ... may well have other results favourable to British interests'. In somewhat non-committal terms, he sympathized with the Duke's desire to go to America after the presidential elections. So long as he remained Prime Minister 'you may surely rely on me ... to do all in my power to serve Your Royal Highness' true interests, and to study your wishes'. Churchill then got to the crux of the matter:

> Sir, may I venture upon a word of serious counsel. It will be necessary for the Governor of the Bahamas to express views about the war and the general situation which are not out of harmony with those of His Majesty's Government. The freedom of conversation which is natural to anyone in an unofficial position, or indeed to a major-general,* is not possible in any direct representative of the Crown. Many sharp and unfriendly ears will be pricked up to catch any suggestion that your Royal Highness takes a view about the war, or about the Germans, or about Hitlerism, which is different from that adopted by the British nation and Parliament. Many malicious tongues will carry tales in every direction. *Even while you have been staying at Lisbon, conversations have been reported by telegraph through various channels which might have been used to your Royal Highness' disadvantage.*† In particular, there is danger of use being made of anything you say in the United States to do injury, and to suggest divergence between you and the British Government. I am so anxious that mischief should not be made which might mar the success which I feel sure will attend your mission. We are all passing through times of immense stress and dire peril, and every step has to be watched with care.
>
> I thought your Royal Highness would not mind these words of caution from
>
> Your faithful and devoted servant
> WINSTON S. CHURCHILL[7]

What were the 'conversations reported by telegraph through various channels' which had been intercepted? It would be interesting to know. According to information made available to the author since the first appearance of this book,‡ it is unlikely that British intelligence were reading any German official communications on this subject at the time. They were, however, intercepting Spanish, Portuguese, Italian and Japanese diplomatic communications; and they were also monitoring the

---

* The Duke had held the temporary rank of major-general since September 1939.

† My italics.

‡ See Appendix VI.

despatches of journalists *en clair*. All one can say is that Churchill, while he was certainly not aware of everything that was going on,* knew enough to realize that there was terrible danger, that the Duke would have to be warned by a man he trusted, that it was imperative he leave the continent without delay. Hence Monckton's mission; in his letter, Churchill told the Duke that Monckton 'would talk over various matters of which you should be verbally informed'.

Although there is no detailed report of what transpired between Monckton and the Duke, it is not difficult to piece together the general sense of what happened from the available sources.

It has been seen that, when Monckton arrived at Cascais on the evening of Sunday 28 July, the Duke was in a highly troubled and bewildered state. He hardly knew whom to trust or what to think. He had the constant feeling of being spied upon, he had witnessed a number of unsettling incidents, and that day he had been warned both by a senior Portuguese police officer and a persuasive Spanish visitor that his life might be in danger if he went to the Bahamas. And then there had been the extraordinary letter of Don Miguel. The Duke therefore told Monckton 'that he had received from various sources, which he was not at liberty to disclose, though he regarded them as reliable, a report that ... there was a plot afoot against his security and that British influence, including probably some members of the Government, were implicated'.† (It was rather typical of the Duke that he did not at this stage reveal the source of this information even to Monckton, or show him Don Miguel's letter.)

Monckton, on the other hand, came with news of a German plot against the Duke. This is what the Duchess of Windsor tells us in her memoirs. 'British intelligence', she writes, 'had picked up information that German secret agents were plotting to kidnap us.' The Duchess goes on to record the following exchange:

> 'But how could we possibly be of any use to them?' David asked, incredulously.
>
> Walter was very serious. 'Winston is convinced that Hitler is crazy enough to be tempted, in the event of a successful invasion of Britain, to try to put the Duke back on the throne in the belief that this would divide and confuse the people and weaken their will to resist further.'
>
> David was flabbergasted. 'Winston couldn't possibly think that,' he replied.

---

* British intelligence knew nothing about Schellenberg's mission, for example – as Schellenberg discovered to his surprise when he was interrogated after the war (*Memoirs*, p. 139).

† See below, p. 211.

'Sir,' Walter said, 'in war Winston is always ingenious and imaginative. He overlooks no possibilities – however unlikely.'[8]

Like so much in this story, this conversation sounds somewhat improbable. But there is partial corroboration for it. The Duchess wanted living persons who were mentioned in her book to be able to check the references to themselves before publication; and so George Allen (who was still then the Windsors' man of business) sent the extract to Monckton for his comment. Monckton replied, on 4 May 1956:

> ... I cannot of course recollect the exact terms of the conversation.... I remember of course that Winston had it in mind, and I certainly told the Duke and Duchess that the Germans might be plotting to keep him in Europe and if possible get hold of him, and that it would be the view of the German Government that if they had possession of him he could be used to endeavour to destroy the unity of the British. At that time, August 1940, it was quite likely that there would be an invasion of England and I certainly thought that if that happened, and if the Duke was in their hands, they would try (though they would not succeed) to make use of him and even to restore him to the Throne. What I cannot remember at this time is whether Winston had gone so far as to speak about the Germans trying to put the Duke back on the Throne, or whether I attributed that idea to him. It had certainly occurred to me as a thing they might plot.[9]

What is certain is that, with Churchill's letter on the one hand and Monckton's news on the other, the Duke was quickly and firmly persuaded to waive his objections to sailing on the *Excalibur*. To calm his fears, Monckton proposed to summon a detective to accompany him and the Duchess to the Bahamas. At 2.24 on the afternoon of Monday 29 July, two telegrams marked 'immediate' were simultaneously despatched to London from the British Embassy in Lisbon. One was from Monckton to Lloyd: 'For reasons which I cannot now disclose, I consider it essential that responsible CID detective be sent to accompany our friends to destination and to remain as long as necessary....' The other was from the Duke to Churchill: 'Monckton has arrived and I agree to sail August 1st as you have arranged.'[10]

His mission apparently fulfilled, Monckton stayed on at Cascais for the remainder of the Duke's time in Portugal. He appears to have enjoyed himself, and to have indulged his taste for pretty women. There are photographs of him at the poolside parties at the *Boca do Inferno*, which still continued daily. 'After the depression of the London black-out and the squalor of wartime London', writes his biographer, 'Walter felt an astonishing and almost guilty sense of liberation when he saw the lights blazing in Lisbon; and the carefree evenings at Estoril with men in white dinner jackets and women *en grande tenue* seemed to belong to another and forgotten world.'[11] But his part in the story was not over.

Meanwhile, elsewhere in Europe, another thread was weaving its way through the complex tapestry. At almost exactly the same moment as the Duke and Monckton were telegraphing London to confirm departure on 1 August and ask for a detective, Stohrer (who still assumed, on the basis of Schellenberg's latest report, that the Duke would not be leaving till 1 September) was telegraphing Berlin to say that the Duchess of Windsor's maid had now left Madrid for Paris. He added: 'She will be held on the return journey by our officials on the Franco–Spanish frontier until I give leave for her to continue.'[12] Somewhat belatedly, the plot to keep the Duke and Duchess in Europe by shanghai-ing their servant and their luggage was on. The Spanish stamps in Mademoiselle Moulichon's passport (there are no German stamps) show that she crossed the Irun–Hendaye frontier on Sunday 28 July.[13] In contrast to her subsequent nightmarish adventures, her rail journey was unexpectedly trouble-free and swift, only made uncomfortable by the chronic lack of food and drink. Tiger had seen her off in Madrid and given her an enormous bag of oranges, which she distributed among the famished passengers in her compartment: gifts which evoked as much suspicion as pleasure.[14]

On arrival in the capital Mademoiselle Moulichon went straight to the house in the Boulevard Suchet, where she was greeted by Fernand the butler and his wife, who had left Paris before the occupation but subsequently returned in a caretaker capacity. Together they packed up all the household linen (even today, Mademoiselle Moulichon the ex-*lingère* is visibly moved as she talks of its splendour) along with sundry other items the Duchess might need in the Bahamas: she recalls that she packed for some reason an enormous quantity of soap. All of this occupied several large trunks. They then directed their attention to the safe whose contents Mademoiselle Moulichon had been instructed to fetch: but this would not open. It yielded neither to the keys nor the combination codes she had been given. Finally a man was summoned from Fichet, the French safe manufacturers; but he could not open it either, and it was decided to seal the safe rather than blow it open. What the safe was supposed to contain remains a mystery; Mademoiselle Moulichon has forgotten, if she ever knew. Possibly it held that part of the Duchess's jewellery she had not taken with her, possibly papers of the Duke, which may have included records of his work for British Military Intelligence. At any rate, the safe was still sealed when its owners returned to it in September 1945.[15]

Her mission accomplished at least in part, Mademoiselle Moulichon directed her thoughts towards returning to Portugal. She booked a place for herself and space for the trunks on the *Sud Express* leaving Paris on the morning of Wednesday 31 July. In the ordinary course of things, this would get her to Lisbon around noon on Thursday, well in time for the sailing of the *Excalibur*. But she was far from sure (as she told the Spanish *Chargé d'Affaires* in Paris) whether the Duke and Duchess would still be sailing on the *Excalibur*.[16]

By this time, however, the Germans had discovered that such was indeed their intention. From his agent network at the *Boca do Inferno*, Schellenberg had not been slow to learn of Monckton's persuasions and the Duke's new resolve to depart on 1 August. The spy-servants had been reporting other things too, and it was obvious that German plans were going very seriously wrong – or rather, that German assumptions had been very seriously mistaken. As Schellenberg wrote in his memoirs, he now had a 'full picture' of the Duke's intentions. It confirmed his private view:

> The Duke of Windsor no longer intended to accept the hunting invitation; he was most annoyed by the surveillance of the British Secret Service; he did not like his appointment to Bermuda [*sic*] and would much have preferred to remain in Europe. But he obviously had no intention of going to live either in a neutral or an enemy country. According to my reports, the furthest he ever went in this direction was once to have said in his circle of Portuguese friends that he would rather live in any European country than go to Bermuda.[17]

29 July, Schellenberg later wrote in his final report, was the day when 'the Spanish plan collapsed completely' – that is, when the supposition that the Duke would go to Spain dissolved. The Duke had still to give his final reply to Don Angel – but it hardly seemed likely that it would be the reply originally expected. In his log for the 29th, Schellenberg summed up the situation in a striking German phrase: *Willi will nicht* – Willi won't play, Willi says no.

Up to this point, the Duke was supposed to be totally unaware of active

Hitler with his Foreign Minister, Joachim von Ribbentrop. Immersed in fantasy and wishful thinking, Ribbentrop persuaded the Führer that the Duke had lost his throne purely because of his pro-German sympathies, and would be happy to recover it through collaboration with the Germans. In the background on the left stands Ernst von Weizsäcker, the brilliant but compliant State Secretary at the Foreign Ministry, in whose files captured in 1945 the documents concerning the Duke of Windsor episode were found.

Walter Schellenberg, the thirty-year-old German spymaster who was sent to the Peninsula to bring the plot to fruition. Clever and self-seeking, he realized that Ribbentrop's design was based on a misconception and could only be realized by the Duke's forcible abduction.

Oswald Baron von Hoyningen-Huene, the non-Nazi but cynical and lethargic German Minister in Lisbon. A friend of the Duke's Portuguese host, he sent secret reports to Berlin about the ex-King and finally passed a message to him from Ribbentrop.

Eberhard Baron von Stohrer, German Ambassador to Madrid and author of most of the famous telegrams. Filled with a profound love of Spain and an equally profound contempt for Ribbentrop, he saw the plot as a game which would enable him to deflect the German Foreign Minister's attention from his schemes to force Spain into the war.

Maria-Ursula, Baroness von Stohrer, who used her dazzling charms to protect her husband from exposure as an opponent of Nazism. Was she responsible for the choice of Miguel Primo de Rivera (who was one of her countless admirers) as an emissary to the Duke of Windsor?

General Franco, the *caudillo*. Following a foreign policy of 'skilful prudence', he wanted to oblige the Germans as much as possible without endangering the independence or security of Spain.

His brother, Don Nicolás, Spanish Ambassador to Portugal. Shrewd and unscrupulous and probably in British pay, he played a strange double game of trying to persuade the Duke to remain in Europe while tipping off the British authorities about what was being planned.

General Franco's brother-in-law Ramón Serrano Suñer, the brilliant but unpopular Spanish Interior Minister. He thought the plot 'puerile' but went along with it partly to please the Germans, partly to buy time for Spain. Portrait by Julio Moisés.

Colonel Juan Beigbeder, the 'neutralist' Spanish Foreign Minister, who proposed to the Germans that they contact the Duke in the Peninsula. Deeply romantic and sentimentally pro-British, he appears to have believed that the Duke held the key to the end of the Second World War. Portrait by Angel Espinosa.

Don Javier 'Tiger' Bermejillo, the jovial Spanish diplomat who had befriended the Prince of Wales and Mrs Simpson in the early 1930s. In the summer of 1940 he was their agent in their ill-advised efforts to rescue their belongings from occupied and unoccupied France.

Miguel Primo de Rivera, an irresponsible playboy with a famous name. An old friend of the Duke of Windsor, he was the first of the Spanish emissaries sent to Portugal to persuade the Duke not to go to the Bahamas. Did he try to use his mission to advance a fantastic conspiracy against the Franco regime?

Angel Alcázar de Velasco, the second Spanish emissary to the Duke. An agent of the *Abwehr* and a friend of Schellenberg, he failed totally in his mission to bring the Duke back to Spain.

Dr António Oliveira Salazar, the anglophile but strictly neutralist Portuguese dictator. Determined that no embarrassment should arise out of the Duke of Windsor's stay in Portugal, he put the ex-King under a regime of virtual protective custody. He later refused a Spanish–German request to detain the Duke in his country.

Captain Agostinho Lourenço, the dreaded (but pro-British) chief of the Portuguese secret police. Having known the Duke as Prince of Wales during the First World War and on his visit to Lisbon in 1931, he resolved that no harm should befall him while under his protection.

Remembrance of Cascais
3-I.II — 1-I.III
1940
Ricardo

The Duke with his Portuguese host, the banker Ricardo Espírito Santo Silva. A man of much persuasive charm but given to fantasy and exaggeration, Ricardo sought to curry favour with the Germans by appearing to help them in their efforts to keep the Duke in Europe.

German interest in him. He was to be persuaded to return to Spain in order to retire quietly from the war, to hunt with his friends, to escape from a British assassination plot, to discuss Anglo–Spanish relations, to launch a personal appeal for peace . . . but without ever realizing that the Germans would be waiting for him at the other end. Now that this tactic had failed, two possibilities remained to the German plotters. One was to abduct him by force. The other was somehow to get in touch with him in Portugal, to find out whether he might be willing to co-operate with them in some way. Hoyningen-Huene was the first to suggest the latter move. In a brief telegram of the 28th he had reminded Ribbentrop that he was 'friendly with the Duke's host', and wondered whether the Duke 'might not be contacted directly'.[18] Now, on the 30th, Schellenberg reported:

> From what I learn it must be taken as certain that Willi is leaving Lisbon on 1 August and travelling out to the Bahamas via New York. . . . All things considered, it seems that the simplest course would be to get a message to Willi to the effect that Germany is interested in making contact with him, but that this could not be realized if Willi were in the Bahamas, where moreover no guarantees could be given for his security.[19]

Meanwhile Winzer had returned to Madrid that morning and confirmed to Stohrer that the Duke seemed to be holding to 1 August, though this might be 'a deceptive manoeuvre'. Stohrer reported this to Berlin in the same telegram as he reported Don Angel's indecisive first meeting with the Duke, adding that Serrano Suñer had instructed his emissary 'to employ anew all his force of persuasion to get W. at least to give up his imminent departure . . .'. He continued, echoing Schellenberg's words:

> In these circumstances and with a view to the possibility that W. holds to his decision to leave, the question arises as to whether we should not to some extent emerge from our reserve. Minister von Huene has, according to the information of Herr Winzer, reported to Berlin that the Duke has on occasion expressed to his host a desire to come into contact with the Führer.* Through Minister von Huene or a Portuguese confidential emissary, perhaps we could urge the banker as on his own volition to put to the Duke without any binding force the question of what he would do if he were afforded the opportunity to get into communication with the German Government. The intermediary would in

---

* The Duke wrote 'No' beside this sentence when he first saw this telegram in 1953. It must be said that, in Hoyningen-Huene's reports to Berlin, there is no mention of the Duke having expressed any such desire. The nearest he had gone was to say that he was in favour of the Anglo-German compromise that Hitler was seeking.

such a situation have to be empowered, in the event of the Duke falling in with this line of thought, to say that in his opinion this desire could be fulfilled if the Duke did not depart but returned to Spain, which was also urgently desirable from the viewpoint of his personal safety.[20]

At noon on 30 July – at roughly the same moment as this telegram was being sent – an event occurred which appeared to dispel the last shred of doubt that the Duke and Duchess intended to sail on the *Excalibur*. For over three weeks – as a result of a request by the British Embassy to the Portuguese authorities – not a word had been written about them in the Portuguese press, and no foreign journalist had been allowed near them. Now the silence was broken, and their departure was announced at a press conference at the British Embassy. Flanked by the Duchess and the Ambassador, the Duke delivered the following impromptu remarks to the assembled pressmen:

> The Duchess of Windsor and I would like to say how much we have appreciated the hospitality of Portugal, where we have had the opportunity of spending three weeks of peace and quiet at this difficult time. Portugal is a country whose beauty and history I have admired ever since I first stepped on her soil in 1931. Although that visit was made under very different conditions, my reception on this occasion has been no less warm and kind than before.
>
> As you know, the Duchess and I are shortly leaving for the Bahamas, where I have been appointed Governor. This will be a new experience for me, as I have never before governed a British Colony, and the Bahama Islands are one of the few parts of the British Empire which I have never visited. But before we leave, we would like to express our heartfelt thanks and greetings to Portugal.
>
> *Adeus! Muito obrigado por tudo*!* I am afraid those are the only words I know of your language. *Muito obrigado. . . .*[21]

A few uncontroversial questions were asked; sherry was served; and the correspondent of Associated Press, Luis Calveri Lupi, thanked the Duke on behalf of the Fourth Estate. Then his words were flashed around the world.

They reached Berlin on the afternoon of Tuesday the 30th, at the same time as the latest despatches of Schellenberg and Stohrer. All spoke of the Duke's imminent departure on the *Excalibur*: and together they can only have come as an unexpected, an appalling shock. Nothing had prepared Ribbentrop for this! Seen from Berlin, everything up till then had appeared to be proceeding splendidly. On the 26th, Schellenberg had

---

* Farewell! Thank you very much for everything!

written of the Duke's 'firm intention' to return to Spain; on the 27th, Hoynigen-Huene had described him as denouncing Churchill and delaying his departure; on the 29th, Stohrer had indicated that he did not mean to leave Europe before 1 *September*. The parallel missions of Schellenberg and Alcázar de Velasco had appeared almost as a quaint formality, a purely technical affair to enable the Duke and Duchess to realize their 'firm intention' to cross the frontier. These illusions fell apart with a vengeance on the afternoon of the 30th. *Willi wollte nicht.* In his memoirs, Ribbentrop's aide Erich Kordt recalled the arrival of a 'shattering telegram'. Up till then, there had been nothing but 'encouraging reports. The Duke, it was said, had expressed approval for German policies, the Duchess was as good as won over.' But now, 'without any hint or warning', the Duke, 'Hitler's crown prince', was preparing 'to vanish with his wife, not into Occupied France [*sic*] but to the Bahamas, where Churchill had appointed him Governor'.[22]

Ribbentrop's cherished scheme hovered on the edge of ruin. There were only two days to go before the sailing of the *Excalibur*. Obviously some drastic action was required if the Duke and Duchess were not to be on it. Would Schellenberg's 'scare-manoeuvres' do the trick? Or Don Angel's persuasive gifts? It seemed very far from certain. Was this then the moment, as Stohrer, Hoynigen-Huene and Schellenberg all counselled, to drop part of the mask and ask the Duke whether he was prepared to deal with the Germans? Meanwhile, a message received from Stohrer on the 28th still awaited reply. It read: 'Schellenberg asks for instructions as to what measures he is to take in the event of the Duke actually deciding to leave for America in spite of scare-manoeuvres' – an event which, as things stood, seemed all too likely.[23]

According to his memoirs, Schellenberg now received an extraordinary telegram. It was from Ribbentrop. It read, quite simply: 'The Führer orders that an abduction is to be organized at once.'[24]

12
An Abduction?
30–31 July

We only have the word of Schellenberg in his memoirs that he received this extraordinary telegram. Neither it nor any direct reference to it appears among the captured diplomatic documents. Nor is it mentioned in Schellenberg's log, where he enumerates his telegrams. Even his final report fails to allude to it – or indeed to the very idea of abduction. Moreover, the chronology he puts forward in the memoirs is wildly inaccurate: he says he received the order to abduct after two weeks in Lisbon, whereas his log shows that he only arrived there on 26 July and stayed eight days in all. Can it therefore be that Schellenberg's introduction of the abduction theme is pure invention? Is it possible that, while recalling an episode which was basically true, his imagination (or that of some editor) ran away with him and tempted him to add a superfluous dash of colour to a narrative which one might have thought already extraordinary enough?

This may be so. Later on, when he became head of Nazi foreign intelligence, Schellenberg was to acquire something of a reputation for doctoring the record in order to make it look more interesting and impressive.[1] On the other hand it is possible that Schellenberg, while not telling the exact truth, is not recounting a total fiction either. The captured documents appear to contain no messages at all addressed to him in the Peninsula – though one imagines there would have been some. It is evident that the use of force was always present in the minds of Hitler and Ribbentrop as something which might have to be contemplated. The original scheme was to lure the Duke to Spain under false pretences and keep him there, by force if necessary; it was but a short step from there to kidnapping him in Portugal and bundling him off to Spain. (The Portuguese Government would be outraged; but what could they do?) By late on 30 July it must have been obvious in Berlin that plans to get hold of the Duke had gone drastically wrong; possibly it seemed in some quarters that only drastic measures could retrieve the situation. According to Schellenberg, Ribbentrop had told him during the original interview: 'Hitler ... has come to the conclusion after serious consideration that if the Duke should prove hesitant, he himself would have no objection to your helping the Duke to reach the right decision by coercion ... [provided] that the Duke and his wife are not exposed to any personal danger.'[2] Once again, the only source for this is the internal evidence of the memoirs. But it does seem entirely plausible that Ribbentrop said such things to Schellenberg.

There is one hitherto unpublished German telegram which does refer to the use of force, albeit indirectly. On the night of 30 July Winzer telegraphed Heydrich to say that all the security arrangements had been made to spirit the Duke across the Spanish frontier.

> Operation Schellenberg running to plan as far as police involvement is concerned. Protective measures in Portugal up to Duke's planned border crossing ... assured under personal direction of our special agent in Portuguese police. After border crossing adequate protective measures to be provided by our own commandos [sic] in addition to Spanish preparations.

However, there was 'no guarantee that planned scare-manœuvres will influence Duke', whose 'final decision' (the reply to Don Angel) was expected that day; and Winzer concluded:

> In the event of his retaining intention to travel to America, Ambassador Madrid suggests that Reich Foreign Minister, through Portuguese intermediary, should ask him in a veiled manner (without revealing source) about his willingness to deal with German authorities, *because it would seem ill-advised to compel Duke to come to Spain under duress in view of political designs we have with regard to him.*[*3]

There is one extraordinary new item here: German 'commandos' were now waiting on the frontier to 'protect' the Duke as soon as he crossed into Spain. Since the Spanish police were not entirely to be trusted, since the Spanish Government had given no guarantees of their willingness to intern the Duke should he prove unco-operative, Winzer and his Gestapo gang at the German Embassy had taken things into their own hands. In effect, the Duke would become a prisoner of the Germans as soon as he left

* My italics.

Portuguese soil. But it would be 'ill-advised' to go a step further and abduct him in Portugal – a course which had evidently been considered.

In Lisbon, Schellenberg too appears to have regarded coercion as highly ill-advised. In his memoirs he describes in detail his reactions to the abduction telegram. It came, he says, as an 'unexpected blow'.

Since the Duke was so little in sympathy with our plans an abduction would be madness. But what could I do? I was quite certain that it was Ribbentrop alone who was behind this order. He had made a completely wrong evaluation of the situation, and had probably distorted my reports in order to persuade Hitler to sanction this ultimate folly.

The Ambassador was as worried as I was, though I assured him at once that I had no intention of carrying out my orders. In the evening I discussed the matter with my Japanese friend. I thought I discerned mild contempt in his eyes. He remained silent for a long time. Finally he said, 'An order is an order. It has to be carried out. After all, the thing should not be so difficult. You will have all the help and support you need, and the element of surprise will be on your side.' After another pause he said, 'Your Führer certainly knows why he wants the Duke of Windsor in his hands. But what do you really wish to discuss with me? How to carry out this order, or how to evade it?' I was somewhat hurt that he had thought it necessary to remind me of my duty. I tried to explain to him that Hitler had reached this decision on the basis of false information.

Finally he said, making a small motion with his hand, 'How you will justify yourself to your Führer is not my affair. Let us not lose any more time, but discuss how you can circumvent the order. You have to save face – that means you have to arrange things so that action becomes completely impossible. There I cannot help you, for I have no influence with those responsible for the Duke's security guards, but these guards will have to be strengthened to such an extent that any attempt at force would be out of question. You can blame a Portuguese police official whom you can say you suspect to be working with the British. You could even go so far as to arrange a bit of shooting – which, of course, would come to nothing. And perhaps, if you are lucky, the Duke will lose his nerve as a result of all this and blame his own people for it.'

Slowly I left the house. We had nothing more to say to each other. It was a lovely night, clear and starry. But I could find no peace. My situation was extremely difficult. All the more so as I could not fathom the attitude of the two companions Heydrich had sent with me.

That evening I had supper with my Portuguese friend in a small restaurant. I felt tired and beaten and really did not want to discuss the matter any more.

But in order to test his reactions I said, 'Tomorrow I have to bring the Duke of Windsor across the Spanish frontier by force. The plan has to be worked out tonight.' My friend awoke from his usual lethargy as I went on, 'How many of you people – who will have to leave the country afterwards – can I count on? And what will the whole thing cost?'

My friend looked terrified. 'I can't be responsible for a thing like that,' he said. 'People might get killed. It would be very difficult – not only here, but at the border.' Nervously he drew geometric figures on the tablecloth with his knife. After a pause he gave his final answer: 'No, I can't help you, and I really don't see what use the Duke of Windsor can be to you if you abduct him by force. Inevitably it would become known, and I don't think the prestige of your country would grow by it. And then the order contains no mention of his wife. But it was Hitler who pointed out her decisive importance in the Duke's life. You are right, it must be Ribbentrop who is behind it. Let's be realistic though: if you feel you must carry out this order, I shan't place any difficulties in your way, but I won't be able to help you any further.'

I now told him that I was completely of his opinion. His relief was obvious, and with great enthusiasm he discussed with me how we could circumvent the order. Next morning he arranged for twenty additional Portuguese police to be assigned to the Duke's guard. This was followed by an immediate intensification of security measures by the British. These two facts I conveyed to Berlin in a long report, and asked for further instructions.[4]

This then is Schellenberg's story – that he craftily sabotaged the abduction with the collusion of C, only a few hours after he had received the order. It is a colourful story, and it is unfortunate that there is nothing whatever to corroborate it. There is no trace of his 'long report' explaining the difficulties of abduction, nor of the reply which he claims to have received after 'two anxious days' (by which time the *Excalibur* would have sailed), leaving him to take 'measures suitable to the situation'. Nor is there anything in the memoirs about the idea of indirect German contact with the Duke, which – as the contemporary records show – had been proposed to Berlin by Hoyningen-Huene, Stohrer and Schellenberg himself as an alternative to the use of force.

A more likely explanation is that Schellenberg's original instructions had specifically charged him with bringing the Duke to Spain by force unless he was willing to go voluntarily. By the 30th it had become clear that he was not so willing (*Willi will nicht*) – but Schellenberg was not at all keen to carry out his contingent instructions. Stohrer and Hoyningen-Huene had expressed horrified opposition to any form of kidnapping; it would be a self-defeating exercise 'in view of political designs we have with regard to him'; and Schellenberg was also doubtless alive to the possibility that the operation might not be an easy one and that he was liable to take the blame if it was bungled or if any serious trouble arose from it. And so – anticipating rather than actually having received the abduction-at-once telegram – he played for time, asking for new instructions, urging upon Berlin the virtues of persuasion rather than force, possibly even tipping off the Portuguese police.

Schellenberg also seems to have dreaded some form of counter-attack by the British secret service. It is, of course, difficult to say for certain, but it is not at all clear that they had much of a role. The fact that it had been necessary to summon a detective from London suggests that there was no local British security officer to look after the Duke. The British authorities seem to have relied for the most part on the Portuguese secret police to protect him, and on such men as Eccles and Monckton to keep an eye on him. Chamberlayne – the member of the Embassy officially responsible for his safety – later swore that he had known nothing of German and Spanish plots to prevent him leaving Europe; his sole fear had been that he might be captured in the course of a German invasion of Portugal.[5] It is, of course, likely that MI6 in Lisbon – run by the 'Financial Attaché' at the Embassy, Richman Stopford – was trying to keep tabs on the Duke through its local network.[6] François de Panafieu, then Secretary at the French Legation, remembers being asked by a friend in MI6 whether he knew anything of the Duke's intentions.[7] But there is no evidence of the great counter-intelligence operation that Schellenberg was expecting. For that matter, there is no evidence that the British intelligence and security services were even aware of Schellenberg's presence in Lisbon.[8]

On the other hand, there can be little doubt that the Portuguese police activity surrounding the Duke did indeed become frantic. Montarco was later told by Portuguese connections that Lourenço had become pretty well aware of Spanish and German machinations in the later stages and made it his duty to frustrate them.[9] Perhaps C had all along been a double agent. At all events, there is no reason to doubt Schellenberg when he writes that, as the departure of the *Excalibur* approached, the Portuguese police 'were in a state of feverish activity and excitement. The ship was searched several times from top to bottom. Security measures were doubled, then redoubled'[10] – all of which, says Schellenberg, helped to confirm his argument that abduction was impracticable. Meanwhile he carried on with his 'scare-manœuvres'. In his report of 30 July he wrote, in true conspiratorial fashion:

> I have considered with the chief Portuguese confidential agent two further and final possibilities which might cause Willi to change his mind about departing by increasing the anxiety-motive.
>
> (1) Harmless firing of shots at one or two window-panes in Willi's residence.
>
> (2) Discovery of an infernal machine [*Höllenmaschine*] two hours before the departure of the ship.
>
> It must however be taken into account that both of these possibilities might equally have the effect of strengthening Willi's resolve to depart, since remaining here would seem so insecure.
>
> In view of this, the first possibility has been dropped, while the second, which will be extremely difficult to carry out, is being prepared in earnest.[11]

Such antics sound absurdly comic; but as Schellenberg explains: 'I had to take some form of action because Berlin was continually demanding reports of progress, and these moves, somewhat dramatized, served as raw material for my reports.' He even considered getting his contacts to arrange for him to meet the Duke; 'but the possibility of anything useful resulting from this seemed so remote that I did nothing.'*[12]

At the *Boca do Inferno*, the Duke and Duchess remained ignorant of whatever real threat may have existed to their personal security. But with the outburst of police activity on the one hand, and Schellenberg's incidents on the other, they were increasingly on edge as the day of their departure approached. The detective requested by Monckton had not yet arrived.

Meanwhile, on the afternoon of Tuesday 30 July, the Duke had had his second interview with Alcázar de Velasco and given his final reply about returning to Spain. Don Angel's report – communicated to Berlin by Stohrer twenty-four hours later – is a document of some importance. It read as follows:

> The Duke and Duchess were strongly impressed by the reports of English intrigues being carried out against them and of danger to their personal safety. They no longer feel secure. They say they cannot take a step without surveillance. Yet the Duke declared he wanted to proceed to the Bahamas. No prospect of peace existed at the moment. Further statements of the Duke indicate that he has nevertheless already given consideration to the possibility that the role of an

* See Appendix iv.

intermediary might fall to him. He declared that the situation in England at the moment was still by no means hopeless. Therefore he should not now, by negotiations carried on contrary to the orders of his Government, let loose against himself the propaganda of his English opponents, which might deprive him of all prestige at the period when he might possibly take action. He could, if the occasion arose, take action even from the Bahamas.

The Duke stated to the confidential emissary that he would probably leave at the end of this week or beginning of next week. However, aside from tomorrow, August 1, there is no immediate possibility of departure. Thus it may be assumed that the Duke made this statement in order to conceal the true date.[13]

Once again Don Angel is able to confirm the autheniticity of this report, and add a few details. He remembers the Duke telling him: 'I'm not Mr Churchill. He alone can decide questions of war and peace.' He remembers that the Duchess came in during the course of the meeting, and he had the impression that the Duke had rehearsed with her what he was going to say. Don Angel did not care for the Duchess.[14] Having received the Duke's reply he returned to Madrid – but not before getting the news to Schellenberg, who wrote in his log on the 30th that it was 'now established for certain that *Willi will nicht*'.

That day the Duke had also had a similar conversation with Ricardo Espírito Santo, who had evidently continued to impress upon him the need to remain in Europe for the sake of peace. As Hoyningen-Huene reported in a *most urgent* telegram on the night of the 30th, the Duke, though still in favour of 'the Führer's policy' (i.e. peace negotiations), considered 'the present moment as inopportune for him to manifest himself on the political scene'. But he added 'that his departure for the Bahamas need not imply a rupture, since he could return within 24 hours' flying time via Florida'. The Duke had told Ricardo that he actually looked forward in a sense to the remoteness of the Bahamas. 'He welcomes the fact that his temporary absence from Europe will tend to push him into the background from which, to his regret, he has recently been hauled out by the press.'[15]

The significance of these two reports cannot be underestimated. Though they confirmed that the Duke had abandoned any intention he may have had of returning to Spain, and that he did not consider there was any role for him in Europe at that moment, they also showed that he believed he might have a part to play in possible future peace negotiations. It was the first time he had spoken definitely of such a possibility, and in so doing he encouraged the Germans and the Spaniards to make a massive, last-minute effort to keep him in Europe. Moreover, in the last forty-eight hours all the Germans involved in the plot in the Peninsula – Hoynigen-Huene, Stohrer, Schellenberg, even the Gestapo attaché Winzer – had been urging Berlin to throw aside the veil and make an approach to the Duke. There had not yet been any response to this suggestion. But the Duke's latest hints – that he might be ready to come forward as a peacemaker when the time was right – made it likely that such an approach would be sanctioned at the last moment.

All was set, therefore, for the last great effort. The immediate object was no longer to bring the Duke to Spain either by persuasion or by force, but simply to stop him sailing on 1 August or, failing that, somehow to keep him within the German circle of communications. But before examining the final plots, let us take a look at the doings of the Duke and Duchess on Wednesday 31 July, which they imagined would be their last day in Europe.

That day, the Duke was busy with pre-departure correspondence. He wrote to his new equerry Vyvyan Drury, telling him to make his own way from England to the Bahamas.[16] He replied to messages of welcome from the Bahamas legislature, assuring them that he was 'looking forward with interest' to his arrival in the islands.[17]

That day, the Duchess sent a telegram to Tiger, expressing her 'disappointment at not seeing you before sailing. A thousand thanks for all you have done and are doing for us. . . . May we all meet very soon.'[18]

That day, the latest flying boat from England brought Evelyn Fyrth, the new maid engaged by Phillips, and Detective-Sergeant Harold Holder of the Special Branch, who would accompany them to the Bahamas.*

That day too, Ricardo Espírito Santo arranged for the Duke to have a private interview with Dr Salazar before sailing on the morrow; he took care to inform Sir Walford Selby that he had done this.

That day, a French journalist, Suzanne Chantal, managed to obtain a short interview with the Duke and Duchess in the gardens of the *Boca do Inferno*. They posed for photographs, and spoke of the beauty and friendliness of Portugal – 'a country', said the Duke, 'which happily does not know the horrors of war'.†[19]

That day, the Duke played his last round of golf with his Portuguese

---

* Sergeant Holder remained the Duke's detective until the summer of 1942.

† This interview – the only one he gave in Portugal which was published – aroused the disapproval of the British Embassy.

friends at Estoril, and presented the Club with a large silver cup embellished with his arms and inscribed with his 'appreciation of their hospitality, July 1940'.*[20]

That day, the wife of a Portuguese official called on the Duchess to express 'anxiety about her husband's position, since if anything happened, he would lose his post'. (This was of course a Schellenberg-inspired 'scare-manœuvre'.) The Duchess responded with 'deepest thanks to the Portuguese lady and the request to remain firm, since the Duke must make the journey'.[21]

That day, the Duke wrote to Winston Churchill to confirm once more that he would be leaving the following afternoon, although it was 'not too convenient' to sail without 'many of our things which we shall need in the Bahamas and which we are trying to recover from France'. He continued:

> I naturally do not consider my appointment as one of first class importance, nor would you expect me to. On the other hand, since it is evident that the King and Queen do not wish to bring our family differences to an end, without which I could not accept a post in Great Britain, it is at least a temporary solution to the problem of my employment in the time of war. . . .
>
> I shall bear your word of counsel in mind, and hope that from time to time, you will let me know your views on the trend of events.
>
> The Duchess joins me in sending you our best wishes, and believe me

Yours very sincerely
EDWARD[22]

And yet, there is evidence that the Duke gave a strange flicker of hesitation that day. According to a report of the Italian Minister, he called 'secretly and alone' at the Spanish Embassy, where he asked Nicolás Franco 'to tell him honestly what he thought of his situation'. Don Nicolás again advised the Duke not to leave. 'A country which finds itself in the difficult position of England', he argued, 'ought to have some force in reserve with which to confront the unknown things of tomorrow. A large part of the English people are with you. The moment may come when England will feel the need to have you once more at her head, and therefore you should not be too far away.'

The Duke considered this advice and rejected it. The time was not ripe, he said, for him to play any role. He was a soldier, and it was his duty to obey. 'The fact is that the Duke is a very troubled man', Don Nicolás told

---

* The Duke of Windsor Cup is still played annually.

Bova Scoppa, 'and for the moment I do not think I have managed to persuade him to resist Churchill's game and not to leave.'[23]

Having apparently overcome this momentary qualm, the Duke prepared to give an eve-of-departure dinner for his Portuguese friends at the Hotel Aviz in Lisbon.

13
Eleventh Hour
31 July–1 August

Having driven four hundred miles through the night, Alcázar de Velasco reached Madrid on Wednesday morning. He went to the house of the Princess Ratibor in the calle de Serrano, where he had arranged to meet Miguel. They telephoned Serrano Suñer, who asked them both to come immediately to his office at the Ministry of the Interior. There Don Angel reported on the outcome of his mission – that the Duke seemed intent on sailing the following day, but that he had 'nevertheless given considera-tion to the possibility that the role of an intermediary might fall to him'. Don Miguel then said to Don Ramón: 'Send me back to Portugal today, and I shall get him here by fair means or foul [*por las buenas o por las malas*].' The Minister replied: 'No, the plan has been a flop and I wish to hear no more about it.'[1]

In the end, however, Miguel had his way. That afternoon, Stohrer conveyed Don Angel's report to Ribbentrop in a long telegram. It continued:

.... The Minister of the Interior is ready to make a last effort to prevent the Duke and Duchess from leaving should there still be time for it, and in spite of his previous objections to sending the same confidential emissary a second time, is now ready to despatch again this afternoon by plane to Lisbon the first confidential emissary, who is especially close to the Duke (the district leader of the Falange here, Primo de Rivera), for the purpose of acquainting the Duke personally with two lines of thought.

(1) According to reports available to the Minister, the decision will very quickly go against England and the English Government and King will soon be forced to leave the country.

(2) From the Bahamas, where the Duke would be in the power of the English Government (even if it should settle in Canada), he would not be free to inter-vene. This would be possible only from a neutral country. Accordingly a return

to Spain is advisable. In order not to create the impression of flight the Duke should at once postpone his journey as now planned and then after 8 or 10 days travel to Spain.[2]

Something is missing here. Had the tactic been abandoned of trying to persuade the Duke that his life was in danger from the British authorities, and that he ought to make for Spain in the interests of his own safety? It would appear that this was not the case, and that Don Miguel would restate this psychological argument on top of all political arguments. Indeed, he could hardly do otherwise after the letter he had written the Duke.

Serrano Suñer has only a vague recollection of Don Miguel's second mission. He insists that by this stage he was doing no more than play a part in a hollow farce mounted by Stohrer, and that neither he nor the Ambassador seriously expected anything to come of the latest plan – although, once again, the fatuous Miguel seemed to take it seriously.[*3]

Three hours later Stohrer sent another telegram to Berlin, to say that Don Miguel was now airborne for Portugal and expected to land there early that evening.[4]

In Paris that morning, Mademoiselle Moulichon had waited at the Boulevard Suchet with her mistress's trunks, listening for the car which the Spanish Embassy (on instructions from Tiger) had promised to send to convey her and her precious cargo to the Lisbon train. A car finally arrived – and out stepped two Germans in plain clothes. They were correct and polite: *gens d'ambassade* rather than police or military, she thought. But they informed her that it would not be possible for her to leave France for the time being.

Mademoiselle Moulichon was stricken. She protested that her royal employers would be unable to sail without her and their trunks. The Germans regretted there was nothing to be done for the moment; but if she left her luggage in Paris, they would be happy to give her a pass to visit her widowed mother in the Nièvre, in the Unoccupied Zone. . . .[5]

---

* Of Don Angel's mission Don Ramón recalls nothing whatever. But the circumstantial evidence for Don Angel having been the second emissary must be regarded as almost conclusive. Quite apart from the fact that he knows things which few people other than the emissary could have learned, there is the *Viktor* code-name and there is the Bova Scoppa telegram (see note on p. 158 above). In his memoirs, published in 1979, Don Angel in fact reveals that his wartime spy missions included '*el rapto del Duque de Windsor*' – but his publisher cut out the ensuing details on the ground that they sounded too improbable! (*Memorias de un agente secreto*, p. 20.)

Despite anxious enquiries, nothing more was heard for several weeks of Mademoiselle Moulichon.

At 11.30 that morning, Hitler held a conference at the Berghof to discuss the coming invasion of Britain. Grand Admiral Raeder announced that the naval preparations would be completed by 13 September – by which time the weather would be uncertain. He would rather the operation were postponed until the spring. Hitler did not like this: eight months might give the British time to regroup. Colonel-General Halder pointed out that, during that time, England might be reduced by aerial and submarine warfare and defeated in the Mediterranean.

Hitler still seemed curiously reluctant to authorize the attack. Already his thoughts were turning to an eventual campaign against Russia. 'Russia is the factor on which England is mainly betting.' If Russia were disposed of, then surely England would make peace? Meanwhile, the course of the war against England would depend on what happened in the air. Halder recorded the Führer's decision in the following strangely negative terms: 'If result of the air war is not satisfactory, then preparations will be halted. If there is impression that English are being smashed and that after a certain time the effect is being felt, then attack.'[6]

Hitler did not yet order the start of the all-out air offensive, however. He merely instructed that preparations were to continue on the assumption that his directive to commence operations would be issued within the next eight or ten days. But what was he waiting for?

A few miles away, at Schloss Fuschl in what had once been the Austrian Alps, Ribbentrop awaited Stohrer's report of Don Angel's second meeting with the Duke. It arrived (along with the news of Don Miguel's new mission) at 6.25 pm. The Foreign Minister was ready for action. Five minutes later the following telegram – which had evidently been prepared in advance for instant despatch – was sent off directly to Hoyningen-Huene in Lisbon.*

---

* In the captured papers, this is Ribbentrop's only communication to Hoyningen-Huene on the subject of the Duke. Everything else – including the correspondence with Schellenberg – had gone through Madrid. Stohrer had been expecting this reply also to go to Madrid, for onward transmission to Lisbon (B15/B002611–12). German communications with Spain were evidently regarded as much safer, and only the urgency of the situation appears to have prompted this direct message to Portugal.

MOST URGENT
TOP SECRET
Special Train, Fuschl, 31 July 1940
Received Berlin, 31 July, 6.30 pm.

No. 19 of 31 July from Fuschl
No. 442 from the Foreign Ministry
Sent 31 July, 6.30 pm.

In connection with the report that the Duke of Windsor will depart for America tomorrow, I request that you inform your Portuguese friend with whom the Duke is living of the following, for strictly confidential communication to the Duke:

Germany truly desires peace with the English people. The Churchill clique stands in the way of such a peace. Following the rejection of the Führer's final appeal to reason, Germany is determined to compel England to make peace by every means of power. It would be a good thing if the Duke were to hold himself in readiness for further developments. In such case Germany would be prepared to co-operate most closely with the Duke and to clear the way for any desire expressed by the Duke and Duchess. The direction in which these wishes tend is quite obvious and meets with our complete understanding. Should the Duke and Duchess have other intentions, but nevertheless be ready to co-operate in the future restoration of good relations between Germany and England, Germany is equally ready to collaborate with the Duke and provide for the future of the Duke and Duchess in accordance with their wishes.

Our Portuguese agent with whom the Duke is living should seriously endeavour to dissuade him from leaving tomorrow, as we have in our hands reliable information that Churchill intends to get the Duke into his power in the Bahamas in order to hold him there for ever, and also because the task of getting into communication with the Duke in the Bahamas at the appropriate time would be attended with the greatest difficulties for us. We are certain that the Duke will be so under surveillance there that he will never again have the opportunity to come to Europe, even by aeroplane, as he suggested to the Portuguese agent.

Should the Duke insist on leaving in spite of everything, there would still be a chance that the Portuguese agent could remain in touch with him and so arrange some channel of oral communication whereby we might continue to keep in contact and, should the occasion arise, negotiate. You may inform the Portuguese agent that the proposed overture comes from an authoritative German source. I assume that your Portuguese friend is discreet and can be relied upon to transmit so secret a communication. I naturally wish you to pass it to him only verbally and in your private presence, and if, contrary to all expectation, an indiscretion should take place, you must of course deny entirely any such statement or any connection with the matter whatsoever.

Please place this telegram personally under lock and key.

RIBBENTROP[7]

After weeks of elaborate secrecy, Ribbentrop was finally authorizing contact with the Duke. But the contact envisaged was still tentative and indirect. Ricardo was only to say that his message came from 'an authoritative [*massgebender*] German source' – and the German authorities, if approached, would deny all knowledge of it. Nothing was to be written down: Ribbentrop was well aware of the dangers of any written communication falling into British hands.

Apart from the decision to approach the Duke in Portugal, nothing had changed. The message to be delivered by Ricardo was almost exactly the same, word for word, as the message included in Ribbentrop's telegram to Stohrer of 11 July, which the Duke was to have been given once he had become an effective prisoner of the Germans in Spain.* It was the same tale – that Germany was about to attack England, that peace depended on the replacement of 'the Churchill clique', that Germany was willing to restore the Duke to the throne (which Ribbentrop still imagined represented his 'obvious wishes') or at least to assure him and his wife a royal existence, that it was hoped they would 'co-operate in the establishment of good relations between Germany and England'. Just as before, Ribbentrop put out a wild story to terrify the Duke into changing his plans. Then it had been that 'the English Secret Service' meant 'to do away with him at the first opportunity'. Now it was that Churchill intended 'to get the Duke into his power in the Bahamas in order to hold him there for ever' – a psychologically cunning allegation, since the Duke was known to be both annoyed and perplexed at not having received a definite assurance from the British Government that he would eventually be allowed to visit the United States from his colonial post.

Was Ribbentrop in the least interested in the Duke's hint of possible future good offices in the event of England one day seeking peace? Or did he rather wish – while the battle was in full progress – to lure him into German power so as to weaken Great Britain's continuing will to resist?

Having arrived at Sintra airport around seven o'clock that evening,[8] Don Miguel made his way to the Spanish Embassy in Lisbon. Nicolás Franco knew where to find the Duke of Windsor. He sent a messenger to the Hotel Aviz to inform him that his old friend had arrived 'with an official

* See above, pp. 98–9.

mandate from the Generalissimo', and to 'urge him to receive him at once and listen to what he had to say'.[9]

As Stohrer and Serrano Suñer had anticipated, the arrival of Don Miguel and the purpose of his mission were soon widely known in the Portuguese capital. 'I have formed the impression', wrote Bova Scoppa to Rome in the following day's despatch, 'that the Spanish Government is trying very hard to influence the Duke and persuade him to remain in Spain and Portugal. The arrival here from Madrid yesterday of the young Primo de Rivera – a friend of the ex-King – should be viewed in the light of this pressure.'[10]

As the Duke's friends remember it, the farewell party at the Aviz was a jolly occasion. It continued late, with numerous toasts and much recipro- cal signing of menus. If the Duke politely excused himself for a while to see some unexpected visitor, no one seems to have taken much notice of the fact. Nobody seems to have remarked any particular anxiety in him towards the end of the evening.[11]

The celebration was still going on at midnight, when an urgent mes- sage was brought to the Duke's principal guest, Ricardo Espírito Santo, asking him to call on the German Minister as soon as possible. Once the party was over Ricardo drove to the German Legation Residence, which was only a few doors from his own house in the fashionable suburb of Lapa.

Hoyningen-Huene explained to Ricardo the new instructions he had just received from Berlin. They 'discussed thoroughly possible further courses of action', and Ricardo 'promised to give the message to the Duke in the course of the morning'.[12] Ricardo also informed Hoyningen-Huene that he had arranged an interview between the Duke and Salazar. The Minister wondered whether, if all else failed, it might not be possible to add the persuasive voice of the Portuguese premier to the growing chorus of those who advised the Duke against leaving. . . .

Schellenberg had little sleep that night. He carefully followed the various plots to keep the Duke in the Peninsula. He noted in his log that Primo de Rivera had seen Willi, that 'Ribbentrop's answer' had arrived, that Hoy- ningen-Heune had 'acted accordingly'. But Schellenberg too had to be seen to be taking measures to prevent the Duke's departure. Throughout the night he planned a final series of 'scare-manœuvres'.

At 7 am he reported to Hoyningen-Huene that a 'seven-point plan' was about to be put in motion. An anonymous warning would be smuggled to the Duchess in a bunch of flowers. The Duke's servants would be bribed to refuse to accompany him to the Bahamas. His bodyguard would be disarmed by the Portuguese police. He would be warned that his fellow passengers consisted of a dangerous gang of Jewish emigrants. He would be informed 'from the highest level' that the operation against England would begin in four days' time. He and the Duchess would learn of the discovery of an 'infernal machine' on the *Excalibur*. If they still tried to leave, their car would mysteriously break down on the way to the ship. . . .[13]

Seven o'clock on the morning of Thursday, 1 August 1940. Less than twelve hours to go before the sailing of the *Excalibur*. During that time, Miguel Primo de Rivera (bearing a strange Spanish message) would warn the Duke not to leave, for the sake of his life. Ricardo Espírito Santo (bearing a strange German message) would warn him not to leave, for the sake of Europe. Don Nicolás Franco had warned him not to leave for the sake of the British Empire – and it was possible that the proverbially wise Dr Salazar would also advise him not to leave.

Mademoiselle Moulichon and her trunks were expected at noon on the *Sud Express*: they would not be on it. The hours before embarkation would be filled with frightening incidents, anonymous warnings, bomb alerts, defective motor cars.

Would the Duke and Duchess be sailing on the *Excalibur*?

LIST OF PASSENGERS

AMERICAN EXPORT LINES

S. S. EXCALIBUR

Captain S. N. GROVES, Commander

STAFF

Chief Officer, G. A. MOLDESTAD
Second Officer, A. W. FALLIS
Third Officer, G. McALLISTER
Jr. Third Officer, J. F. MARCHANT

Chief Engineer, H. G. STRINER
1st Asst. Engineer, J. FINESTEIN
2nd Asst. Engineer, J. YOUNG
3rd Asst. Engineer, S. MIRTICH
Jr. 3rd Asst. Engineer, L. TAPRAHANIAN

Purser, JOHN F. WALKER
Asst. Purser, C. M. McANENY

Surgeon, M. M. EXLEY, M.D.

Chief Steward, M. PARMAN
Second Steward, C. MILDE

LIST OF PASSENGERS

BERMUDA

H.R.H. The Duke of Windsor
The Duchess of Windsor

Captain George J. Wood
Miss Isabelle Pons
Mr. Harold Holder

Mrs. George J. Wood
Miss Evelyn Fyrth
Mr. Alastair Fletcher

NEW YORK

Mr. Hermann Apt

The Hon. A.J. Drexel Biddle Jr.
Mrs. A.J. Drexel Biddle Jr.
Mr. Hale Benton
Mr. Henry Berger
Mr. Lucien Brouha
Mrs. Elizabeth Brouha
Mr. Walter Brannon
Mr. William Bryan
Miss Mersedes Bucher

Mr. Francisco Cambo
Miss Helene Cambo
Miss Pearl Carruthers
Mr. Donald Coster
Miss Esmerayda Cuella

Mr. Jacques Demarquette
Mr. Hans Ditisheim
Mr. Harry Ditisheim
Miss Marion Ditisheim
Mr. Arthur Doble
Mrs. Georgie Doble
Mr. Daniel Doyen
Mrs. Renee Doyen
Miss Jeanne Doyen
Master Jacques Doyen
Mr. Charles Dyar
Mrs. Isabel Dyar

Mrs. Lise Eliacheff
Miss Alexandra Eliacheff

Miss Mary Eastman
Mr. Howard Elkinton
Mrs. Bertha Emshemer

The Hon. George A. Gordon
Mrs. George A. Gordon
Captain John Gade
Mr. Andre Gaillot
Miss Suzanne Ghisletti
Mr. Hanns Gleichman

Mr. Leopold Haas
Mrs. Else Haas
Mr. Walter Haeberli
Mr. Elias Haim
Mr. Mauricio Haim
Mr. Willy Heinberg
Mr. Jose Hernandez
Mrs. Maria Hernandez
Mr. Carlos Hernandez
Mr. Jorge Herrera
Mrs. Margarita Herrera
Miss Teresa Herrera
Miss Julia Herrera
Miss Leonor Herrera
Mr. Arnold Hildesheimer
Mrs. Ella Hildesheimer
Miss Marie Hildesheimer
Miss Vera Hildesheimer
Miss Lillian Hog
Miss Freida Hotterman

Mr. Emil Humble
Mrs. Hanny Humble

Mr. Alfred Jacob
Mrs. Norma Jacob
Master Piers Jacob
Miss Teresa Jacob
Mr. Royal Jordan
Mrs. Tatiana Jordan
Master Robert Jordan

Mr. Frances Kargl
Captain Monroe Kelly
Miss Lina Knoll

Lady F. Lindsay Hogg
Master W. Lindsay Hogg
Mr. Erwin Lang
Mrs. Emma Lang
Mr. Leon Levy
Mrs. Freida Levy
Mrs. Louise Lanz

Miss Mercedes Mallol
Mr. Raymond Marshall
Mr. Enrique Martin
Mrs. Olga Meyers
Miss Maud Mills
Mr. Georgio Minerbi
Mr. Emilia Minerbi
Master M. Minerbi

Miss Vittorino Nacamulli
Mr. Rene Nordmann

Mrs. Ellen Orosdi
Miss Eliane Orosdi

The Hon. William Phillips
Miss Beatrice Phillips
Mr. Horry Prioleau
Mr. Adolph Pestalozzi

Mr. Percy Robinson
Mrs. Olive Robinson
Mr. Roger Rodoti
Mr. Leo Rossel
Mrs. Maria Rossel
Mrs. Maida Roussel

Mr. Victor Sax
Mrs. Sylvia Sax
Mrs. Klara Saxer
Mr. Theodore Schneider
Mrs. Leona Schneider
Mr. Bruno Serrano
Miss Alice Shaffer
Mr. Donald Sherman
Mrs. Ginette Sherman
Master Robin Sherman
Master Patrick Sherman
Mr. Harry Sherman Sr.
Mr. Isaak Stein
Mrs. Wicia Stein
Miss Gisia Stein
Mr. Michel Steinberg
Mrs. Mariya Steinberg

Mrs. Regina Thurliman

Mr. Alfredo Vasquez

Mr. Hans Wertheimer
Lt. Arthur Wilson
Mr. Ernest Wittmann
Mrs. Rose Wittmann
Mr. Richard Wormser
Mrs. Erna Wormser
Miss Maria Wormser

Mr. Noritake Yosheoka
Mrs. Tazuko Yosheoka

Mrs. Bernice Zdunek
Mr. Albert Zuppinger

The passenger list of the *Excalibur*

14
The Reports
August 1940

I: On the Departure of the Duke and Duchess

From the British Ambassador in Portugal to the Foreign Office[1]

Lisbon, 2 August 1940

En clair from Sir Walford Selby.
Duke and Duchess of Windsor sailed last night.

From the German Ambassador in Spain to the Reich Foreign Minister[2]

MOST URGENT   Madrid, 2 August 1940
TOP SECRET   Received 2 August 1940, 1.25 pm
For Reich Foreign Minister
No. 2632 of 2 August 1940

Schellenberg has just telephoned from Lisbon that ducal couple sailed last night on American steamer 'Excalibus' [*sic*]. Further report about final unhappily vain attempts to restrain W. from departing follows.
STOHRER*

---

* A similar telegram was sent by Winzer to Heydrich.[3] Were these the first indications which Berlin had had of the Duke's departure? The question may be of some importance; for the day the Duke sailed was also the day that Hitler finally issued his Directive No. 17 'for the conduct of air and naval warfare against England', giving the go-ahead to the Luftwaffe 'to overcome the English Air Force with all means at its disposal and in the shortest possible time'. When Hitler signed this order (which he did after so much hesitation), did he already know that the Duke of Windsor had sailed (or was with certainty about to sail) from Europe? It would be interesting to have information on this point.

In his memoirs, Schellenberg wrote:

On the day of the Duke's departure I was in the tower room of the German Embassy, watching the ship through field-glasses. It appeared so close that I seemed almost able to touch it. The Duke and Duchess went on board punctually, and I recognized Monckton too.* There was some excitement about the hand luggage. The Portuguese police in their zeal insisted on searching that too. Finally the ship cast off, and moved away down the broad mouth of the Tagus. Slowly I returned to my house. The chapter was closed.

II: The Report of Oswald Baron von Hoyningen-Huene[4]

MOST URGENT   Lisbon, 2 August 1940, 3.46pm
SECRET   Received 2 August, 8.55 pm
No. 800 of 1 August
For the Reich Foreign Minister personally.

With reference to your telegram No. 442 of 31 July.

(1) In accordance with the telegraphic instructions which arrived shortly before midnight, I immediately got in touch with our confidant the Duke's host, the banker Ricardo de Espírito Santo Silva, who happened to be at the ducal couple's farewell reception at a hotel here. After the end of this affair he visited me at my residence, where we discussed thoroughly possible further courses of action. I would note at this point that the person concerned is an unobjectionable individual, who has never denied his friendly attitude towards Germany and whose discretion is beyond doubt. The confidant promised to give the message to the Duke in the course of the morning.

(2) Every effort made to detain the Duke and Duchess in Europe (in which connection I refer particularly to Schellenberg's reports) was in vain. Their departure took place this evening.† The decision of the Duke was influenced during the last days by his close friend Sir Walter Monckton, who had come to Lisbon expressly for the purpose of indicating to the Duke the serious objections which existed to a further postponement of his departure. Monckton told the confidant verbally that, while the Duke was no doubt the most popular man in England, the whole of England today still stood behind Churchill.

* According to contemporary newspaper reports the Duchess arrived first without the Duke and was escorted on board by Monckton. The Woods had already gone on board with the servants. The Duke (who had presumably been held up by his interview with Salazar) arrived half an hour later with the Espírito Santos in their red three-seater. There was a crowd of several hundred to see them off. The ship sailed at 6.40 pm.

† That is, on the evening of 1 August. This telegram was evidently drafted that night but for some reason only despatched the following afternoon.

(3) On the other hand the message which was conveyed to the Duke made the deepest impression on him and he felt appreciative of the considerate way in which his personal interests were being taken into account. In his reply, which was given orally to the confidant, the Duke paid tribute to the Führer's desire for peace, which was in complete agreement with his own point of view. He was firmly convinced that if he had been King it would never have come to war. To the appeal made to him to co-operate at a suitable time he gladly consented. However, he requested that it be understood that at the present time he must follow the official orders of his Government. Disobedience would disclose his intentions prematurely, bring about a scandal, and deprive him of his prestige in England. He was also convinced that the present moment was too early for him to come forward, since there was as yet no inclination in England for an approach to Germany. However, as soon as this frame of mind changed, he would be ready to return immediately. To bring this about there were two possibilities. Either England would yet call upon him, which he considered to be entirely possible, or Germany would express the desire to negotiate with him. In both cases he was prepared for any personal sacrifice and would make himself available without the slightest personal ambition. He would remain in continuous communication with his former host and had agreed with him upon a code word, upon receiving which he would immediately come back over. He insisted that this would be possible at any time, since he had foreseen all eventualities and had already initiated all the necessary arrangements. The statements of the Duke were, as the confidant stressed, supported by firmness of will and the deepest sincerity, and had included an expression of admiration and sympathy for the Führer.

HUENE

III: The Report of Walter Schellenberg[5]

MOST URGENT   Lisbon, 2 August 1940, 10.00 pm
No. 808 of 2 August*   Received 3 August, 6.35 pm
For the Reich Foreign Minister personally.

At the time of ...† to Madrid I had to assume that the Duke of Windsor, as a result of the mediation of the Ambassador and the highly

* See also Schellenberg's log for 1 August, Appendix III below.
† Note on original: 'one word missing'.

influential Spanish confidential emissary, had given up the intention to travel to the Bahamas and was trying instead to return to Spain. (I refer to taking advantage of the hunting excursion on the frontier.)

Principal tasks in Lisbon:

(1) Creation and organization of a personal protective service for the Duke and Duchess.

(2) Preparation of security for the automobile journey of the Duke and Duchess from Lisbon by way of Guarda to Villa Formosa [sic], 320 kilometres.

(3) Security for hunting excursion.

(4) Security for border crossing.

(5) Security in Spain.

Good connections were soon established with the main confidential agent on the Portuguese side (the director of counter-espionage in Portugal) and with the Portuguese collaborator made available by him. The superior of the principal Portuguese confidential agent works very closely with the Intelligence Service and Scotland Yard through the British Embassy. It was nevertheless possible to secure compliance with almost all of our requests.

After only 2 days there was established a protective service of 18 agents working for us. One to three agents were constantly active in the immediate vicinity of the Duke. In connection with the preparations for the journey, security at the frontier, etc., the reports which came in soon made it evident (and this was confirmed from the beginning by the Minister here) that the Duke was giving up the return to Spain and had even expressed himself unfavourably about it within his intimate circle. After the appearance of Monckton accompanied by members of the I.S. and Scotland Yard a change of tactics seemed advisable, since the Duke fell completely under their influence.

Through the efforts of a high Portuguese police official who visited the Duke and Duchess personally, it was possible to interfere with the plans of the Duke and Duchess to move to a hotel under I.S. surveillance. The hints dropped on the occasion of this visit about the impending danger to the Duke and Duchess from I.S. activities, Jews and emigrants produced a very strong effect.

From 29 July onwards the principal object was to prevent the departure of the Duke and Duchess by making use of all the means available suitable to the nature of the mission.

(1) Since the Spanish plan collapsed completely, the Portuguese host

of the Duke and Duchess was employed in closest co-operation with the Minister here, in a manner which is evident from the personal reports of the Minister on the subject.

Attention is called particularly to the Minister's last report of 1 August,* where it is noted how every effort was made, even in a political way, to influence the Duke in our direction. The result expresses entirely the Duke's mentality and is strikingly characteristic of the situation I found here.

(2) In order to increase the anxiety-motive and to determine the Duke and Duchess to remain in Europe, they were kept constantly aware – through the influence of various personal connections of the principal Portuguese confidential agent – of the danger of a surprise attack by Churchill and of I.S. activity. It is certain that the Duke and Duchess had real feelings of anxiety. However, Monckton was evidently able to dispel the anxiety as it arose. As the preparations for departure became more active, the strongest methods were brought into use by us. These were as follows:†

(a) Complete uncovering through police activity of the known I.S. members here. (Thus, for example, the Scotland Yard officer Holder and the operatives Evelyne Forth‡ and Catherine Fox did not receive their firearms before departure of the ship because of uncertainty in interpretation of customs regulations.)

(b) Since the Duke was especially impressed by the Jewish peril, the principal private secretary of the Duke, Philipps [sic], was furnished with a list of Jews and emigrants sailing on the same ship, and it was stressed that the counter-espionage police could make no guarantees.

(c) Call on the Duchess by the wife of a Portuguese official. (Reason for visit: anxiety about her husband's position, since if anything happened he would lose his post. Reaction: deepest thanks to the Portuguese lady and a request to stand firm, since the Duke must make the journey.)

(d) Anonymous gift of flowers with a greeting card containing a warning.

(e) Anonymous letter to the Duchess also emphasizing the gravity of the danger in a psychologically suitable form.

(f) Bribing of the second (English) driver who refused to go along to the Bahamas on account of the danger. The chauffeur could not go along and

* No. II above.

† Against the following list, the Duke wrote when first shown this telegram in 1953: 'Very interesting.'

‡ Evelyn Fyrth was the Duchess's new maid, whom Gray Philips had engaged in London.

will for the time being be taken care of by the principal Portuguese confidential agent.

(g) On the day of departure a paid agent was arrested on the ship for lacking a passport and at his hearing he stated that he had seen suspicious persons on the ship and he actually led the Portuguese authorities to a spot where traces of an infernal machine and tools for building such a machine were found. The affair was bruited about in the company of the Duke and Duchess as a most serious sort of warning, yet without result, since the Duke stressed that because of political prestige he had to make the journey.

(h) Sabotage against the motor car which was driving to the ship with luggage. The luggage only reached the ship after an hour's delay.

A firing of shots (harmless breaking of bedroom window) scheduled for the night of 30 July was omitted, since the psychological effect on the Duchess would only have been to increase her desire to depart. Because of the opposition of the aforementioned chief of the Portuguese alien police no trouble would have been made for the I.S.

However, through steady undermining of their sense of security, and open and concealed references to the activity of the I.S., the Duke and Duchess were strongly influenced, and this led, according to the admission of the principal private secretary Philipps, to personal steps on the part of the Duke which resulted in the establishment of a protective service by proved and devoted friends of the Duke.

(3) In order that no possibility should be overlooked, the so-called Spanish plan was out of necessity taken up again on 29 and 31 July and 1 August. As already reported, the Spanish Minister of the Interior sent the district leader of the Falange in Madrid, Primo de Rivera, out to the Duke. His intervention too was without success. On 1 August, five hours before the departure of the ship, the attempt was made, with the aid of the Minister here, to send the Spanish Ambassador (the brother of the Caudillo) to see the Portuguese Premier Salazar, to get him to persuade the Duke and Duchess, when they made their farewell call, to remain at least in Portugal.* Ambassador Nicolás Franco and Salazar spoke of official Spanish and Portuguese wishes, etc. Even this final manoeuvre could not prevent the departure of the Duke. I am leaving with my party for Madrid on 3 August and, should there be no other instructions, I shall seek to reach Berlin by the quickest possible means, where I can give a

* See IV and V below.

205

complete report verbally. I should be particularly grateful if you would inform the Head of the Security Police.

Schellenberg's log shows that, after brief stops in Madrid and Rome, he returned to Berlin on 6 August. In his memoirs he gives the following account of his final interview with Ribbentrop:

> He received me rather coolly, his expression distant, his handshake perfunctory. It was obvious that he was dissatisfied. He said curtly, 'Please report.' I remained calm and spoke quietly, my verbal report following very closely the written reports I had sent from Lisbon. When I had finished he stared in front of him for quite a while, then said in a monotonous and tired voice, 'The Führer has studied your last telegram thoroughly and asks me to tell you that in spite of his disappointment at the outcome of the whole affair, he agrees with your decisions and expresses his approval of the manner in which you proceeded.'

> In the afternoon I reported to Heydrich. He listened quietly, nodded several times, and finally said, 'A rather disjointed affair. Please don't get yourself involved too closely with Ribbentrop. I feel that you should not have accepted this assignment in the first place. Obviously you realized from the beginning how it would probably end. I must say that you carried it off rather shrewdly.'[6]

IV: The Report of Dr Luis Teixeira de Sampaio[7]

Ministry of Foreign Affairs
General Secretariat
Minute of Interview   Lisbon, 1 August 1940

On the afternoon of 1 August 1940 the Spanish Ambassador asked to see me as soon as possible. I received him immediately.

Don Nicolás told me that the Duke of Windsor would be received by Dr Salazar before embarking for America. This was to be at five o'clock. (I pretended not to know about this, as the President of the Council* had told me it was confidential and had been arranged at the last moment.) The Ambassador wanted Dr Salazar to have the following before he received the Duke of Windsor:

> It has always been my impression that the Duke, despite his temperament, might be a *trump for peace*; I still feel he might have a role to play today, provided he is not too far away. The trumps for peace are not so numerous that they may be disregarded or allowed to be destroyed.

---

* Salazar's official title as Premier.

It was most advisable for Dr Salazar to know this before receiving the Duke.

I promised the Ambassador that I would pass this on to the President of the Council, whom I had already told about an earlier conversation in which Don Nicolás had expressed the same views unofficially.*

As the Ambassador seemed to be hinting at the possibility of the Duke's seeking or receiving advice from Dr Salazar about whether he should leave or stay, I told him that in my view Dr Salazar would not pronounce on such a matter. I gathered this from what had happened when another royal personage sought advice about the expediency of staying or departing. The President had said that he would never advise leaving, which might be interpreted as an indirect limit on the duration of Portuguese hospitality; nor would he advise staying, since that would be to assume a responsibility which did not fall to him, besides being a pronouncement on the political bearing of other countries, or on political affairs which did not concern Portugal.

The next day I spoke to the British Ambassador and told him, on behalf of the President, that the interview had been requested as a personal matter through Dr Ricardo Espírito Santo, and that was why he, the Ambassador, had not been told of it. Fortunately I spoke rather vaguely for the Ambassador cut me short, saying that Dr Ricardo Espírito Santo had told him on Wednesday, that is on the 31st, that an interview had been arranged between the Prince and Dr Salazar. He did not seem in the slightest disturbed by the fact. He asked me whether Dr Ricardo Espírito Santo had been present at the interview. He seemed pleased when I answered in the negative, and likewise very pleased when I said that the newspapers would not be told of the interview.†

He alluded to speculations about the Prince which had arisen from certain statements which he, Selby, had asked him to avoid: 'He doesn't see traps, he falls into them.' He did not conceal his displeasure at the interview given to the journalist Chantal,‡ but still less did he conceal his

---

* See above, p. 133.

† Ambassador Alberto Franco Nogueira, Salazar's official biographer and the only historian so far to have had access to his private papers, says that he found no record of the interview other than an entry in the dictator's engagement book.

‡ See above, p. 189. In this interview, as well as praising Portugal as 'a country which does not know the horrors of war', the Duke described the Hotel Palacio with its multilingual refugees as 'a Tower of Babel', and expressed his fears that the continuation of the war and consequent disruption of trade might impede 'the great task' of Salazar (*Diario de Notícias*, 1 August 1940).

satisfaction at seeing the Duke leave amid references to his kindness and friendliness.

TEIXEIRA DE SAMPAIO

V: The Report of Renato Bova Scoppa[8]

To the Royal Minister of Foreign Affairs, Count Ciano
Secret, by bag, 412/048   Lisbon, 2 August 1940

Following my telegram . . . of yesterday's date.*

As expected, the Duke of Windsor sailed yesterday 1st August on the steamer *Excalibur* bound for New York, from where he will proceed to the Bahamas. Right up to the last moment the Spanish continued to put pressure on him to show a more resolute attitude and give up his departure.

On the evening of 31 July, while the Duke was giving a farewell dinner for his friends, Ambassador Franco sent his Military Attaché, the Count of Almina, to inform him that Primo de Rivera had arrived from Madrid and urge him strongly to receive him at once and listen to what he had to say, thus making it clear that the Marquis of Estrela† had an official mandate from the Generalissimo.

Not content with this, Ambassador Franco sought the help of Dr Salazar in interceding with the Duke and persuading him to remain in Portugal. Franco's thesis – which Salazar accepted, leaving aside the Duke – was that it would not be in the interests of Spain and Portugal that England should fall into anarchy following a disastrous military defeat. The only reserve force which really existed was that represented by the ex-King. There was clearly a case for him to refuse to leave or at least to delay his departure, and this would be evident not just to British public opinion but to the world. The post of Governor of the Bahamas was not consistent with the dignity of one who had been King of England and Emperor of India. Salazar found these arguments valid but replied to Franco that for obvious reasons, given his position with regard to England, he was not willing to take any initiative of this kind or involve himself in a delicate affair which did not concern him.

The Marquis of Estrela for his part sought to put the same points directly to the Duke. But the latter, showing his usual irresolution, replied

---

* Reporting the Duke's meeting on 31 July with Don Nicolás Franco. See above, pp. 190–91.

† Don Miguel's marquisate was in fact of *Estella*.

with the arguments he had already given Franco – that the situation had not reached the stage where he could hope that the English people might recall him to the throne, that he was a soldier and had to obey the orders of the King of England, that he had already received a number of messages asking him when he was going to leave, and a further delay would only have caused the British Government to be even more suspicious of what his real intentions were. The situation in his country was already difficult enough without his complicating it further by indecision and delaying tactics which would have been hard to justify. He thanked his Spanish friends for the proofs of trust and friendship they had given him but he thought it best to leave. He also believed that the example of obedience he would be giving would have a salutary effect on British public opinion.

And so, on the date of 1 August which had already been fixed (as I informed you in my telegram no. 269 of 25 July), the Duke and Duchess embarked for New York, accompanied by their ADC Captain Wood and his wife.

Franco mentioned a detail to me which is worth passing on, and which gives an idea of the relationship currently existing between the British Government and the ex-King. The passports of the Duke and Duchess were sent by the British Embassy to the Spanish Embassy with the request that visas be made out in the name of his Royal Highness the Duke of Windsor 'and his party', without mentioning the Duchess. In fact it is believed in London that the Duke's reluctance to leave was due to the attitude of 'the American woman', who, by speaking of a 'second Saint Helena' for her husband and bitterly criticizing the measures taken by Churchill, has incurred the rage and disgust of the latter.

According to Franco, the Duke also had fears that old Churchill, who had given such clear proof of his unscrupulousness, would have him assassinated if he did not decide to leave. And so, in spite of the resistance of his wife, the recommendation of his friends and of the Spanish Government, his personal conviction that he might be able to pull his country back from the precipice by hurling Churchill and his gang into the sea [sic], the ex-King took the road to political isolation and exile.

Off the record, the German Minister tells me that he has asked Berlin for instructions with regard to the possible establishment of contact with Windsor but has received no reply.*

R. BOVA SCOPPA

---

* This conversation must have taken place before the evening of 31 July.

VI: The Report of Don Miguel Primo de Rivera[9]

MOST URGENT   Madrid, 3 August 1940
TOP SECRET   Received 4 August, 12.25 am
No. 2663 of 3 August
For the Reich Foreign Minister

I have just heard from the Spanish Minister of the Interior that his
confidential emissary has telephoned him from Lisbon, using agreed
phraseology, to say that he spent a considerable amount of time with the
Duke and Duchess on the day of their departure. The Duke hesitated
right up to the last moment. The ship had to delay its departure on that
account. The influence of the Duke's legal adviser, Sir Walter Turner
Monckton, was again successful, however, in bringing him around to
leave. The confidential emissary added that the Duke had clearly per-
ceived that it would have been better to remain here so as to be able to
step in at the decisive moment. The Duke believed, however, that it
might be possible for him to do this from the Bahamas. For this purpose
an arrangement was reached concerning which the confidential emissary
did not wish to say anything over the telephone.

Schellenberg, who has just returned from Lisbon, is reporting about
all his numerous and extremely circumspect measures taken to prevent the departure. His account with regard to the influence of Sir Walter
is in accord with the report of the Spanish confidential emissary.
Schellenberg also made certain arrangements which ought to make
possible resumption of relations with the Duke.

STOHRER*

---

* On the same evening as he despatched this telegram, Stohrer departed for Berlin, whither he had
been urgently summoned by Ribbentrop. He had originally proposed to await Don Miguel's return to
Madrid, but had learned that this would not take place before the 5th (B15/B002640 & 136/74251).

VII: The Report of Sir Walter Monckton[10]

Ministry of Information,
Senate House,
London University Building,
Malet Street,
London WC1.

Confidential   *8 August 1940*

My dear Prime Minister,

 I do not want to trouble you to give me time to make a personal report on my journey to Lisbon, but there are three matters upon which I ought to make you a short note.

. . . .*

 (3) There was considerable difficulty in keeping him to the date fixed for departure from Lisbon. He was due to start on Thursday, 1st August. On the previous Tuesday† he told me that he had received from various sources, which he was not at liberty to disclose, though he regarded them as reliable, a report that he would be in danger if he went to the Bahamas. What he was told was that there was a plot afoot against his security and that British influence, including possibly even some members of the Government, were implicated. It was in order to persuade him to go in spite of this warning that I asked Lord Lloyd to send a responsible detective to go with them. This was enough to keep him to his plans until the day of his departure, when a distinguished Spaniard flew from Madrid specially to repeat the warning and to urge him to delay his departure for two or three weeks, in the course of which the full facts could be ascertained so that he could decide whether to undertake the risk or to give up his appointment. I was allowed to see the Spaniard and to discuss the matter both with and without the Duke. The Duke and the Spaniard wished me to telegraph to you advising the postponement of his departure for two or three weeks in view of dangers which I could not disclose at that stage. I said that this was impossible and that what was required was some concrete evidence of the existence of such a plot, for which I could see no possible purpose. I was told at once that it was not possible to give me any facts or names at the moment, but that in ten or

---

 * Monckton's first two matters concern the Duke's desire to visit America after the presidential elections, and his willingness to declare his dollar securities under the Exchange Control Regulations.

 † It was in fact on Monday 29 July. See above, p. 176.

twelve days they would certainly be forthcoming. I pointed out that if I were to advise the Duke or the Government to postpone his departure without any further material I should be faced on my return to England with the suggestion that it could not be to Great Britain's interest, though it certainly would be to Germany's, for the Duke to remain in Europe, and that one could not resist the suspicion that the report of the plot had a German origin. In the end the Duke accepted the position that he must leave as arranged, on the understanding that he could be stopped in Bermuda unless enquiries showed that it was safe for him to proceed. I told the Spaniard that if, as he anticipated, he was in the possession of material establishing the authenticity of the report within ten or twelve days, I should be prepared to come out again to Lisbon to collect the material and have it investigated.*

I have mentioned this matter both to Lord Lloyd and to Sir Philip Game,† who are both of the opinion that there can be nothing in the suggestion, and Sir Philip Game pointed out that the only possible danger might be that the Germans might make an attempt on the Duke's life and say that it was done by the British. He did not suggest that this was probable, but if it is a danger to be guarded against he would need to send a second detective to the Bahamas. I understand the Duke is likely to arrive in Bermuda today or tomorrow. I have had no more news from Spain about the alleged plot. I think I ought to telegraph to the Duke at Bermuda saying that the matter of the alleged plot has been brought to the notice of all the relevant government departments here and that the heads of these departments are satisfied that there is no foundation for the allegation and that accordingly they are anxious that he should proceed to the Bahamas in accordance with the arrangements which they have already made. I am asking Lord Lloyd's private secretary to inform me what precisely these arrangements are. It may well be that I shall need a telegram from a higher authority than myself to persuade him to leave Bermuda at an early date, particularly because of the fact that he

---

* Monckton referred to these events more briefly in a memoir which was quoted in his official biography. 'The Marqués de Estella, a son of the old Dictator Primo de Rivera, flew over from Madrid to persuade the Duke not to go to the Bahamas on the ground that he had information of a plot by the British Government to have him killed there. It sounds fantastic, but he managed to impress the Duke and Duchess.' Monckton's 'long and bizarre' conversation with Don Miguel took place in the garden of the Duke's villa (Lord Birkenhead, *Walter Monckton*, p. 180).

† Metropolitan Police Commissioner.

has a troublesome wisdom tooth which he wants to have extracted while he is in Bermuda, by a doctor whom he will get out from New York!*

Yours ever,
WALTER MONCKTON

> 10, Downing Street,
> London S.W.1.
> *9 August 1940*

My dear Monckton,

   Thank you very much for your letter. It was very lucky you were on the spot to dissipate strange suspicions. I do not think it matters if he stays on at Bermuda for a little while. The climate is much better than at Nassau at this time of year. . . .

   Once more thanking you for the trouble you took and the service you rendered,

yours sincerely,
W.S.C.

---

* The *Excalibur* reached Bermuda on 9 August. The Duke at once telegraphed Monckton: 'Have arrived. Impossible continue journey until we hear from you.' Monckton replied the following day: 'After enquiries here am satisfied no foundation for allegations which reached us in Lisbon. Accordingly do not think any need to delay continuance of your journey.' The Duke sailed with the Duchess for the Bahamas on the 15th, arriving in Nassau to take up his governorship on the 17th.

Epilogue:
The Solution

The plot – the plot to bring the Duke of Windsor under German power in Europe – had failed. But had it ever any chance of success? For an astonishing fact emerges. With a single exception, none of the conspirators – Stohrer, Hoyningen-Huene and Schellenberg in the German camp; Beigbeder, Don Ramón, Don Miguel, Don Eduardo, Don Nicolás and Don Angel in the Spanish camp; Captain Catela and Ricardo Espírito Santo in the Portuguese camp – appear to have believed in Ribbentrop's plan. They did not think it likely to come off. Furthermore, most of them did not want it to come off. But they all had their reasons for going along with it, for pretending to take it seriously, for appearing confident of its success.

First, the German envoys. Stohrer and Hoyningen-Huene are very different men: Hoyningen-Huene the cold, rationalistic former state prosecutor and constitutional lawyer, the childless, *fin de race* aristocrat, the cynical, jaded cosmopolitan, the trimmer who will do anything for a quiet life; Stohrer a far more vigorous and energetic character, a massive, earthy South German whose family have quite recently become rich and titled, a man with ideas and convictions, courageous enough to take risks on behalf of Jews and others but skilful enough to stay where he is. But they react to the plot in the same way. Stohrer thinks it 'idiotic'. Hoyningen-Huene bursts out laughing when he tells Teixeira de Sampaio that the Duke is to be 'our first President of the Great British Republic'. Both are fearful of a scandal which may harm Germany's comfortable relations with Spain and Portugal; but they cannot ignore their instructions. They take measures designed more to illustrate their zeal than to further the plot, which they describe in reports of a kind they have become quite used to writing in the past few years – couched in the prevailing jargon and full of details likely to appeal to the peculiar mentality of their master.

Hoyningen-Huene, to be sure, only reports on the matter when he has to – when Lisbon is buzzing with rumours after the announcement of the Duke's appointment, when Schellenberg appears. Stohrer on the other hand sends a regular stream of reports; his aim is to spin things out and so keep Ribbentrop's mind off even more nefarious schemes; and yet, amidst all the optimism and high drama of his telegrams, he manages never to say anything whatever on the point which is at the core of the matter – the willingness of the Spaniards to hold the Duke by force. So long as they are judged only by their telegrams, the envoys are safe. The awful moment for them is when Schellenberg comes on the scene. Will they be caught out, and will things now be for real?

But, as it happens, Schellenberg too has a vested interest in the failure of the plot. A clever young man on the make, living in a world of ceaseless conspiracy and in-fighting, he at first finds himself in a complicated position: Ribbentrop will not forgive him if he fails, his own boss Heydrich will not forgive him if he succeeds, his enemy Canaris will take advantage if he makes a mess of things. But Schellenberg quickly realizes that Ribbentrop is virtually alone when it comes to the abduction side of the plot. He suspects (rightly, as it turns out) that Hitler has only been half-persuaded to sanction the use of force if deceit and persuasion fail. He senses the mood of Ribbentrop's own diplomatic agents in the Peninsula. When it becomes clear that only by snatch-and-grab will the Duke be brought to Spain, Schellenberg – while fobbing Berlin off with reports of his 'scare-manœuvres' – connives at the failure of his own mission. In the memoirs, this leads to some bizarre exchanges: Schellenberg asking his Portuguese agent Catela (who is a double agent anyway) to step up the local security and so help him fail respectably; Heydrich finally remarking on the affair that Schellenberg 'carried it off rather shrewdly' – congratulating him, in effect, on failing so well.

Schellenberg and the envoys are united in their contempt for Ribbentrop. All recognize his plan as the product of a mind immersed in fantasy – as do the Foreign Minister's own entourage as represented by Erich Kordt.* Schellenberg knows that the scare-manœuvres are just the sort

---

* It would be particularly interesting to know about Weizsäcker's reactions. His diaries – probably edited and rewritten towards the end of the war – maintain a discreet silence on the subject. But neither the diaries nor his memoirs are silent on the subject of Ribbentrop, for whom no terms of scorn are too great, and who 'served up to Hitler jargon which would not be out of place in an historical novel' (*Memoirs*, p. 108).

of thing which will impress a man like Ribbentrop (whereas Heydrich, who receives copies of the reports, will see through them). In his dream world, Ribbentrop is strikingly isolated. He barks out orders, but is incapable of seeking advice or of discussing the matter with anyone. No one is allowed to contradict him, but no one trusts or respects him apart from Hitler. Stohrer can talk about the affair with his local friend Serrano Suñer, a man with whom he shares certain cultural and intellectual values, in a way in which he never could with the bombastic and irresponsible wine merchant in Berlin.

Serrano Suñer and Beigbeder are again very different men: Beigbeder the soldier-mystic, the daring romantic, a legend for his eccentricities and beloved of all Madrid's diplomats; Serrano Suñer the cold intellectual, the much-feared post-Civil War police minister, the admirer of Mussolini who is obsessed by public order, seen by his numerous enemies as Franco's sinister *eminence grise*. Once friends, they are now rivals in Spain's internal politics. Serrano Suñer wants the Germans to win; Beigbeder does not. Beigbeder appears to have a certain admiration for the Duke of Windsor and to harbour some hopes of him as an eirenicon; Serrano Suñer does not. Beigbeder sets the whole thing off by suggesting to the Germans that they get hold of the Duke in Spain. By the time the Germans get serious, however, they no longer trust Beigbeder; they fear (with some reason) that anything they tell him will get back to the British Ambassador. So they turn to Serrano Suñer. But the reactions of the two ministers are the same. Both are Spanish patriots; both are alarmed to see Europe's most powerful army arrive on their frontier; both recognize in Germany's obsession with the Duke of Windsor a useful means of appeasing the Germans and keeping the war out of Spain. For both of them the plot is a means to an end, and neither takes his role in it very seriously. Don Ramón finds it all 'puerile'; he willingly goes along with Stohrer's (or, as he suspects, the Baroness von Stohrer's) plans for the despatch of emissaries (and what emissaries!), but looks upon the whole proceeding as a charade. Beigbeder, out to ingratiate himself with the Germans who are already wary of him, promises that he will do 'everything possible' to keep the Duke in Spain; he goes so far as to offer the Duke indefinite Spanish hospitality, but after that he just pretends. He allows the Duke to slip safely out of Spain, concocting a cock-and-bull story to explain his 'escape'. He claims to have urged the Duke not to go to the Bahamas, through Bermejillo and Nicolás Franco. But Tiger in fact ridicules the idea that the Duke will be in danger in the Bahamas, while

Don Nicolás is playing an outrageous double game – telling the Italians and the Portuguese of his efforts to dissuade the Duke from leaving Europe, while making sure that the British also know what is going on.

The main concern of the Spanish ministers is that there should be a steady flow of reports to Berlin recounting their zeal in accommodating the Germans. The same is probably true of Ricardo Espírito Santo. He too is out to curry favour with the Germans, for business rather than political reasons. He therefore keeps Hoynigen-Huene informed of the Duke's table talk; he encourages the Duke to stay on at his house (which will also redound to Ricardo's social prestige); and he makes some effort (or backs up other people's efforts) to persuade the Duke not to leave. By passing the German message to the Duke just before his departure, he obliges his friend the German Minister and notches up a great favour with the Nazis. But he exaggerates: when the Duke finally sees the German telegrams, nothing will surprise him more than the role they give Ricardo. In truth, one wonders how much Ricardo counts on the success of German plans. He is close not only to Hoynigen-Huene, who takes a cynical view of the plot, but also to Salazar,* who will not tolerate anything happening to the Duke in Portugal. And Ricardo has no interest in the war coming to a rapid end. He is making a fortune out of it. So long as it continues and Portuguese neutrality is maintained, he will become one of the richest men in Europe.

Of all the people in the plot, only three would be really happy to see it succeed – Don Miguel, Don Angel, and Eduardo de Montarco. These men are friends, 'old shirt' *falangistas*, bound together by their early days in the movement, their Civil War experiences (all having tasted both prison and the battlefield), and by a *machismo* illustrated by their common interest in drinking, womanizing and bullfighting. They hope for and are confident of an Axis victory – and they would be delighted to see the Duke of Windsor on the Axis side, however he might be got there. They believe that 'the Prince thinks like us'. With their fascist creed, they are prepared to contemplate unorthodox solutions to the world's problems; believing that the end justifies the means, they have no scruples about luring the Duke into their hands by deceit. They want to replace the Franco régime with one more to their own liking; the success of the plot, they feel, may somehow serve their cause. And yet, for all their idealistic enthusiasm, at least two of them are not lacking in scepticism as to the

* According to Franco Nogueira they met once a week, Salazar relying heavily on Ricardo for information about foreign countries.

chances of success. Montarco – who is also a hard-headed landowner and Serrano Suñer's aide – wonders whether the Duke will do anything so unpatriotic as to abandon his own side. He has no illusions as to the persuasive powers of Miguel. He thinks it all a bit of fun which will probably not result in anything; he gladly lends his house to the plot, but does not even bother to go and get it ready for guests who may never come. As for Alcázar de Velasco, he starts off full of optismism but, possessing a typical 'spy-complex', immediately begins to suspect hostile intrigues from every side – from Don Nicolás who is a British agent, from the Duchess of Windsor who is an American agent, from his own chief Canaris, from the spy-mistresses who will doubtless be squeezing secrets out of everyone else involved.

There remains Don Miguel. Of all the conspirators, only he seems suffused with blithe confidence. He throws himself heart and soul into the plot in the excited expectation that it will realize its aims – and his own. With his mood of drama and intrigue, his faith in his 'historic mission', his secret meetings with his cronies in Madrid, his grandiose plan for the Duke to issue a peace manifesto in Spain, his gallant touch in getting his mistress included in the plot, his absurd dream that the Duke's installation as England's royal dictator will lead to his own ascent in Spain, he thinks and behaves like a character in a boy's adventure story. And in truth, Miguel is no more than a dreamy adventurer, 'a great silly lovable irresponsible child'. If the Stohrers propose him for his role, if most of the others are delighted to see him in it, it is largely because his involvement is liable to reduce the affair to the level of a harmless joke.

With the men required to carry it out either lukewarm or sceptical or incompetent, what is really surprising about the plot is not that it fails but that it gets as far as it does. For a moment, it is facilitated by the state of mind of the Duke of Windsor.

According to the evidence which it has been possible to discover and which is presented in this book, there is little if anything to support the view that the Duke 'flirted' or 'intrigued' with the Nazis in the summer of 1940. Somewhat unwisely, he obtained through Spanish offices the dispensation of the occupant of Paris in two domestic matters; and somewhat indiscreetly, he talked in private of his preference for a negotiated peace. But that preference was dictated not by love of the enemy but by fear that his country would be defeated; and so long as the war continued, he wished above all to serve his country. Hence his reluctance to return to England as 'a refugee with nothing to do'; and hence his unhesitating acceptance of the

Bahamas governorship. By the time that appointment is announced, however, the Duke finds himself oppressed by the atmosphere of Portugal, by the intensive security with which he is surrounded, by his virtual confinement over a period to a remote seaside villa. He feels 'almost a prisoner' and 'surrounded by spies'. He is beginning to experience classic symptoms of paranoia induced by anxiety and isolation. The seemingly endless cataclysm of war fills him with depression. What he perceives as the vindictiveness of his family and his inability to return to his country continue to prey upon his mind. His original euphoria about going to the Bahamas has evaporated; he now regards that prospect 'with profound gloom and despondency'. At least he is able to keep his mind occupied with all the preparations for his new post (very royal and somewhat over-elaborate preparations); and he has one thing to look forward to. On the way to 'Saint Helena', he and his wife will be passing through New York, still gay and neutral, which she has not seen since 1933 and he not since 1928. That will be a treat for them before they are exiled for the duration to a third-class island colony.

Then, on 18 July, comes news from London. The Duke will not be allowed to pass through America on his way to the Bahamas. Nor will he be allowed to re-enlist his batman. (It is difficult for non-royal persons to understand the importance royalty attaches to having the right retainers and being properly dressed in their public life. It is similar to the importance the actor attaches to his make-up, costume and props.) For the Duke, whose current mental state distorts his view of the world, this is the final straw. He feels 'messed around long enough', 'sorely tempted to chuck the whole project and retire entirely from the contest'. And it is at this moment – when the Duke is wondering whether he can face going to the Bahamas – that Miguel restates the Spanish Government's offer of a refuge in the South of Spain. True, Miguel is a silly person and much of what he says is not to be taken too seriously. He speaks of restoration in the event of Axis victory, which the Duke rejects out of hand.* He puts

* Miguel thinks the Duchess may be interested in the idea of a German-sponsored restoration; she seems to 'look thoughtful' when the idea is mentioned. On the other hand, Don Angel thinks she is trying to influence her husband in exactly the opposite direction. In fact it is unlikely that the Duchess affected the Duke's judgment in the matter one way or the other. She exercised great authority over him, but it was authority of a purely domestic nature. His great personal choices he made alone: she had been unable to dissuade him from making the most important decision of his life. The Duchess's role in this story is a subordinate one. The Germans were not interested in her, except in so far as they realized that he was devoted to her and was unlikely to go anywhere or do anything without her. She is mentioned by name in less than half the German telegrams. And yet she has a considerable indirect influence. It is largely because of her equivocal status (a

forward his peace manifesto project: if the Duke thinks about this, he does not do so for long. But Don Miguel also brings news of secret information possessed by his Government concerning a British plot against the Duke's safety. Such is the Duke's state of mind, such are his current feelings concerning the British authorities, that he is sufficiently alarmed by this news to be swayed for an instant by Miguel's suggestion that only in Spain will he be safe.

Meanwhile Hitler has made his *Friedensrede* at the Reichstag. This gives the Duke food for thought (though one may question whether he writes to the King to suggest the dismissal of the existing British Government, as Axis propaganda claims and Hitler apparently believes). He longs for peace. He is in favour of Anglo–German negotiations. He regards Great Britain's continued resistance as a dangerous gamble which may result in prolonged misery and final disaster. Up to now he has done no more than express his views (no doubt too freely) to friends; but now he begins to wonder whether he may not have a role to play. This notion is encouraged by the plausible Nicolás Franco, who assures him that, in the event of England's defeat, only he can save the British Empire. Don Nicolás urges the Duke to return to Spain so as to be at hand to fulfil this destiny, and helps him obtain travel papers for Spain (which the Duke has in fact applied for some days earlier in connection with a projected visit to La Cröe which he has since abandoned).

The Duke has no idea that the Germans will be waiting for him if he comes to Spain: this is something which Miguel never reveals to him (if he knows himself). He is in the dark about Ribbentrop's plan to confront him in the Peninsula – which Ribbentrop is determined he should not suspect until actually in German hands. It cannot possibly occur to him that a mission such as Schellenberg's is in preparation, that it is planned to put him under the 'protection' of German commandos as soon as he crosses the frontier, that there is a notion of having him imprisoned in Spain if he proves unco-operative or even of abducting him if he remains in Portugal. All he knows is that the hospitable Spanish Government have offered to put at his disposal a mediæval *palacio* in the Andalusian mountains. This he sees as a possible refuge where he may 'retire entirely from the con-

matter which means infinitely more to him than to her) that he does not return to England that summer. Her obsession with recovering the contents of her two houses leads to all kinds of complications. Above all, her angry reactions to events – enshrined in the letter she writes to her aunt on 15 July – encourage the Duke in his sense of grievance.

test', where he may 'keep himself outside events, following developments from afar'. In the vision which is hesitantly forming in his muddled brain, and will hover there for a few days before vanishing, Spain represents not danger but a safe haven, not entanglement with the Germans but an opportunity of putting himself beyond both sides in the affray, of making himself a free agent who may possibly come forward eventually as a go-between. If one thing spoils this prospect, it is the danger that Spain may abandon her neutrality and join the Axis; but he is promised that, in such case, he would be able to move on to 'England or any neutral country'.

In these circumstances, the Duke gives Don Miguel and Don Nicolás to understand that he *may* be prepared to go to Spain. But he does not commit himself (as strikingly evidenced by the fact that he carries on with his preparations for the Bahamas). Instead he demands more information – on his position if Spain enters the war, on the secret information which the Spanish Government possess about his safety, on where and how he may cross the Spanish frontier. Miguel writes to reassure him on these matters and urge him to take to flight without delay; but the despatch of the letter is held up while Schellenberg sets up his operations. By the time Don Angel delivers the letter, it is too late. The moment of hesitation has passed. Everything has changed. The Duke's row with the British Government has resolved itself. He has come to the conclusion that there is 'no possibility' of his 'intervening in political events, as he would only come forward if he were convinced that there was overwhelming support for him to do so'. Having planted his spies at the *Boca do Inferno*, the first thing Schellenberg learns is that the Duke has abandoned any intention he may have had of going to Spain: *Willi will nicht*. Meanwhile Don Nicolás has been busy betraying the plot to Eccles, while Catela has probably been betraying it to Lourenço: the British and Portuguese authorities have thus been alerted. Monckton is about to arrive, to warn the Duke of the dangers which surround him and make sure he sails on time.

The plotters carry on plotting, as they must be seen to. Don Angel and Don Nicolás attempt to reason with the Duke – but to no effect. Schellenberg carries out his scare-manœuvres – these ensure that the Duke and Duchess will have no peace while they remain in Portugal, but do not affect their resolve to sail. Miguel comes on his second mission – but his exhortations are nullified by those of Monckton. Hardly any time now remains. Only two possible measures are left which may still bring the

Duke into German hands – direct invitation or abduction. The idea of abduction is seriously considered. The Duke is saved by Schellenberg's cold feet; but he also saves himself. For at the last moment, in his talks with Don Angel and Ricardo, he drops the very hint the Germans have been waiting for all along – that he has 'given consideration to the possibility that the role of an intermediary may fall to him'.

But what in fact does the Duke say? He holds out the prospect of participation in negotiations – but at once makes it clear that this is a vague and distant prospect, that he believes 'the present moment inopportune for him to manifest himself on the political scene'. Only if two conditions are satisfied will he consider playing a role. First, his country must be ready for negotiations – and at the moment, as he tells Don Angel, 'the situation is by no means hopeless', therefore 'no possibility of peace exists'. Secondly, he must have the full confidence of his country in whatever role he is to play. He will not carry on 'negotiations ... contrary to the orders of his Government'; to do so would lose him 'all prestige'. Only if he does his duty – if he goes to serve in the Bahamas as he has promised – can he command the respect which will be essential if one day he is to perform greater tasks. He is a soldier and must obey. Patriotism may one day impel him to return to Europe; for the moment it obliges him to go to the Bahamas. And if one day he is to be the man to restore peace to the continent, all the more reason for his leaving it now.

That Britain desire talks and give him 'overwhelming support' to conduct them – such were the only circumstances under which the Duke saw himself as a peacemaker. They were circumstances which would never materialize. Britain fought on and survived. In the summer of 1940 she was saved by the weather, by German dilatoriness in attacking, by the morale of her people and the heroism of her pilots. In the summer of 1941 she was saved by Hitler's decision to attack Russia. By 1942 the United States too was at her side; and though the Allies came perilously close to disaster that year, theirs now was the long-term advantage. By the end of 1943 their victory was inevitable: their war aim was Germany's unconditional surrender.

But what if things had been different? What if some accident had befallen Churchill, and his successor had lacked his rock-like determination? What if Roosevelt had been defeated for the presidency in November 1940, and America had returned towards isolationism? What if Hitler had decided not to attack Russia in 1941? Without Churchill, without allies, without Lend–Lease and the American convoys, without her

Middle East oil supplies which would soon have been overrun, Britain could not have continued to resist for long. Sooner or later she would have been forced to sue for peace.

Would the Duke of Windsor have been a suitable man to negotiate that peace on behalf of England? This is a speculative question which everyone must answer for himself. But one fact cannot be doubted. Hitler did not cease to regard the Duke as destined to bring about a peaceful settlement between England and Germany. On 14 October 1941 Major Hayne D. Boyden, US Naval Attaché at Havana, sent an intelligence report to Washington to say that

> at a conference at the German Legation on 1 October 1941, in discussing the Duke of Windsor, they said 'He is no enemy of Germany'. When he was in Germany he had contact with Hitler and he is the only person with whom Hitler would confer in any negotiations of peace or armistice when it became necessary. Hitler well knows that Edward at present cannot work in a matter that would appear to be against his country, and he does not urge it. But when the proper moment arrives he will be the only one person capable of directing the destiny of England.[1]

In Germany, it had long been the order of the day that the Duke was the one Englishman whose name was to be free from all attack. In May 1941, Goebbels had come across some recently reported remarks of the Duke (to the effect that in modern warfare there were no victors) which he immediately recognized as having great anti-British propaganda value. 'We shall not use it', he wrote in his diary, 'to avoid discrediting him.'[2] That was just before the invasion of Russia. But as late as the autumn of 1943 Hitler, in his private notes, could still write:

> England for the good of the world must remain unchanged in her present form.
> Consequently, after final victory, we must effect a reconciliation.
> Only the King must go – in his place the Duke of Windsor. With him we will make a permanent treaty of friendship instead of a peace treaty.[3]

Such were German hopes of the Duke.* But what of the Duke's own intentions? To what extent, if at all, did he see himself in the role which

---

* The Duke was seen as a peace hope not just by the Nazi leaders but also by some members of the anti-Nazi resistance. In August 1941, Ulrich von Hassell, one of Nazism's most passionate secret opponents (also a friend of Eberhard von Stohrer), visited like-minded friends in Hungary and asked the Archduke Albrecht – earmarked as that country's future Regent – how he thought the war would end. 'He banks on the Duke of Windsor,' recorded Hassell, 'who he believes is holding himself in readiness.' (Haddell, *Zum anderen Deutschland* [Zurich, 1946], p. 225.)

Hitler envisaged for him? In order to answer this question, one must examine his reaction to the only communication (and it was an unsolicited and indirect communication) which he is known to have received from the Germans during the Second World War – the message claiming to come 'from an authoritative German source' which was delivered to him by Ricardo just a few hours before he sailed, urging him to remain in Europe to facilitate 'the restoration of good relations between England and Germany', holding out the prospect of restoration to the throne, and asking him, should he 'insist on leaving in spite of everything', at least to maintain 'some channel of oral communication' through Ricardo 'whereby we might continue to keep in contact and, should the occasion arise, negotiate'. For want of better evidence, one must analyse Hoynigen–Huene's report of 1 August which contains the Duke's purported reply to Ricardo – a suspect document to be sure, a third-hand account.

As revealed by this report, the Duke's attitude at first appears to be unchanged from recent days. He will not remain in Europe at the Germans' request. Nor does he appear to be interested in restoration. He is willing 'to co-operate at a suitable time in the establishment of peace', but there is 'as yet no inclination in England for an approach to Germany'. He must therefore 'follow the orders of his Government', otherwise there will be 'a scandal' which will 'deprive him of his prestige in England'. But the report then goes on to say that, should a climate arise in England favourable to peace, the Duke

> would be ready to return immediately. To bring this about there were two possibilities. Either England would yet call upon him, which he considered to be entirely possible, or Germany would express the desire to negotiate with him. In both cases he was prepared for any personal sacrifice and would make himself available without the slightest personal ambition. He would remain in continuous communication with his former host and had agreed with him upon a code word, upon receiving which he would immediately come back over.

Such is the consoling message which Ricardo claims to have heard from the Duke and with which Hoynigen–Huene concludes his otherwise disappointing report to Ribbentrop. How is one to reconcile it with the Duke's other reported statements at that moment – that England's position is 'not by any means hopeless', that as a soldier he must obey, that he cannot conduct negotiations behind his Government's back, that he can only talk peace at his country's behest, and only so long as he has kept his hands clean by avoiding all association with his country's enemies? If he is prepared to return to Europe later on at the German request, why is he leaving now when the Germans are requesting him to stay? Or is he merely saying something he does not really mean in order to dupe the enemy and make a safe escape? Or does he say nothing of the sort, the words being put into his mouth either by Ricardo in order to ingratiate himself with the Germans, or by Hoynigen–Huene in order to conceal from Ribbentrop the total failure of the plot? It is impossible to know exactly what passed that 1 August between the banker and the ex-King. Nevertheless, if one considers that encounter in the context of the story as a whole, a pattern emerges – a pattern which may provide the key to the mystery.

From the moment the Duke arrives in Madrid to the moment he sails from Lisbon, suggestions are made to him concerning his future by neutrals who are either personal friends of his or important official personages. It is suggested that he remain in Spain rather than return to England, that he return to Spain rather than go to the Bahamas, that he flee to Spain for his own safety, that he stay in Europe in order to restore peace to the continent, that he make a public announcement calling for an end to the war, that he prepare to be restored to the English throne. Only the last of these suggestions does he reject outright. In all the other cases he begins with an equivocal reply, which encourages his interlocutor to hope that he may be prepared to go along with what is proposed. He does not say yes – but he does not say no. He reacts in this way (which for him is typical) for a whole host of probable reasons. First, because his royal training has conditioned him to respond to whatever is said to him (however ridiculous) with a polite air of sympathetic interest. Secondly, because in the dangerous atmosphere of July 1940 it may be prudent to humour all comers. Thirdly, because he is still something of an *enfant terrible* who is inclined to keep everyone guessing about his intentions until the last moment. Fourthly, because his perplexed and anguished mood at that moment makes him vaguely and briefly amenable to suggestions to which he would not normally give much thought. Finally, there is the fact that the future is wholly uncertain. No one can know quite what will happen – and it is as well to be prepared for all events. Just as at the beginning of July, when he leaves Spain for Portugal, he is unsure as to whether he will be returning to England, so at the beginning of August, when he sails for the Bahamas, he has no means of knowing whether, in a few weeks time, his country will be free and undefeated, or *in extremis* and suing for peace. Therefore it is as well not to reject categorically certain possibilities which, however unacceptable they may seem at the moment, may have a positive value should certain eventualities arise. It is these factors, in my view, which jointly form the underlying motive of the Duke's responses, and which jointly explain the apparent enthusiasm with which he greets Beigbeder's offer of the Palace at Ronda, the apparent seriousness with which he considers the exhortations of Don Miguel, Don Angel and Don Nicolás, the fact that he ruminates for forty-eight hours upon the plan for flight before rejecting it. Equally they explain the fact that, confronted by Ricardo's 'German message' on 1 August, he seems in effect to reply: 'Under the circumstances which exist, my duty must be to leave now for the Bahamas; but should circumstances change, I may have to ask myself again where my duty lies.'

By nodding and looking thoughtful and interested and saying that he will reflect upon the ideas which are put to him – a procedure which is second nature to him – the Duke keeps everyone happy and keeps his options open while committing himself to nothing. But the agents who are responsible for the success of the plot cannot afford to report these insubstantial responses for what they are. They must be seen to deliver the goods, at the risk of wholesale exaggeration and distortion. In the telegrams, therefore, the vaguest comments are seized upon and magnified into the most categorical assertions. Thus it is that the Duke's friendly but non-committal assurances, designed to string along his Spanish and Portuguese acquaintances, become translated into bold declarations of intention which wildly raise German hopes. As Erich Kordt writes in summing up the affair: 'Who had duped whom?'

It is in this sense that the episode assumes a place of importance in the history of the Second World War. By providing raw material for sanguine reports, the Duke unwittingly encouraged Hitler's hopes and illusions concerning him in a remarkable degree; and his presence in Europe, while it lasted, appears to have had a tantalizing effect on Nazi policy. The consequences may possibly have been fateful. Throughout that July, Hitler hesitated to order the attack on Great Britain – thus giving the British a chance to regroup their forces and survive. Were his hopes of the Duke one of the principal causes of his hesitation? What one can say for certain is that it was not until 1 August – the day that the Duke sailed from Europe – that the Führer issued his Directive No. 17 ordering the Luftwaffe 'to overcome the English Air Force with all means at its disposal and in the shortest possible time'; and that it was not until 2 August that Ribbentrop ordered Stohrer to work for 'Spain's early entry into the war'. And one must remember too that Hitler's guiding motive in switching the brunt of his force against Russia in 1941 was his conviction that, with Russia defeated, England – the country he most wanted as an ally – would come to terms. Would he have held this view had he not continued to harbour such hopes of the Duke of Windsor?

There is one further and final piece of evidence which must be considered. It is the last of the German telegrams on the subject of the Duke of Windsor in the summer of 1940; and it too is a despatch of Hoynigen-Huene reporting an account of Ricardo. Dated 15 August – the day the Duke and Duchess sailed to the Bahamas from Bermuda – it reads:

> The confidant has just received a telegram from the Duke in Bermuda, asking him to report as soon as it may become necessary for him to act. Should anything be sent in reply?[4]

If true, this makes no sense. For why should the Duke take the risk of sending Ricardo a telegram from Bermuda – with that colony's enormous and vigilant censorship and intelligence establishments – merely in order to repeat to him something he had already told him less than two weeks before? If, on the other hand, Ricardo had been distorting the truth on 1 August when he assured the Germans that the Duke would return on receipt of 'a message', one can well see why he might resort to a second distortion in order to back up his earlier story – why he might, for example, try to put an outlandish meaning on a telegram which in fact concerned another subject.

For the strange fact is that the Duke *was* at that moment 'in continuous communication with his former host' about a certain matter – and would continue to be so for many weeks to come. It was a matter which obsessed him on his departure from Europe – to such an extent that he left Gray Phillips behind in Portugal to try to sort it out. Concerning the same matter he was in constant touch with Tiger at the Spanish Foreign Ministry, and throughout the autumn would beg the assistance of numerous Spanish, Portuguese, English, American and French officials. But that matter had nothing to do with the peace of Europe, still less with the Duke's political future. Just as in 1936 the Nazis found it unimaginable that the sovereign destined to bring about Anglo–German *rapprochement* should give up his throne for love, so in August 1940 they would have found it impossible to believe that the mind of the man earmarked as 'our first President of the Great British Republic' was preoccupied by ... the problem of getting the chef with the trunks from La Cröe, and the maid with the linen from Paris, to Lisbon and thence to the Bahamas.

There was no mystery about the Pinaudiers: they were stuck at Antibes, unable to move with their cargo owing to the petrol shortage, waiting for the lorry which Tiger was trying to have sent out from Spain. But what had happened to Mademoiselle Moulichon? Prevented by the Germans from leaving Paris for Portugal at the end of July, she had been deprived of her trunks and sent off to visit her mother in a remote part of unoccupied central France. Not until mid-August was she able to return to the capital. She had learnt that her employers had sailed without her and she had received no message, but she was nevertheless determined to fulfil the mission with which she had been entrusted, to convey the Windsor linen to Lisbon for shipment to the Bahamas. She demanded that the Germans release her baggage and allow her to proceed on her journey. After some days, a distinguished German called to see her with a large official car and a van containing the trunks, explaining that he was to escort her to the Spanish frontier; she imagined this to be some German cousin of the Duke of Windsor. They set off in silence for Bordeaux, where they spent the night at a house. On waking the next morning, Mademoiselle Moulichon found the gentleman gone, the car and van gone, and the house deserted. But the trunks were still there, and somehow she managed to make her way with them to the border at Hendaye, 120 miles distant.

By this time, Gray Phillips and Ricardo in Lisbon and Tiger in Madrid had finally succeeded in getting the Pinaudiers to Portugal with the trunks from La Cröe; but of Mademoiselle Moulichon they had heard nothing. Endless enquiries had produced no result. Early in September Phillips sailed to join his master, leaving Tiger to continue the search. Anxious telegrams arrived from the Bahamas: 'Please ask your friends to release Marguerite quickly as maid situation desperate.' Tiger went north to San Sebastian to conduct investigations on the spot.

Mademoiselle Moulichon had meanwhile arrived at Hendaye at the same moment as the private train of King Carol of Romania, who had abdicated and was in flight with his mistress Lupescu. With her tale of royal baggage, Mademoiselle Moulichon was taken to be an errant member of his party; she was detained, she was released, she was put on a train to Paris without her luggage, she managed to get off it and return to Hendaye, where she was reunited with the trunks but still unable to cross the frontier. Further days of miserable waiting followed. Then, one afternoon, an official called out: *'Laissez passer la femme de chambre de la Duchesse de Windsor!'* – and there was Tiger to escort her over the bridge to Spain. 'You cannot know how much I have suffered over the whole thing,' wrote Tiger to the Duke from Madrid after he had safely put maid and trunks on a train for Portugal. 'Anyhow all is over now thank God!'

On arrival in Portugal Mademoiselle Moulichon's papers were found not to be in order and she was flung into prison. Two days later Ricardo discovered her whereabouts and telephoned the British Embassy, who sent an official to have her released and a van to take the luggage. In Lisbon, she was given permission to remain for thirty days; after a desperate search for a sea passage, she and the trunks sailed for New York on the thirtieth day, arriving in the Bahamas at the end of November, a bizarre postscript to a phantasmagorical tale of wartime conspiracy.[5]

Appendix I
The Publication of the German Documents

In the latter stages of the Second World War, the bulk of the archives of the German Foreign Ministry were evacuated to safe hiding-places in the Harz Mountains. In April 1945 over 400 tons of these archives (which their guardians had been ordered but refused to destroy) were captured by the advancing US First Army under General Hodges. They were amassed at Marburg Castle, where a team of experts rapidly sifted through them, bringing any material which seemed to be of particular sensitivity or importance to the attention of General Eisenhower's headquarters. Among such material were the telegrams of June–August 1940 concerning the Duke of Windsor affair. These were examined by Eisenhower's intelligence staff, who concluded 'that there was no possible value to them, that they were obviously concocted with some idea of promoting German propaganda and weakening Western resistance, and that they were totally unfair to the Duke'. It was therefore decided to remove them from Marburg and give them to the US Ambassador in London, John G. Winant, for transmission for safe keeping to the British Government.

In London, the file was given the most secret classification and regarded by the few who knew about it, in the words of the new Foreign Secretary Ernest Bevin, as 'a 'ot potato'. It was studied by Churchill, by Attlee who had just succeeded him in the premiership, and by King George VI. The King contented himself with the reflection that, if the documents were ever to be made public, his brother should be given due warning. The politicians took a sterner view. 'Although clearly little or no credence can be placed in the statements made', Attlee wrote to Churchill on 25 August 1945, 'nevertheless I feel sure that you will agree that the publication of these documents might do the greatest possible harm.' Churchill did agree: he 'earnestly trusted' that it would be possible 'to destroy all traces of these German intrigues'. When, therefore, an Anglo–American agreement was signed in June 1946 providing for the publication of selections of captured German diplomatic documents 'on the basis of the highest scholarly objectivity', the file on the Duke was not included in the

230

archive given over to the British and American historians entrusted with the task.

There things might have rested but for the efforts of John Wheeler-Bennett, the British editor-in-chief of the German documents. Having strong secret service links, he got wind of the held-back material; and he was determined (as he revealed in a volume of memoirs published after his death) that it should be released and published. With the connivance of three men – Bevin, his Permanent Under-Secretary Sir Orme Sargent, and the King's Principal Private Secretary Sir Alan Lascelles (who detested the Duke of Windsor and who, Wheeler-Bennett tells us, proved 'entirely co-operative') – he managed to have a microfilm made and sent to his American counterpart, Ray Sontag.* Thus it was that, in 1953, the British Government learnt with great alarm that the documents which it had been imagined were safely out of reach in the most secret of archives were proposed to be published in the near future in the volume of *Documents on German Foreign Policy* dealing with the summer of 1940 – a volume whose editorship had been entirely entrusted to the Americans.

Churchill was now Prime Minister again and Eisenhower was President of the United States. On 27 June 1953 Churchill wrote to Eisenhower asking him 'to exert your power to prevent . . . publication' of the documents, which represented 'a Nazi-German intrigue to entangle and compromise a Royal Prince' and the 'historical importance' of which was 'negligible' since their allegations 'rest only on the assertions of German and pro-German officials in making the most of anything they could pick up'. If published, they might give the impression 'that the Duke was in close touch with German agents', whereas in fact 'it was because I foresaw that the Germans would try to entrap him verbally or even kidnap him' that Churchill had arranged the Bahamas post – which the Duke had accepted 'not without some personal risk', embarking for Nassau 'in spite of many threats'. Churchill urged the President 'to prevent the United States . . . from inflicting distress and injury upon one who has so long enjoyed their hospitality'. Eisenhower replied that he was 'completely astonished' to learn that a microfilm had been made of the documents he had taken such care to keep secret in 1945, and promised to look into the matter. In August 1953 Churchill brought the matter to the attention of the Cabinet, to whom he circulated a confidential print containing translations of the principal telegrams. He wanted to 'propose that publication be postponed for at least ten or twenty years' on the grounds that the papers would give 'pain to the Duke of Windsor' and an impression 'entirely disproportionate to their historical value'.

Churchill's solution was not possible, for by this time too many people knew about the documents and were talking. The general view of the Cabinet was that

* *Friends, Enemies and Sovereigns* (London, 1976), pp. 80ff. Wheeler-Bennett went on to become King George VI's official biographer, in which he displayed none of the mania for exposing the embarrassments of royal persons which he had displayed a few years earlier. He was made GCVO.

publication would be a lesser evil to endless public speculation. The voice which carried most weight was that of the Marquess of Salisbury, Lord President of the Council, who gave the opinion:

.... I must confess that I find them very harmless. The Duke was subjected to very heavy pressure from men, personal friends of his, who used every means of persuasion at their disposal, his personal resentment at his treatment by England, the Duchess' fears of the perils of a wartime journey across the Atlantic, and so on; yet he never allowed himself to be diverted from his determination to go to the Bahamas and take up an official position there. So far as the intense propaganda to which he was subjected influenced him at all, it was by skilfully flattering him into a belief that he could play an important part in restoring peace. But he never showed himself, even in the biassed reports of German agents, favourable to the victory of Germany. Personally, I should let the papers be published. I think that, by suppressing them, Her Majesty's Government will only give the impression that they are more damaging than they in fact are.

Apart from Churchill, two members of the Cabinet had special cause to know of the events described in the papers – Sir David Eccles, now Minister of Works, and Sir Walter Monckton, now Minister of Labour. Monckton was charged with going to Paris to apprise the Duke of the matter. It appears to have come to him as a complete surprise, and it was with astonishment that he seems to have read the telegrams, which he did later that year in the Cabinet Room at 10, Downing Street.

It proved possible to delay publication of the volume in question for four years. When it finally appeared on 29 July 1957, the British Government issued a statement to say that the German documents were 'necessarily a much-tainted source' and that the Duke had 'never wavered in his loyalty to the British cause'. The Duke put out his own statement to say:

While I was in Lisbon certain people, whom I afterwards discovered to be pro-Nazi sympathizers, did make definite efforts to persuade me to return to Spain and not to take up my appointment as Governor of the Bahamas. It was even suggested to me that there would be a personal risk to the Duchess and myself if we were to go to the Bahamas. At no time did I ever entertain any thought of complying with such a suggestion which I treated with the contempt it deserved.

Almost unanimously at that time, in England and in America, the press came out in support of the Duke of Windsor.

Appendix II
The Schellenberg Memoirs

There appears to be something of a controversy over the genuineness of Schellenberg's published memoirs, which David Irving describes as 'mutilated and ghostwritten'.* It is not easy to see why. There can be no doubt that Schellenberg started to draft memoirs in the last days of the war; that he continued to write or at least mentally plan them in the years that followed, during much of which time he was in captivity; and that in 1951, when he was released from prison and signed a contract with a Swiss publisher, he had a draft 'almost a thousand pages long'.† He subsequently received a certain amount of 'literary assistance' from two German journalists, Klaus Harpprecht and Gita Petersen, both of whom have written of their collaboration with him,‡ and whose task was to help him revise the form and not the substance of his recollections. The next version of the memoirs took account of their suggestions but was still in Schellenberg's own words, which were dictated daily into a tape recorder and then transcribed into a typescript. There is a record by a visiting journalist of Schellenberg reading out long passages from this typescript.§ Plans for further revision and early publication were dashed by Schellenberg's death from cancer in March 1952 at the age of forty-two: he had been at liberty for only nine months, hardly long enough, one might have said, for the wholesale rewriting of a large work. After a protracted interval a typescript purporting to be Schellenberg's materialized in London, where it was first published in a translated edition by André Deutsch in the autumn of 1956. A more heavily edited German edition was subsequently prepared by Gita Petersen, who was able to confirm that the German typescript now circulating appeared to be identical to the one on which she had briefly worked with Schellenberg six years earlier – except for one chapter concerning the last stage of the war. This typescript is now in the *Institut für Zeitgeschichte* in Munich under the reference ED 90. Those pages of the typescript which

* *Hitler's War* (London, 1977) p. xxii.
† Alan Bullock's introduction to *The Schellenberg Memoirs*, p. 16.
‡ In prefaces to the German edition (Cologne, 1959).
§ André Brissaud, *The Nazi Secret Service* (London, 1972).

concern the Duke of Windsor episode do not differ in any significant way from the published chapter in the English edition, except that the published version has been abbreviated by the removal of a small amount of circumstantial detail. As for Schellenberg's original handwritten draft, this is not easily decipherable, but there too the story appears to run along identical lines.

Assuming then that *The Schellenberg Memoirs* are truly the memoirs of Schellenberg, how much reliance can be put on them? All writings of professional spies are suspect – those whose careers involve the ceaseless practice of deception tend to have somewhat peculiar notions of truth – and Schellenberg is no exception. He had a decided talent for invention and fantasy. There is proof of a number of occasions when he rewrote his agents' reports before showing them to his superiors in order to make them sound better; and in the summer of 1945 he tried to persuade the Allies that Himmler had poisoned Hitler. But such things were done with a purpose; and what purpose would Schellenberg have had for distorting the record in his memoirs, memoirs which (as Alan Bullock has eloquently pointed out) represent an attempt not at self-exculpation but at reliving past glories?

The Duke of Windsor chapter is a useful test, for there are contemporary sources against which many statements can be checked – the telegrams, the Log and the final report. And two kinds of discrepancy are at once noticeable. First, the chronology of the memoirs is seriously wrong; Schellenberg describes as taking place over several weeks events which in fact (so the Log reveals) took no more than eight days. This is a common trick of memory. Secondly, when Schellenberg mentions very small details (details one might be expected to forget), he nearly always gets them wrong. In his memoirs, for example, he tells us that his flight to Madrid in July 1940 was by way of Lyons and Marseilles; in fact it was via Bourges. Here one feels Schellenberg is resorting to invention in order to fill gaps in his memory.

On the whole, however, the general tenor of the memoirs is convincing and borne out in many respects by the documents. Writing some years later without any access to papers, and with so much having happened in between, he describes with substantial accuracy the immediate aims of the plot, the plan to get the Duke to Spain, and the campaign of scare-manœuvres. If his chronology is false, his sequence of events is very nearly correct. There is really only one significant fact which appears in the memoirs but of which there is no trace in the documents – the abduction order. Even here (as I suggest in Chapter 12) the distortion may not be so great as one might imagine: even if Schellenberg was not expressly ordered to abduct, abduction was in the air, and he would surely have given thought (possibly long and anxious thought) to the problem of how to deal with (and possibly evade) an order if one came.

Finally, Schellenberg writes with an unerring touch when he comes to describe the characters of those with whom he has to deal. His portrait of Stohrer – the unhappy ambassador whose fight seems to be more against his own superiors than his country's enemies – is both vivid and accurate. His account of his first interview with Ribbentrop carries the ring of truth both in tone and content. Here is the summary of Ribbentrop which Schellenberg gives at the end of his chapter; it could hardly be bettered:

> Ribbentrop was a most peculiar type. I had an especially strong impression that day* that everything about him was studied and unnatural, without the slightest spontaneity. The rigidity of his expression, the visible effort it cost him to smile, the artificiality of his gestures, all this gave the impression of a man who had put on a mask, and I wondered what really went on behind it. It was completely impossible to move him or to convince him by logical discussion. If one attempted it, one soon had the feeling that he was not listening at all. Perhaps this sprang from a feeling of insecurity – a fear that he would not be able to maintain his own position and his own viewpoint. I knew that I would never be able to establish any real contact with this man.

* The day of the final interview at the end of the mission.

Appendix III
Schellenberg's Log, 24 July to 6 August 1940

[Document no. R 58/572 in Bundesarchiv, Koblenz]

Berlin, 7.8.40

Wednesday 24.7.40
Given assignment by Reich Foreign Minister.

Thursday 25.7.40
Take-off from Berlin-Staaken 10.00. Stopover at Bourges 13.50, resume flight 14.45. Arrive Madrid 18.00. Immediate discussion with v. Stohrer, who gets in touch once more with Spanish Interior Minister. Winzer is put in the picture. Dinner with Ambassador and discussion of further details. Short telegram to Reich Foreign Minister.

Friday 26.7.40
Exhaustive report to Berlin on proposed plan. Telegram to Lisbon. R.R.*Schellenberg flies at 4 from Madrid to Lisbon. Arrival there 19.00. Immediate contact with C as arranged by Winzer. C in full agreement and declares that he is able to guarantee security for 'Willi'. Interview with v. Hühne [*sic*]. Heineke and Böcker leave Madrid by car 15.30 and arrive 22.00 Badajoz where they spend the night.

Saturday 27.7.40
[Heineke and Böcker] leave Badajoz 8.30, Lisbon 13.30. Winzer arrives in Lisbon 19.00. Exhaustive discussion with C about protective service etc. for 'Willi'. Telegram to Madrid with request that it be repeated to Berlin. Winzer brings with him Spanish plan. (Frontier). Discussed with C.

Sunday 28.7.40
'Viktor' expected. Telegram to Madrid; 11.00 to Berlin. Two possibilities pointed

* *Regierungsrat* (Government Counsellor) – Schellenberg's civilian cover.

236

out and instructions requested. Discussion with C and Winzer. 'Viktor' saw 'Willi'. The latter asks for 48 hours to reflect.

Monday 29.7.40
Discussion with C and 'Willi'. Report via Madrid to Berlin. *'Willi' will nicht.* At 12.00 Madrid forwards report which Stohrer has given Berlin.

Tuesday 30.7.40
Winzer returns to Madrid at 8. Telegram to Berlin via Madrid 16.00 about the two above-mentioned possibilities, it now being established for certain that *Willi will nicht.* Build an infernal machine with C.

Wednesday 31.7.40
Short a.m. conference with Hühne. Winzer communicates 10.30, nothing of importance. Stohrer gives news of the things he has put in motion. Wife of high police official visits wife of 'Willi'. Primo de Rivera sees 'Willi'. Ribbentrop's answer arrives. v. Hühne acts upon it. During night of 1.8.40 7 point plan is elaborated – bunch of flowers, arrest of suspicious person on ship, list of fellow passengers to be handed over to Philipps [*sic*], information from highest level that offensive to begin in 4 days.

Thursday 1.8.40
Discussion with v. Hühne at 7 in the morning. Philipps will be attended to by one of our men. As a result of our initiative Willi's long-standing chauffeur will refuse to travel with him. Discussion with C. Suspect will be arrested on ship, who will let on about the bomb. The 7 point plan is put into effect. Holter* will be relieved of his gun by the Spanish [*sic*] police. Galde [?]. Miss Fox (San Sebastian). R.R. Schellenberg has discussion with v. Hühne and C. v. Hühne has discussion with F [?]. F has discussion with S [?], L [?] and Menkton [*sic*]. Primo de Rivera has meeting with Willi. Ship 'Exagilbur' [*sic*] sails 18.30.

Friday 2.8.40
Discussion with v. Hühne who reports on what has happened. Report of R.R. Schellenberg to Berlin (see telegram).

Saturday 3.8.40
Leave Lisbon by motor car 6. Cross frontier 11. Madrid 18.30. Brief discussion with v. Stohrer.

---

* Presumably the CID detective Holder.

Sunday 4.8.40
Winzer receives 1,000 escudos.

Monday 5.8.40
Take off Madrid 9.50. Barcelona arr. 11.45, dep. 12.50, Rome 4.15 [*sic*]. Kappler, Brüning, Gärtner, Dollmann.

Tuesday 6.8.40
Take off Rome 8. Venice arr. 9.50, dep. 10.25. Munich arr. 12.55, dep. 13.10. Berlin arr. 15.40.

Appendix IV
The Duke-Meets-Germans Stories

As the evidence presented in this book shows, the often-repeated accusation that the Duke of Windsor 'intrigued' or 'flirted' with the Nazis in the Peninsula has no sound basis in fact. He was closely involved with four Spaniards, one of whom was an ambassador, two of whom were old friends of his, and all of whom went to see him on behalf of their own Government; he talked somewhat freely to his Portuguese host and other neutrals about his desire for peace; and, through Spanish offices, he obtained German dispensation in two matters which were purely domestic. Through no initiative of his own, he received just before departure an informal message purporting to come 'from an authoritative German source', to which he gave an informal reply. Before he received that message there is nothing to show that he had engaged in any political contact with the Germans or even knew of their interest in him: Ribbentrop was determined that he should not know, and he was 'astonished' when Miguel suggested that they might want to restore him to the throne. Nor is there any proof that, when he briefly entertained the notion of returning to Spain, it was with the idea of meeting Germans there; on the contrary, he wished to be assured that, if Spain joined the Axis, he would be able to leave for 'England or any neutral country'. It is therefore misleading to say the least that Frances Donaldson, the Duke's somewhat hostile biographer, should have entitled her chapter on the subject 'Encounter with the Germans'; or that Sir John Wheeler-Bennett, the man most responsible for the release of the telegrams, should have described those telegrams in his memoirs as concerning 'the relations which had existed between the Nazis and the Duke of Windsor in Madrid and Lisbon during the summer of 1940'.*

However, rumour knows no bounds, and much talk continues to circulate to the effect that, not only did the Duke make active efforts to get in touch with the enemy that summer, but that he physically encountered Germans then. It has specifically been alleged that he met Hoynigen-Huene† and that he met Schellenberg.‡

* Wheeler-Bennett, *Friends, Enemies and Sovereigns*, p. 80.
† G. Bocca, *The Life and Death of Harry Oakes* (London, 1959).
‡ Peter Allen, *The Crown and the Swastika* (London, 1983).

Credence is lent to the Hoynigen-Huene story by the fact that no less a person than Ricardo Espírito Santo was fond of claiming in later years that he had organized a conference at the *Boca do Inferno* consisting of the Duke, the Minister and himself. This is what he told a journalist in the 1950s (though he later retracted the story); and this is what he also told one of his daughters at some stage. There are also a number of persistent witnesses in Lisbon who claim to have seen the Duke wander in broad daylight into the German Legation there – which then happened most conveniently to be only a few hundred yards from the British Embassy.*

Such a meeting would no doubt have been interesting. All one can say is that there is no hint of it in the Minister's reports to Berlin (and we seem to have all of them, judging by the fact that each telegram refers to the previous despatch on the same subject); that it would have been absolutely contrary to Ribbentrop's instructions (which were that under no circumstances was the Duke to be alerted to German interest in him); and that the advantage of such a meeting (and it is hard to see what) would have been outweighed by the risk of exposure both for the Minister (who was under the surveillance of the Gestapo) and the Duke (who was under the surveillance of the British and Portuguese secret services). It is of course possible that Ricardo later imagined he had organized the discussion at his villa; of his reliability as a witness enough has been said.

As for Schellenberg, he writes in his memoirs that he 'considered getting my friends to arrange for me to meet the Duke, but the possibility of anything useful resulting from this seemed so remote that I did nothing.' The only evidence to the contrary is his Log entry for 29 July 1940, which begins: 'Discussion with C and Willi'. The meaning of Schellenberg's impersonal police language is often hard to fathom; but can this mean that Schellenberg had a meeting with C and Willi? There is no hint of this in his final report. The Log, though an interesting source, is a scrappy document, apparently consisting of notes hastily scribbled at the time and typed up afterwards, with various misspellings and grammatical errors; one wonders whether 'Willi' here is a mistype for some other name such as 'Winzer', or whether Schellenberg means to say that the discussion was merely *between* C and Willi. At all events, if Schellenberg did meet the Duke on the 29th (and one tends to agree with him that such a meeting would have been from his point of view purposeless), there was little comfort for the plot: for on the next line of the Log we read *Willi will nicht*.

The evidence is that Hoynigen-Huene and Schellenberg, if not concerned to see the Duke leave safely, were both at least highly unenthusiastic about their orders to keep him in Europe by trickery. Had they got in touch with him, it might well have been not to tempt but to warn him. Such meetings and warnings offer splendid material for the novelist: it is unfortunate for the historian that they do not seem to have occurred.

* Nicholas Shakespeare, *The Men Who Would Be King* (London, 1984).

Appendix V

Baden Denazification Commission   No. U IV/N 843
[*Badisches Staatskommissariat für politische Saüberung*]

Tribunal at Freiburg

JUDGMENT

In accordance with Article 20 of the *Landsverordnung* of 29 March 1947, the Tribunal in its session of 26 April 1949 has decreed that HERR EBERHARD VON STOHRER, born 5 February 1883, Ambassador of Germany, member of the NSDAP and of the National Socialist Welfare Organization from 1 September 1936 to 1945, charged under clauses II/D/4 and II/K/1 of Schedule A of Directive 38,* is to be classed in the category of EXONERATED PERSONS.

No punishment is to be applied.

Grounds for decision:

According to the sworn statements presented by Stohrer† and the investigations which have been made, it is established that Stohrer only joined the National Socialist Party in 1936 as a result of pressure brought to bear upon him from the Foreign Ministry, to which he had belonged since 1909. At the time of the seizure of power by the NSDAP Stohrer was Minister in Cairo. According to the evidence presented and annexed to the file, Stohrer sought to prevent Nazi propaganda in the German colony of Cairo; for this reason he entered into opposition to the Nazi Party, but he also rendered outstanding service to German interests in Egypt. During the Italo–Abyssinian conflict Stohrer was known not to be on the side of Fascism. He managed moreover to maintain the unity of the German

---

* These clauses made it an offence to have obtained public office or promotion therein solely or mainly on account of Nazi allegiance.

† Stohrer presented affadavits whose signatories included former Egyptian prime ministers, eminent Jews, and former colleagues of his who had become refugees from Nazism.

colony in Cairo in a remarkable way; he got rid of class differences formerly underlined by the existence of the Hansa Club by creating a 'German Union' to which all Germans were admitted without distinction of wealth or rank. Stohrer moreover did everything possible to mitigate the consequences of the Nuremberg 'racial laws', of which he was an open enemy. Jewish representatives of German businesses in Cairo were not boycotted and did not have to give up their agencies. . . .

In Spain too Stohrer quickly entered into opposition to the Party. His predecessor, General Faupel, had surrounded himself with those party members who comprised the Press Department. These were party fanatics, men with failed careers and no knowledge of the world who gave free rein to their hatred of the Jews and the Church and who interfered in Spain's internal affairs without being authorized to do so. Stohrer immediately reduced the Press Department to powerlessness, put an end to all attacks on the Church. . . . A local party chief, the schoolmaster Fleischmann, was removed because of his coarse antisemitic outbursts. Stohrer also concerned himself with the inventory and evaluation of losses suffered by German Jews during the Spanish War of 1936–9; he thus saved many claims. General Faupel had entirely neglected to carry out this duty. But the struggle of the Party against Stohrer did not cease. The Party incited speeches on the race question and even declared that the Spaniards were inferior from the racial point of view! Stohrer firmly opposed himself to all this. He also intervened in the prosecution of Counsellor von Waldheim for being a friend of the Jews. . . .

According to the evidence of Dr Paul Schwarz of New York,* Ribbentrop, while Minister of Foreign Affairs, once spoke of Stohrer in the following terms: 'Things cannot go on with the Ambassador in Madrid. He carries out his own policies and could not care less about us.' Stohrer for his part called Ribbentrop an incompetent politician and a cold-blooded cad [eiskalter Schuft]. . . . Stohrer was out of favour with the Party and Ribbentrop because of his efforts to keep Spain out of the war. He believed – and with reason – that Spain had been so weakened by the Civil War as to be incapable to withstanding a long struggle. Stohrer was thus responsible for the failure of the projects of Hitler and Goering to occupy Spain with a view to seizing Gibraltar. . . . So great became the uncertainties of his position and the pressures upon him both from the Party and the Foreign Ministry that Stohrer resigned from his Madrid post. He was at first put on the reserve list, but then retired at his own request. He moved to Switzerland. But the Foreign Minister wanted to lure him back to Germany. Ribbentrop assured him that he would be able to leave Germany again, but the Minister broke his word. Stohrer however managed to flee from Konstanz,

---

* Ribbentrop's worst enemy, who had been German Consul-General in New York in 1933 and there obtained political asylum.

where he was staying towards Christmas of 1944*, just as the Gestapo were coming to arrest him. . . .

In resisting Hitler's policy with regard to Spain, Stohrer set himself against the National Socialist régime in an area which at that moment was of the utmost significance in German politics. He did so in running a grave personal risk; he faced the consequences of his brusque recall. Stohrer therefore actively resisted the National Socialist tyranny to the extent of his powers and thereby suffered disadvantages.

In view of the foregoing the Tribunal considers the conditions of Article 6† fulfilled and classifies Stohrer in the category of

EXONERATED PERSONS

The President: STRUPP
An assessor: ACKERMANN

---

* More likely 1943. By the end of 1944 Stohrer was a hunted man, having been a close friend of von Hassell and other plotters against Hitler.

† Directive No. 38 of the Allied Control Council for Germany, promulgated on 12 October 1946, decreed that all who had served the Third Reich were to be tried and classified into five categories: major offenders, offenders, lesser offenders, followers and exonerated persons. An exonerated person was defined in Article 6 as 'anyone who, in spite of his formal membership or candidature or any other indication, not only showed a passive attitude but actively resisted the National Socialist tyranny to the extent of his powers and thereby suffered disadvantages'.

Appendix VI
Could Churchill Have Read the German Telegrams in July 1940?

In the original edition of this book, I suggested (as Martin Gilbert did in his great biography of Churchill) that British intelligence may have intercepted, and Churchill may have read, some of the German secret communications in July 1940 concerning Operation Willi. I deduced this from the fact (revealed in Professor F. H. Hinsley's official history of wartime intelligence) that some *Abwehr* and SD ciphers were being read at this time; from the line in Churchill's letter to the Duke of 27 July that 'conversations have been reported by telegraph through various channels which might have been used to Your Royal Highness' disadvantage'; and from Attlee's letter to Churchill of 25 August 1945 enclosing the German file on the Duke, 'with the contents of which you should already be familiar'.

I am grateful, however, to Lord Dacre of Glanton (formerly Professor Hugh Trevor-Roper), who wrote to me on 13 November 1984 pointing out why it was in fact improbable that Churchill had seen any of the *German* official communications on this subject at the time. I quote from his letter:

> It is true that *Abwehr* hand-ciphers were being read at that time, but these hand-ciphers (as far as the Peninsula was concerned) were only used between Madrid and its out-stations in Spain and Spanish Morocco, none of which would have been involved (even if the *Abwehr* itself was involved; which seems not to be the case) in this affair. *Abwehr* communications between Madrid and Berlin, Madrid andLisbon, Lisbon and Berlin, were *always* in Enigma, and these were not read in 1940. The first *Abwehr* Enigma was broken on 25 December 1941 (I have special reasons for remembering the date). So no *Abwehr* communications relevant to this affair could have been read at that time.

> Some SD communications were read, but the SD did not then operate in Spain and Portugal. Schellenberg, as you make clear, was sent on a special mission by Ribbentrop, and would have reported through diplomatic channels.

> The German diplomatic cipher was *never* broken. We did have German ambassadors' reports at a later stage in the war, but not by interception. They were texts *en clair*, known to us as 'Wood' material, and were brought to Switzerland (to OSS – Allen Dulles) by a member of the German Foreign Office.

They came at fairly rare intervals, when 'Wood' was able to travel, so were never 'hot': but they were useful. In any case they did not come till later (I forget the date when they began, but I think it was in 1943).

For these reasons I do not think that the German plans in this matter can have been known at the time (though they may have been surmised), and I presume that Churchill's statement, in the letter carried by Monckton, that conversations at Lisbon had been reported by telegraph *cannot* refer to German official secret communications. It might refer to casual indiscretions of the Duke reported by *non-German* diplomats whose ciphers we read. More probably, I suspect, it refers to gossip sent *en clair* by journalists. (I doubt if Churchill would have made even a general reference to anything deciphered. In his *Memoirs* he never does, but ascribes it to 'our agents' in Germany.)

Sources

The following list refers only to sources casting direct original light on the main subject of this book – the sojourn of the Duke and Duchess of Windsor in Spain and Portugal in the summer of 1940 and the intrigues to bring them under German power there. Background material is referred to where necessary in the notes to the chapters.

1. Official Archives

A. PUBLISHED DOCUMENTS

Documents on German Foreign Policy, Series D, Volume X (London & Washington, 1957)

Dez anos de politica externa (Portuguese White Book), Volume VII (Lisbon, 1971)

Documenti Diplomatici Italiani, Series IX, Volume V (Rome, 1965)

Foreign Relations of the United States, 1940, Volume III (Washington)

B. UNPUBLISHED DOCUMENTS

In Public Record Office at Kew: FO 371/24249

In *Politiches Archiv des Auswärtiges Amtes*, Bonn (copies on microfilm at Library and Records Department of Foreign Office, London): Series B15, June–August 1940; Document E035156

In *Bundesarchiv*, Koblenz: R58/572 (Schellenberg's Log)

In archives of Italian Foreign Ministry, Rome: file classed originally under *Gran. Brit. I/c*, consisting of telegrams from Madrid and Lisbon for onward transmission to Berlin (discovered by David Irving, who possesses copies)

In National Archives, Washington: 844E.001/51–2

2. *Personal Archives*

Files of Duke and Duchess of Windsor in possession of Maître Suzanne Blum, Paris
Papers of 1st Earl of Avon in Public Record Office (FO 954/33)
Papers of Lord Beaverbrook in House of Lords
Papers of Don Javier Bermejillo in possession of Sr J. Chapa, Madrid
Papers of 1st Earl of Halifax in Public Record Office (FO 800/326)
Papers of 1st Viscount Monckton of Brenchley in Bodleian Library, Oxford
Papers of Mademoiselle Jeanne-Marguerite Moulichon in her possession in Paris
Papers of Herbert C. Pell in Roosevelt Library, Hyde Park NY
Papers of Don Miguel Primo de Rivera in possession of Duque de Primo de Rivera, Madrid
Papers of F. D. Roosevelt in Roosevelt Library
Papers of Walter Schellenberg in *Institut für Zeitgeschichte*, Munich
Papers of Sir Walford Selby in possession of Ralph Selby, Hayling Island
Papers of Dr Eberhard von Stohrer in possession of Maria-Ursula von Stohrer, Ischia
Papers of Sir Ronald Storrs in Pembroke College, Cambridge
Papers of Viscount Tempelwood in Cambridge University Library
Papers of Alexander Weddell in archives of Virginia Historical Society, Richmond Va.

3. *Accounts by Witnesses*

A. PUBLISHED ACCOUNTS AND REFERENCES

Angel Alcázar de Velasco, *Memorias de un agente secreto*, (Madrid, 1979)
Suzanne Blum, *Vivre sans la Patrie* (Paris, 1975)
Ronald Bodley, *Flight into Portugal* (London, 1942)
David Eccles, *By Safe Hand*, (London, 1983)
Generaloberst Halder, *Kriegstagebuch*, Volume II (Stuttgart, 1963)
Erich Kordt, *Nicht aus den Akten* (Stuttgart, 1949)
Walter Monckton's notes in Lord Birkenhead, *Walter Monckton* (London, 1969)
The Schellenberg Memoirs (London, 1956)
Sir Walford Selby, *Diplomatic Twilight* (London, 1953)
Interviews with Sir Walford Selby and Viscount Templewood in *Daily Express*, etc., 2 August 1957
Duchess of Windsor, *The Heart has its Reasons* (London, 1956)
Articles by Duke of Windsor in *Sunday Express* and *New York Daily News*, December 1966

B. UNPUBLISHED MANUSCRIPT ACCOUNTS

Draft memoirs of Herbert C.Pell at Columbia University, New York (Oral History Project)
Draft memoirs of Dr Eberhard von Stohrer in Stohrer Papers
Chapter entitled 'A Deep-Laid Plot' from Lord Templewood's unfinished work *Spain in the Second World War* (Templewood Papers, XXIII/1–2)
Unedited draft of Duchess of Windsor's memoirs in Windsor Papers, Paris

C. INTERVIEWS, ETC.

Angel Alcázar de Velasco, Madrid, October 1983
Duque de Baena y de San Lucar Mayor, Biarritz, May 1983
Nuno Brito e Cunha, Estoril, July 1983
Viscount Eccles, London, September 1983
Vera Espírito Santo Silva, Paris, May 1983
Hon. Neil Hogg, April 1982
Conde de Lancastre, Madrid, May 1983
Susan Lowndes Marques, Estoril, June 1983
Conde de Montarco, Madrid, June 1983
Mademoiselle Marguerite Moulichon, Paris, August 1983
Ambassador A.Franco Nogueira, Lisbon, May 1983
François de Panafieu, Paris, October 1983
Tomás Pinto Basto, Cascais, May 1983
Ramón Serrano Suñer, Marbella, December 1982 and Madrid, May 1983
Reinhard Spitzy, December 1983
Berthold von Stohrer, London, March 1984
Maria-Ursula von Stohrer, Ischia, March 1984
Zacarias Berenguel Vivas, Lisbon, July 1983
Alda Wright, Lisbon, May 1983

4. *Other Accounts containing Original Information*

Geoffrey Bocca, *She Might Have Been Queen* (London, 1955): the relevant chapters of this otherwise thin and unreliable work contain information obtained from Mrs George Wood, Ricardo Espírito Santo Silva, and the driver Ladbrook.
Martin Gilbert, *Finest Hour* (London, 1983): the sixth volume of the official Churchill biography contains much important new information.
Nicholas Shakespeare, *The Men Who Would Be King* (London, 1984)

Further material of value may be expected in the following forthcoming publications: David Irving's work on Churchill; John Charmley's biography of Lord Lloyd of Dolobran; Professor D.L.Wheeler's book *Safe House* dealing with wartime intelligence operations in Portugal.

5. Newspapers

The Times	*Informaciones*, Madrid
The New York Times	*Diario de Notícias*, Lisbon
ABC, Madrid	*O Século*, Lisbon

Notes to the Chapters

German Foreign Ministry documents are cited by the letters AA followed by a serial number and a frame/folio number, according to the system used by the Allies in microfilming captured material after the war (e.g. AA–B15/B002531). Where a document has been published in translation in *Documents on German Foreign Policy*, there follows in brackets the letters GD and then the series, volume and document references (e.g. GD D/X/2). Where the original document has not been consulted, the published reference alone is given.

'Italian Documents' refers to the file discovered by David Irving in Rome, mentioned in *Sources* above.

The letters FO refer to classes with that designation at the Public Record Office, Kew.

DAPE stands for *Dez anos de politica externa*; *DDI* for *Documenti Diplomatici Italiani*; *FRUS* for *Foreign Relations of the United States*.

Prologue

1. Ernst von Weizsäcker, *Memoirs* (London, 1951), p. 213
2. Sir Samuel Hoare to Lord Halifax, October 1940 (Templewood Papers, XIII/20)
3. AA–136/74250 (GD D/X/274)

1: The Duke and the Germans

1. Geoffrey Bocca, *She Might Have Been Queen*, pp. 189–90; interview with Mademoiselle Moulichon
2. For flight to Spain: Bocca, pp. 190–2; interview with Mademoiselle Moulichon; Dodds's report to Lord Halifax of 23 June, FO 800/326 f.193; Duchess of Windsor, *The Heart has its Reasons*, pp. 334–6
3. FO 800/326 f.187
4. *New York Times*, 21 June 1940, p. 9; *ABC* (Madrid), morning edition of 22 June, p. 6
5. AA–B15/B002531 (GD D/X/2): Stohrer to Ribbentrop, No. 2051 of 23 June, arr. Berlin 9.40 pm, 'very confidential'

6. Erich Kordt, *Nicht aus den Akten*, p. 399
7. AA–B15/B002532 (GD D/X/9): Ribbentrop to Stohrer, No. 6 of 24 June 1940, arr. Madrid 4.05 pm 25 June, 'urgent'
8. Duke of Windsor, *A King's Story* (London, 1951), p. 79
9. Quoted in Kenneth Rose, *King George V* (London, 1983), p. 229
10. Duke of Windsor, p. 96
11. Prince of Wales to James Patterson, 4 April 1913 (Windsor Papers, Paris). In his diary the Prince remarks more briefly (17 April): 'I don't care much about the Germans.'
12. Windsor Papers, Paris
13. Duke of Windsor, pp. 100–1
14. Quoted in Duke of Windsor, p. 107
15. Quoted in Duke of Windsor, pp. 123–4
16. GD C/IV/27
17. Frances Donaldson, *Edward VIII* (London, 1974), pp. 194–6
18. GD C/IV/510
19. GD C/IV/531
20. Robert Rhodes James (ed.), *Victor Cazalet: A Portrait* (London, 1976), p. 209
21. Fritz Hesse, *Hitler and the English* (London, 1954), p. 22; GD C/V/77
22. Duke of Windsor, p. 322
23. Interview with Ramón Serrano Suñer
24. Weizsäcker, p. 284
25. Quoted in Alan Bullock's introduction to *The Ribbentrop Memoirs* (London, 1954), pp. xiv–xv
26. Hesse, pp. 31–2
27. *Ibid.*, pp. 32–3
28. AA–3164/674689 (GD C/VI/84): Ribbentrop to Hitler and Neurath, No. 304 of 10 December 1936, arr. Berlin 1.20 am 11 December, 'top secret'
29. Robert Rhodes James (ed.), *Memoirs of a Convervative* (London, 1969), p. 417
30. Kordt, pp. 156–61
31. *Aufzeichnung über die Unterredung zwischen dem RAM mit dem Prinzen Cyrill und dem Regenten Filow in Steinort am 19 Oktober 1943.* Aufz. RAM 48/43 gRS, 4–6. PA des AA, Buero Reichsminister, Handakten Dolmetscher Schmidt, 1943 (Teil II), ff.49423–5. (Copy made available by David Irving.)
32. Duke of Windsor in *Sunday Express*, December 1936
33. Interview with Sir Dudley Forwood
34. For AA reactions, GD C/VI/529 and 553; for FO reactions, FO 954/33 ff.60 *et seq.*
35. FO 954/33 f.69: Phipps to Eden, 4 October 1937
36. W. Shirer, *Berlin Diary* (London, 1941), pp. 76–7
37. Paul Schmidt, *Hitler's Interpreter* (London, 1951), p. 75
38. Martin Gilbert (ed.), *Winston Churchill: Companion Volume V*, Part III (London, 1982), pp. 819–21
39. Ilse Hess to Schwiegermutter in Alexandria, 3 November 1937: intercepts in FO 371/26566
40. Ribbentrop's report of 2 January 1938 on his London mission

(Nuremberg Document TC75), quoted in *The Ribbentrop Memoirs*, pp. 202–8

41. Correspondence between Walter Monckton and Philip Guedalla, September 1938 (Monckton Papers)
42. GD D/VII/485
43. Duke of Windsor's military intelligence reports in WO 106/1678, PRO
44. Draft letter of June 1943 in Windsor Papers, Paris
45. GD D/VIII/580
46. GD D/VIII/621
47. GD D/VIII/648
48. Letter in author's possession
49. Quoted in Martin Gilbert, *Finest Hour*, p. 327
50. Windsor Papers, Paris
51. Dodds's report in FO 800/326 f.193
52. Duchess of Windsor, p. 334
53. Malcolm Muggeridge (ed.), *Ciano's Diary* (London, 1947), pp. 266–7
54. This extraordinary episode was first revealed by Prytz himself in a Swedish wireless broadcast (*The Times*, 9 September 1965). The Swedish documents have now been published in W. M. Carlgren, *Sveriges Utrikespolitik, 1939–45* (Stockholm, 1973); and an analysis of other evidence is to be found in Bernd Martin, *Friedensinitiativen und Machtpolitik im Zweiten Weltkrieg, 1939–42* (Düsseldorf, 1974), pp. 271–3.
55. AA–B15/B002533 (GD D/X/9n): Stohrer to Ribbentrop, No. 2088 of 25 June 1940, arr. Berlin 7.20 am 26 June

2: *Nine Days in Madrid*

1. FO 800/326 f.185
2. Viscount Templewood, *Nine Troubled Years* (London, 1954); J. A. Cross, *Sir Samuel Hoare: A Political Biography* (London, 1977)
3. Templewood, *Ambassador on Special Mission* (London, 1976); David Eccles, *By Safe Hand*, pp. 100–4
4. Templewood, *Nine Troubled Years*, pp. 218–19
5. *Ibid.*, pp. 219–21; Duke of Windsor, pp. 339–40
6. Hoare to Churchill, 27 June 1940 (Templewood Papers, XIII/16/29)
7. FO 800/326 f.191
8. DAPE, VII/892: Salazar to Portuguese Ambassador London, 21 June 1940
9. Information provided by Dr C. M. Josten and Berthold von Stohrer; *The Times*, 11 March 1953; *Genealogisches Handbuch des Adels: Adelige Haüser* B/XI (1974); *Wer Ist's*, 1935
10. Interviews with Ramón Serrano Suñer and Pedro Sainz Rodriguez
11. Draft memoirs of Eberhard von Stohrer in Stohrer Papers (see note on p. 15 above)
12. Interviews with Berthold von Stohrer and Maria-Ursula von Stohrer
13. For Beigbeder: Templewood, *Ambassador on Special Mission*, passim; *Enciclopedia Universal Ilustrada*, Suplemento 1957–8, p. 187; Charles Halstead in *Revue*

de l'Histoire de la 2ème Guerre Mondiale, Volume 21 No. 83 (1971), pp. 31–60

14. GD D/IX
15. Halstead, cited article
16. Interview with Duque de Baena
17. Templewood, *Ambassador on Special Mission*, p. 51
18. AA–B15/B002556 (GD D/X/160): Stohrer to Ribbentrop, No. 2342 of 12 July 1940, arr. Berlin 1.30 pm 13 July
19. Hoare to Halifax, 3 September 1940, in FO 371/24516
20. Interview with Don Javier Chapa Bermejillo, and papers of Javier Bermejillo in his possession
21. Drafts in Bermejillo Papers
22. Duchess of Windsor, p. 338
23. FO 800/326 f.190
24. *Ibid.*, f.196
25. Templewood Papers, XIII/20
26. Templewood Papers, XIII/16/29
27. Stohrer draft memoirs
28. AA–B15/B002538 (GD D/X/86): Stohrer to Ribbentrop, No. 2182 of 2 July, arr. Berlin 12.04 am 3 July
29. The text of this telegram remains closed in Lord Halifax's correspondence, but is described in the index (FO 800/327) under the reference H/XLI/18
30. AA–B15/B002536 (GD D/X/66): telegram signed *Schmidt*
31. Italian Documents: telegram to Berlin No. 18687 of 3 July 1940 transmitting telegram from Lisbon of 28 June
32. See note 54 to Chapter 1
33. Gilbert, *Finest Hour*, p. 412
34. See note 18
35. Gilbert, *Finest Hour*, p. 418
36. Duchess of Windsor, p. 339
37. *FRUS* 1940/III, Weddell to Cordell Hull, 2 July 1940
38. Templewood, *A Deep-Laid Plot* (Templewood Papers, XXIII/1–2)
39. Hardinge to Churchill, 28 June 1940, quoted in Gilbert, *Finest Hour*, p. 614
40. FO 800/326 f.198: Churchill to Duke, 25 June 1940
41. Duke of Windsor, article in *Sunday Express*, December 1966
42. Quoted in Gilbert, *Finest Hour*, p. 613
43. Duchess of Windsor, pp. 340–1
44. Quoted in Gilbert, *Finest Hour*, p. 614
45. See note 28
46. Duchess of Windsor, pp. 339–40
47. *Ibid.*
48. *Ibid.*
49. *New York Times*, 1 July 1940, p. 9
50. Templewood, *A Deep-Laid Plot*, p. 12
51. *Ibid.*
52. FO 800/326 f.202: Hoare to Foreign Office, 1 July 1940
53. *Ibid.* f.203 (sent concurrently with foregoing)
54. Templewood, *A Deep-Laid Plot*, p. 13
55. ALS in Weddell Papers
56. Duchess to Mrs Merryman, 1 July 1940 (Windsor Papers, Paris)
57. AA–B15/B002545 (unpub.): Stohrer to Ribbentrop, No. 2298 of 9 July, arr. Berlin 2.20 am 10 July
58. Italian Documents: telegram to Berlin No. 19187 of 8 July 1940 transmitting telegram from Lisbon of 3 July

59. Templewood, *A Deep-Laid Plot*, p. 14
60. Hoare to Halifax, 1 July 1940 (Templewood Papers, XIII/20)
61. Hoare to Churchill, 5 July 1940 (Templewood Papers, XIII/16/37)

3: The Bahamas Appointment

1. See note 28 to Chapter 2
2. Kordt, p. 399
3. AA–B15/B002537 (unpub.): Gardemann to Abetz of Dienststelle Ribbentrop, No. 2180 of 2 July, arr. Berlin 1 am 3 July, 'secret'
4. Professor Bernd Martin to author, 12 October 1983
5. Hon. Neil Hogg to author, 6 April 1982
6. Eccles, p. 128
7. Memoir of Wing-Commander Chamberlayne, contained in letter to Sir Walford Selby of 29 September 1957 (Selby Papers)
8. *Ibid.*
9. *Ibid.*
10. Selby, *Diplomatic Twilight*, p. 43
11. Eccles, pp. 172–3
12. *DAPE* VII/892
13. Quoted in Gilbert, *Finest Hour*, pp. 613 and 698
14. Draft letter from Duke to Churchill, October 1940 (Windsor Papers, Paris)
15. Referred to in Gilbert, *Finest Hour*, p. 699 in note 7
16. Eccles, p. 142
17. Interview with Lord Eccles, 13 September 1983
18. Interview with Ambassador A. Franco Nogueira, 31 May 1983
19. Eccles, p. 128
20. FO 371/24249 f.148
21. See Michael Bloch, *The Duke of Windsor's War*, Chapter 6; Gilbert, *Finest Hour*, p. 699
22. Diary of Sir Ronald Storrs in Pembroke College, Cambridge, 14 July 1940
23. FO 371/24249 f.155; National Archives Washington, 844E.001/51
24. Interview with Eccles
25. See note 14
26. Interview with Eccles
27. Duchess of Windsor, p. 342
28. Eccles, p. 132
29. Interview with Eccles
30. FO 371/24249 f.149
31. Interview with Eccles

4: In the Jaws of Hell

1. Interview with Conde de Montarco
2. Nigel West, *MI6* (London, 1983), p. 185; interview with Nigel West
3. Interview with Eccles
4. Chamberlayne's memoir
5. Interview with Franco Nogueira; Douglas L. Wheeler, *In the Service of Order: The Portuguese Political Police and the British, German and Spanish Intelligence, 1932–45* in *Journal of Contemporary History*, Volume 18 (1983), pp. 1–25. Wheeler cites 'the protection of the Duke and Duchess of Windsor' as one of five 'secret intelligence operations' in which the Portuguese police

co-operated more with Allied than Axis interests' (pp. 6–7).

6. Interview with Vera Espírito Santo Silva, 14 May 1983

7. Interview with Tomás Pinto Basto, 29 May 1983

8. Interviews with Vera Espírito Santo Silva, Tomás Pinto Basto, Alda Wright, Conde de Lancastre, Nuno Brito e Cunha

9. Interview with Nuno Brito e Cunha

10. Interview with Susan Lowndes Marques

11. The fight, at the end of which the bull was 'dedicated' to the Duchess, is described in Bodley, *Flight into Portugal*, pp. 117–23

12. Articles of S. Chantal in *Diario de Notícias*, 1 August 1940

13. Eccles to his wife, 17 July 1940 (*By Safe Hand*, pp. 139–40)

14. Italian Documents: telegram to Berlin No. 20944 of 27 July 1940 transmitting telegram from Lisbon of 25 July

15. Pell to Roosevelt, 17 July (Pell Papers)

16. Interview with Eccles; Sir A. Hardinge to Churchill, 9 July 1940, quoted in Gilbert, *Finest Hour*, p. 702

17. Nicholas Shakespeare, *The Men Who Would Be King*, pp. 16–17

18. Interview with Susan Lowndes Marques

19. Italian Documents: telegram to Berlin No. 20094 of 19 July 1940 transmitting telegram from Lisbon of 8 July

20. Information provided by Ralph Selby from guest lists kept by his mother

21. Interview with Eccles

22. Italian Documents: telespresso 2565/990 Lisbon to Rome, 22 July 1940

23. Hoare to Halifax, 26 June 1940 (Templewood Papers, XIII/20)

24. Hoare to Churchill, 27 June 1940 (Templewood Papers, XIII/16/29)

25. FO 371/24249 ff.152 and 154

26. *Ibid.*, f.159

27. *Ibid.*, f.166

28. *The Times*, 11 July 1940

29. Original returned by Mrs Merryman's executors and now in Windsor Papers, Paris

30. Original returned by A. G. Allen on his retirement and now in Windsor Papers, Paris

5: The Plot

1. Italian Documents: telegram to Berlin No. 19849 of 15 July 1940 transmitting telegrams from Lisbon of 10 and 11 July

2. AA–B15/B002548 (unpub.)

3. For Hoynigen-Huene: *Freiherrliche Haüser*, B/II (1957); *Wer Ist's*, 1935; private information obtained in Portugal

4. Interview with Tomás Pinto Basto

5. Douglas Wheeler, *Safe House* (to be published)

6. *DAPE* VII/1047: note by Teixeira de Sampaio of discussion with Spanish Ambassador, 24 July 1940

7. AA–B15/B002549 (GD D/X/152): Hoynigen-Huene to Ribbentrop, No. 661 of 10 July 1940, arr. Berlin 4.10 am 11 July, 'secret'

8. Transcription of Tippelskirch Diary in possession of David Irving
9. Kordt, p. 399
10. AA–B15/B002549–51 (GD D/X/152): Ribbentrop to Stohrer, No. 1023 of 11 July, 'most urgent'
11. Weizsäcker, pp. 127–8
12. AA–E035156 has, for example, been transcribed in this manner
13. Interview with Maria-Ursula von Stohrer, 3 March 1984
14. Berthold von Stohrer to author, 13 December 1983
15. GD D/X/87: Stohrer to Ribbentrop, Political Report 1496g of 2 July 1940, 'top secret'
16. Ramón Serrano Suñer, *Entre les Pyrénées et Gibraltar* (Geneva, 1947), p. 72
17. AA–B15/B002552–5 (GD D/X/159): Stohrer to Ribbentrop, No. 2339 of 12 July, arr. Berlin 10.55 pm, 'most urgent', 'top secret'
18. Interview with Ramón Serrano Suñer, 31 December 1982
19. Interview with Angel Alcázar de Velasco
20. Interview with Duque de Baena
21. Interview with Marqués de Santo Floro
22. Interview with Serrano Suñer
23. *Idem*
24. Interview with Serrano Suñer, May 1983
25. *Idem*
26. AA–B15/B002561 (unpub.): Stohrer to Ribbentrop, No. 2358 of 13 July, arr. Berlin 8.45 pm, 'urgent'

6. *Preparations for Exile*

1. 'She has a remarkable talent for housewifery, as the great ladies of earlier centuries conceived it. Cooking, decorating, flowers, clothes, all come into her idea of home making, and are a part of the hospitality for which she has genius.' Rosita Forbes, *Appointment with Destiny* (London, 1946), p. 192
2. AA–B15/B002545 (unpub.): Stohrer to Ribbentrop, No. 2298 of 9 July, arr. Berlin 2.20 am 10 July
3. Windsor Papers, Paris
4. Interview with Tomás Pinto Basto
5. AA–B15/B002560 (unpub.): Stohrer to Ribbentrop, No. 2354 of 13 July, arr. Berlin 4.25 pm, 'urgent'
6. *Contabilidad* dated 16 October 1940 in Bermejillo Papers
7. AA–B15/B002562 (GD D/X/223): Stohrer to Ribbentrop, No. 2384 of 16 July, arr. Berlin 11.04 pm, 'very confidential'
8. *Ibid.*
9. AA–B15/B002563 (unpub.): Stohrer to Ribbentrop, No. 2390 of 16 July 1940, arr. Berlin 11.55 pm, 'top secret'
10. Bermejillo Papers
11. *Ibid.*
12. Interview with Mademoiselle Moulichon
13. *Idem*
14. Draft letter in Bermejillo Papers
15. AA–B15/B002580 (unpub.): Stohrer to Ribbentrop, No. 2451 of 22 July 1940, arr. Berlin 3.15 pm

16. Windsor Papers, Paris
17. See pp. 226–8 below
18. FO 800/326 f.205
19. FO 371/24249 f.156
20. *Ibid.*, f.206
21. *Ibid.*, f. 208
22. *Ibid.*, f.157
23. *Ibid.*, f.209
24. *Ibid.*, f.205
25. Windsor Papers, Paris
26. FO 371/24249 f.162
27. *Ibid.*, f.210
28. Pell to Roosevelt, 17 July 1940, in Roosevelt Papers (Official File 48)
29. *Ibid.*, Roosevelt to Pell, 7 August 1940: 'This Government, as well as the British Government, shared the views you expressed to me. . . .'
30. National Archives, Washington, file 844E.001/52 on diversion of *Excalibur*
31. FO 371/24249 f.212
32. Gilbert, *Finest Hour*, p. 702
33. FO 371/24249 f.161
34. *Ibid.*, f.163A
35. *Ibid.*, f.164
36. *Ibid.*, f.166
37. *Ibid.*, f.172
38. *Ibid.*, f.170
39. *Ibid.*, f.171
40. *Ibid.*, f.175
41. Quoted in Gilbert, *Ibid.*, p. 703
42. FO 371/24249 f.176
43. *Ibid.*, f.181
44. *Ibid.*, f.184
45. *Ibi.d.*, f.187
46. Windsor Papers, Paris

7: Persuasions

1. Part of draft cited in note 14 to Chapter 6, Bermejillo Papers
2. Archives of Spanish Ministry of Foreign Affairs and Don Miguel Primo de Rivera searched by Rafael Blázquez Godoy
3. Duke of Windsor to Templewood, 15 August 1958 (Templewood Papers, RF3)
4. Interview with Serrano Suñer
5. AA–B15/B002582–3 (GD D/X/211): Stohrer to Ribbentrop, No. 2474 of 23 July 1940, arr. Berlin 9.50 pm, 'most urgent', 'top secret'
6. Annotated copy of Cabinet Print C.63 Confidential of August 1953, *Publication of Captured Enemy Documents*, Windsor Papers, Paris
7. AA–B15/B002588 (GD D/X/290): Stohrer to Ribbentrop, No. 2495 of 25 July 1940, arr. Berlin 2.40 pm, 'urgent', 'strictly confidential'
8. Interview with Conde de Montarco, 8 June 1983
9. *Idem*
10. FO 371/24249 ff.162–4, 173, 177–9
11. *Ibid.*, f.189
12. Duke to Allen, 20 July 1940
13. AA–B15/B002586 (unpub.): Stohrer to Ribbentrop, No. 2492 of 24 July, arr. Berlin 8.20 pm, 'urgent', 'top secret'
14. *DAPE* VII/1047: minute of interview, 24 July 1940
15. *Ibid.* for Teixeira de Sampaio's account of this meeting; for the Italian Minister's: telegram 20944 to Berlin of 27 July 1940 transmitting Lisbon telegram of 25 July, Italian Documents
16. Interview with Eccles, 13 September 1983

17. Eccles, p. 143
18. Interview with Eccles
19. Information supplied by Ralph Selby
20. FO 371/24249 f.186
21. *Ibid.*, f.185
22. *Ibid.*, f.186

8: In Berlin

1. Quoted in note on p. 226 of GD D/X
2. GD D/X/177
3. *The Times*, 20 July 1940
4. Generaloberst Halder, *Kriegstagebuch*, Volume II, pp. 30–1
5. *The Times*, 23 July 1940
6. Leonidas Hill (ed.) *Die Weizsäcker Papiere 1933–50* (1974), p. 215
7. *Ibid.*
8. *The Schellenberg Memoirs*, p. 130
9. *Ibid.*, p. 21
10. Alan Bullock in Introduction to *The Schellenberg Memoirs*, pp. 9–11
11. Hugh Trevor-Roper, *The Last Days of Hitler* (London, 1946), pp. 28–30
12. *The Schellenberg Memoirs*, pp. 127–31
13. Schellenberg's Log (B. Arch. R58/572), quoted in Appendix III

9: New Schemes in Madrid

1. See note 5 to Chapter 7
2. Interview with Serrano Suñer, 31 December 1982
3. AA–B15/B002585 (GD D/X/216): Stohrer to Ribbentrop, No. 2488 of 24 July 1940, arr. Berlin 7.30 am, 'urgent', 'top secret'

4. Interview with Conde de Montarco
5. Interview with Zacarias Berenguel Vivas
6. AA–B15/B002590 (unpub.): Stohrer to Ribbentrop, No. 2506 of 25 July 1940, arr. Berlin 2.40 pm, 'most urgent', 'top secret', refers to Ribbentrop's telegram No. 1121 of 24 July (not found)
7. *The Schellenberg Memoirs*, pp. 132–3
8. *Ibid.*, pp. 133–4
9. *Ibid.*, pp. 134–5
10. *Ibid.*, pp. 135–6
11. AA–B15/B002591–2 (GD D/X/235): Stohrer to Ribbentrop, No. 2520 of 26 July 1940, arr. Berlin 6.50 pm, 'most urgent', 'top secret'
12. *The Schellenberg Memoirs*, p. 136; Schellenberg's Log
13. He has written of these events in *Los Siete dias de Salamanca* (Madrid, 1976)
14. See e.g. *Evening Standard*, 20 February 1941
15. Interview with Alcázar de Velasco, Madrid, 2 October 1983
16. Interview with Conde de Montarco

10: Schellenberg in Lisbon

1. *The Schellenberg Memoirs*
2. *Ibid.*, p. 136
3. Interview with Franco Nogueira
4. *The Schellenberg Memoirs*, pp. 137–8
5. *Ibid.*, pp. 136–7
6. AA–B15/B002597 (unpub.): Hoynigen-Huene to Ribbentrop, No. 749 of 26 July 1940,

arr. Berlin 4.25 am
27 July

7. *The Schellenberg Memoirs*, p. 137
8. Schellenberg's Log
9. AA–B15/B002601 (unpub.):
Stohrer to Ribbentrop, No. 2547
of 27 July 1940, arr. Berlin
9 pm, 'most urgent', 'top
secret'
10. Schellenberg's Final Report
11. *The Schellenberg Memoirs*, p. 138
12. *Ibid.*
13. Schellenberg's Log
14. Bermejillo Papers
15. FO 371/24249 f.186: Selby to
Halifax, No. 487 of 25 July 1940,
arr. London 8.25 am 26 July,
'immediate'
16. AA–E035156 (unpub.): transcript
of Stohrer to Ribbentrop, 28 July
1940
17. *Ibid.*
18. *Ibid.*
19. AA–B15/B002603 (unpub.):
Stohrer to Ribbentrop, No. 2554 of
29 July 1940, arr. Berlin 7.40 pm,
'most urgent', 'top secret'
20. AA–E035156
21. Interview with Angel Alcázar de
Velasco, 4 October 1983
22. Windsor Papers, Paris
23. AA–B15/B002611 (GD D/X/257):
Stohrer to Ribbentrop, No. 2576 of
30 July, arr. Berlin 3.35 pm, 'most
urgent', 'top secret'
24. Interview with Alcázar de Velasco

11: The Monckton Mission

1. Wheeler, cited article, at p. 12.
The agent's name was Corte Real.
2. AA–B15/B002610 (GD D/X/254):
Stohrer to Ribbentrop, No. 2564
of 30 July 1940, arr. Berlin
4.45 am, 'most urgent', 'top
secret'
3. *The Schellenberg Memoirs*,
p. 141
4. AA–B15/B002608 (unpub.):
Hoynigen-Huene to Ribbentrop,
No. 775 of 29 July 1940, arr. Berlin
4.25 pm 30 July, 'most urgent'.
Somewhat surprisingly, this
information had been published in
London by the *Exchange
Telegraph*.
5. Lord Birkenhead, *Walter
Monckton*, pp. 73–6
6. Information provided by Martin
Gilbert
7. Quoted in Gilbert, *Finest Hour*,
pp. 704–5
8. Duchess of Windsor, pp. 342–3
9. Windsor Papers, Paris
10. FO 371/24249 ff.190 and 233
11. Birkenhead, p. 180
12. AA–B15/B002603 (unpub.):
Stohrer to Ribbentrop, No. 2554 of
29 July 1940, arr. Berlin 5.16 pm,
'most urgent', 'ultra top secret'
13. Passport of Mademoiselle
Moulichon dated 31 March 1939
14. Interview with Mademoiselle
Moulichon
15. *Idem*
16. AA–B15/B002643 (unpub.):
Schleier (Paris) to Ribbentrop,
No. 334 of 3 August
17. *The Schellenberg Memoirs*,
p. 138
18. AA–B15/B002602 (unpub.):
Hoynigen-Huene to Ribbentrop,
No. 764 of 28 July 1940, arr. Berlin
7.40 pm, 'most urgent', 'secret'

19. AA–B15/B002614 (unpub.):
Stohrer to Ribbentrop, No. 2588 of
30 July 1940, arr. Berlin 2.00 am
31 July, 'most urgent', 'top secret'
20. AA–B15/B002611–12 (GD
D/X/257): Stohrer to Ribbentrop,
No. 2576 of 30 July, arr. Berlin
3.45 pm, 'most urgent', 'top secret'
21. *O Século* and *Diario de Notícias*,
31 July 1940, front-page articles
22. Kordt, p. 400
23. AA–E035157
24. *The Schellenberg Memoirs*, p. 139

12: An Abduction?

1. For Schellenberg's mythopoeia,
Trevor-Roper, *op. cit.*; Ladislas
Farago, *The Game of the Foxes*
(London, 1972)
2. *The Schellenberg Memoirs*,
pp. 129–30
3. AA–B15/B002613 (unpub.):
Winzer to Heydrich, Madrid
telegram No. 2587 of 30 July 1940,
arr. Berlin 2.00 am 31 July, 'top
secret'
4. *The Schellenberg Memoirs*,
pp. 139–41
5. Chamberlayne's memoir
6. Interview with Nigel West
7. Interview with François de
Panafieu. The agent was Roger
Mitchell.
8. Interviewed after the war,
Schellenberg had the impression
that nothing had been known
about his mission (*The
Schellenberg Memoirs*, p. 139)
9. Interview with Montarco
10. *The Schellenberg Memoirs*,
pp. 141–2

11. AA–B15/B002614–15 (unpub.):
Stohrer to Ribbentrop, No. 2588 of
30 July, arr. Berlin 2.00 am
31 July, 'most urgent', 'top secret'
12. *The Schellenberg Memoirs*,
p. 139
13. AA–B15/B002619–20 (GD
D/X/264): Stohrer to Ribbentrop,
No. 2598 of 31 July 1940, arr.
Berlin 6.25 pm, 'most urgent', 'top
secret'
14. Interview wtih Alcázar de Velasco
15. AA–B15/B002609 (unpub.):
Hoynigen-Huene to Ribbentrop,
No. 783 of 30 July, arr. Berlin
3.10 am 31 July, 'most urgent'
16. FO 371/24249 f.239
17. *Ibid.*, f.244
18. Bermejillo Papers
19. *Diario de Notícias*, 1 August 1940
20. Shown to author July 1983
21. Schellenberg's Final Report
22. Quoted in Gilbert, *Finest Hour*,
p. 708
23. *DDI*, IX/V/340, Bova Scoppa to
Ciano, No. 288 of 1 August 1940,
arr. Rome 9.15 am 2 August

13: Eleventh Hour

1. Interview with Alcázar de
Velasco
2. AA–B15/B002619–20
(GD D/X/264): Stohrer to
Ribbentrop, No. 2598 of 31 July
1940, arr. Berlin 6.25 pm, 'most
urgent', 'top secret'
3. Interview with Serrano Suñer
4. AA–B15/B002631 (unpub.):
Stohrer to Ribbentrop, No. 2599 of
31 July 1940, arr. Berlin 9.20 pm,
'most urgent', 'top secret'

5. Interview with Mademoiselle Moulichon
6. Halder, pp. 46–50
7. AA–B15/B002617–18 (GD D/X/265)
8. See note 4
9. *DDI*, IX/V/346, Bova Scoppa to Ciano, 2 August 1940
10. *Ibid.*, No. 340
11. Interviews with Vera Espírito Santo Silva, Mrs Walter Kerr, Conde de Lancastre, Alda Wright
12. See *The Reports*
13. Schellenberg's Log and Final Report

14: The Reports

1. FO 371/24249 f.245 (sent 1.10 pm, received 3.40 pm)
2. AA–B15/B002629 (unpub.)
3. AA–B15/B002630 (unpub.): Winzer to Heydrich, No. 2637 of 2 August 1940, arr. Berlin 4.32 pm, 'top secret'
4. AA–B15/B002632–3 (GD D/X/276)
5. AA–B15/B002635–8 (GD D/X/277)

6. *The Schellenberg Memoirs*, pp. 142–3
7. *DAPE*, Volume VII, Doc. No. 1080
8. *DDI*, Series IX, Volume V, Doc. No. 346
9. AA–B15/B002641–2 (GD D/X/285)
10. Copies of this correspondence exist both in Churchill's and Monckton's papers

Epilogue

1. National Archives, Washington: 862.20241/56
2. F. Taylor (ed.), *The Goebbels Diaries 1939–41* (London, 1982), pp. 344–5
3. Quoted in John Toland, *Adolf Hitler* (1976)
4. AA–B15/B002655 (GD D/X/276n): Hoynigen-Huene to Ribbentrop, No. 884 of 15 August 1940, 'secret'
5. Bermejillo Papers; letters written from Bahamas by Duchess of Windsor to Mrs D. Buchanan Merryman; interviews with Mademoiselle Moulichon

Index